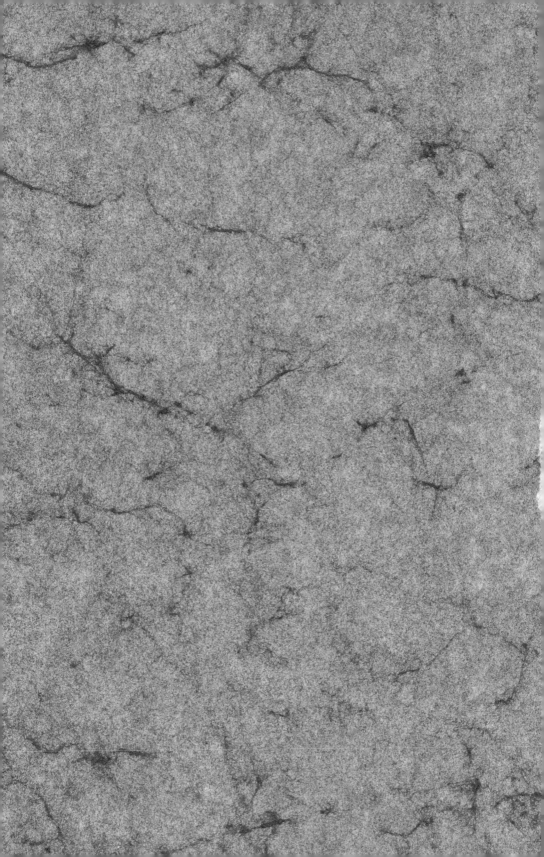

PROOF

U.S. **10**¢

Robert Frost

AMERICAN POET

Commemorative postage stamp honoring Robert Frost, issued on 26 March 1974 by the United States Postal Service. From a pencil drawing by Paul Calle modeled by Frank J. Waslick and engraved by Arthur W. Dintaman. *Courtesy of the United States Postal Service.*

PROOF
4

THE YEARBOOK OF

AMERICAN

BIBLIOGRAPHICAL

AND TEXTUAL

STUDIES

Edited by Joseph Katz

J. Faust & Co., *Publishers*

Copyright © J. Faust & Co. 1975

EDITORIAL ASSISTANTS

Brent L. Kendrick

George H. Jensen

Manuscripts offered for publication in *Proof* must be accompanied by a self-addressed return envelope and unaffixed return postage. Acceptance for publication is made on condition that the contribution will not be reprinted by its author until at least three years after date of the volume in which it appears. Publication decisions are made within a relatively short time during the period October–May, but take longer during the period June–September. *Proof* is edited in The Proof Editorial Offices at the University of South Carolina. The editor hereby acknowledges support of The Proof Editorial Offices and other contributions to *Proof* by the University of South Carolina. *Proof* is a major component of Faust's Journals Program. Essays on British bibliographical and textual studies may be addressed to *Costerus* in care of J. Faust & Co. News, notes, queries, and work-in-progress may be addressed to The *Editorial Quarterly* in care of J. Faust & Co. The publisher also will consider full-length works and monographs — bibliographies, critical editions, and textual studies — in the field.

Address orders to Order Department *(Proof)*, J. Faust & Co., Publishers, Box 5616, Columbia, SC 29205.

Address all other correspondence to Joseph Katz, The Proof Editorial Offices, University of South Carolina, Columbia, SC 29208.

1 2 3 4 5 6 7 8 9 0—85 84 83 82 81 80 79 78 77 76 75

International Standard Book Number: 0–915188–04–X

Library of Congress Catalog Card Number: LC 70–158622

FOR
FREDSON THAYER BOWERS

CONTENTS

Twilight is Robert Frost's first book. It was printed in the fall of 1894—nineteen years before the publication of *A Boy's Will*—but until now was never published. Frost had two copies of *Twilight* made as an aid in his courtship of Elinor White: she was to have one, he the other; with the book to be symbolic of the bond between them and of his potential success as a professional poet. But his presentation ceremony at the door of her boarding house turned into a debacle. Enraged, Frost destroyed his copy. Later, when Elinor finally became Mrs. Robert Frost, her copy of *Twilight* came with her. By then, however, Frost saw it not as the love gesture he had planned it to be, but as a reminder of a bitterly disappointing episode he preferred to forget. Several months after Elinor's death, Frost released the unique copy of *Twilight* to a collector. Twenty years later, at Frost's request, Clifton Waller Barrett acquired it for the Barrett Library at the University of Virginia.

Twilight is first published in a facsimile reproduction of the unique copy.

Contents

Twilight
My Butterfly
Summering
The Falls
An Unhistoric Spot

CONTENTS

ILLUSTRATIONS

PROOF

TWILIGHT:
Robert Frost's First Book

CLIFTON WALLER BARRETT

Twilight IS ROBERT FROST'S FIRST BOOK. FOR REASONS THAT WILL become clear shortly, although it was printed in the fall of 1894 it was never published. Frost had the book printed because there were two things in his mind then: the profession of poetry and the courtship of Elinor Miriam White. He had met her almost exactly three years earlier, while they both were in their final year at the Lawrence High School in Massachusetts; during the next several months their relationship had developed to the point where, in the summer of 1892, they privately exchanged wedding rings. But soon after Elinor left for Canton, New York, to attend St. Lawrence University that fall, she seemed to be drifting away from Frost. When he pressed for a public wedding, she asked how he expected to support her. She saw him drifting through life, teaching occasionally and with poetry as his only ambition. Where, she wondered, was the future? He had no immediate answer to that question—at least none that would satisfy her. By the fall of 1894 Frost was desperate for something to sway her his way. *Twilight* was the result of his desperation.

The late Lawrance Thompson told as much of its story as he could piece together, in *Robert Frost: The Early Years, 1874–1915* (New York: Holt, Rinehart and Winston, 1966), but it is worth summarizing here. In March 1894 Frost had made his first sale: $15 from *The Independent* for 'My Butterfly'. He told Elinor about it when she returned on summer recess from the university, but she was properly unimpressed. She did say, however, that if he had established himself by the time of her accelerated graduation in June of 1895, she would marry him. But Frost decided to press again, this time in a way that should show her that the profession of poetry could provide them both with a tangible future. He selected five poems, including 'My Butterfly', took them to a job printer in Lawrence, and had them made into a book. It was a special book: printed on fine linen paper and bound in brown, pebble-grain leather with the word 'TWILIGHT' in gold on the front, only two copies were made — one for Frost, the other for Elinor. Late in October or early in November 1894, when the two copies were ready, he took them on the train from Lawrence to Canton, so that he could make a personal presentation. The story of the presentation, and the destruction of the remaining copy has been written by Frost himself: 'I had two copies of Twilight printed and bound by a job printer in Lawrence Mass in 1894. . . . One copy I kept for myself and afterward destroyed. The other I gave away to a girl in St Lawrence University to show to her friends.' Although Elinor White accepted her copy of *Twilight,* her reception was so cool as to be a humiliating rebuff to Frost. As he walked along the railroad tracks back towards Lawrence, he tore his copy of *Twilight* into little pieces and scattered them away.

A few days later, he headed for the Dismal Swamp in Virginia, vaguely entertaining thoughts of suicide. He did not kill himself, of course, and on 19 December 1895 he managed to marry Elinor. Her copy of *Twilight* — now unique — came with her. But it was a memento of an experience he remembered with regret and bitterness. Elinor died on 20 March 1938. On 8 January 1940, Frost sold the book to Earle J. Bernheimer, a California collector — without the flyleaf on which Frost had written an inscription to Elinor, but with a new inscription to Bernheimer in explanation of the book's history. Bernheimer, who had gathered the largest collection of Frost's original manuscripts in existence, disposed on the entire collection at auction in 1950 at the Parke-Bernet Galleries in New York. I was there and luckily managed to make a clean sweep of the manuscripts. However, *Twilight* fell to a Chicago collector, Roy V. Thornton, on a bid of $3,500. Mr. Thornton, a discriminating collector, assembled a fine Frost library. He resisted steadfastly every attempt to part him from *Twilight*. I thought I had lost it forever.

Then, ten years later, in the winter of 1960, Frost visited me in New York, where I resided at that time. He inquired about the possibility of adding *Twilight* to the Frost collection which would be prominently displayed at the dedication of the Barrett Library of the University of Virginia scheduled for April of that year. I explained that Mr. Thornton had consistently declined to dispose of the cherished little volume. Frost then said, cryptically, 'Try again — I think the chances are better.' In the meantime, Thornton had moved to Arizona. A telephone call elicited the information that he would not sell *Twilight,* but would consider an offer for the entire collection. An offer was made in a subsequent conversation; and when he hesitated, he was told that Robert Frost would be happy to see the collection go to the University of Virginia. Mr. Thornton then, very graciously, agreed to carry out Frost's wishes.

The crowning sight at the ceremonies dedicating the Barrett Library was the noble head of the great poet bent over his first book, printed sixty-six years before.

Robert Frost's *Twilight:* binding front of the unique copy in the Clifton Waller Barrett Library of the University of Virginia.

TWILIGHT

ROBERT FROST

CONTENTS

I had two copies of Twilight printed and bound by a job printer in Lawrence Mass in 1894 probably out of pride in what Blein Barney and Maurice Thompson inadvertently the poem in it called My Butterfly. One copy I kept for myself and afterward destroyed. The other I gave away to a girl in 8th avenue I unwarily to show to her friends... It had no return and deserved none. But it unaccountably surviving and has lately leaped into prominence as my first. It few scattered lines in it are as much mine as any I was ever to write. I deliver it into your care my dear Bernheimer with the last request that you be not too fondly selfish with it, but consent to lend it once in a long long time to some important exhibition of my works as of the Jones & Library or the hunt or the Baker at Dartmouth Boston February 1 1940 Robert Frost

Sexty years later signed
over to my friend
B V Thornton
at Chicago.
Robert Frost

TWILIGHT

TWILIGHT

Why am I first in thy so sad regard,
O twilight gazing from I know not
  where?
I fear myself as one more than I guessed!
Am I instead of one so very fair?—
That thou art sorrowful and I oppressed?

High in the isolating air,
Over the inattentive moon,
Two birds sail on great wings,
  And vanish soon.
(And they leave the north sky bare!)

The far-felt solitudes that harbor night,
Wake to the singing of the wood-bird's
  fright.

By invocation, O wide silentness,
Thy spirit and my spirit pass in air!
They are unmemoried consciousness,
  Nor great nor less!
And thou art here and I am everywhere!

MY BUTTERFLY

Thine emulous fond flowers are dead,too,
And the daft sun-assaulter, he
That frighted thee so oft, is fled or dead:
    Save only me—
     Nor is it sad to thee—
    Save only me
There is none left to mourn thee in the
    fields.

The gray grass is scarce dappled with
    the snow,
Its two banks have not shut upon the
    river,
    But it is long ago,
    It seems forever,
Since first I saw thee glance
With all thy dazzling other ones,
    Precipitate in love,
    In airy dalliance,
Tossed, tangled, whirled, and whirled
    above

Like a limp rose-wreath in a fairy dance.
When that was, the soft mist
Of my two tears hung not on all the land,
But I was glad for thee and glad for me,
    I wist.

Did you think, when you tottered wan-
    dering on high,
Fate had not made you for the pleasure
    of the winds,
With those great careless wings?
    'Twas happier to die,
    And let the days blow by—
    These were the unlearned things.

It seemed God let thee flutter from His
    gentle clasp,
Then fearful he had let thee win
Too far beyond him to be gathered in,
Snatched thee o'er-eager with ungentle
    grasp,
    Jealous of immortality.

O I remember me
How once conspiracy was rife
    Against my life
(The languor of it,) and
The whirling grasses dizzied me of
    thought,
The breeze three odors brought;
And a gem-flower waved in a wand.
Then when I was distraught,
    And could not speak,
Sidelong, full on my cheek,
What should that reckless zephyr fling
But the wild touch of your dye-dusty
    wing!

I found that wing withered to-day—
    For you are dead, I said,
    And the strange birds say—
I found it mid the withered leaves,
    Under the eaves.

SUMMERING

I would arise and in a dream go on—
Not very far, not very far—and then
Lie down amid the sunny grass again,
And fall asleep till night-time or next
    dawn.

In sleepy self-sufficiency I'd turn;
I'd seek new comfort and be hard to
    please—
Far in a meadow by an isle of trees,
All summer long amid the grass and
    fern.

Forests would have to be all round about,
And the mead silent, and the grasses
    deep,
Else I might not gain such a tireless
    sleep!
I could not slumber if the wains were
    out!

THE FALLS

'Tis a steep wood of rocks,
With the fern grown everywhere;
But with no birds—not a wing!
And the falls come down there.

Even an Indian trail
Would swerve to a haunt so fair!
One used to—there were the ferns
And the falls came down there.

AN UNHISTORIC SPOT.

Ah passionate is rest when to the earth
I yield in full length contact of sweet
    pain !
Here just within the bars in the chill
    grass,
And the great shadow of a fruitless tree,
I at once sleep and am awake in joy.
And when I sit half-conscious on the
    slope,
And lean upon one grass-wrought hand
    and gaze,
The lone thrush gurgles nectar in his
    throat,
On some green spire, adjusting his
    furled wings,
The local cricket quavers to the wind,
And every one that passes looks at me.

Sway of trees chafing interlocking
And a woodpecker knocking.

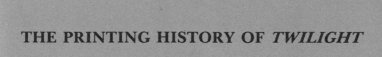

THE PRINTING HISTORY OF *TWILIGHT*

JOAN ST.C. CRANE

NEITHER ROBERT FROST NOR HIS BIOGRAPHERS HAVE SAID MUCH ABOUT the printing facts of *Twilight.* However, a connective thread of evidence makes it possible to conjecture the identity of the *Twilight* printer. In 1891 Frost was editor of the Lawrence High School *Bulletin* and, facing deadlines with little copy to meet them, he frequently spent hours in its printer's office writing articles sufficient to fill the eight three-column printed pages of the *Bulletin.* For that reason one must explore the possibility that when Frost wanted a special job of printing two and one-half years later he turned to the *Bulletin* printer.

Unfortunately, the *Bulletin* for 1891–1892 bears no printer's imprint. It does carry, however, only one advertisement by a printer in its advertisement section. That printer is the American Printing House, job printers for the American Publishing Company of Lawrence and also publisher of the Lawrence *Daily American.* (For a short time in 1895 Frost worked as a reporter for the *Daily American.*) It is reasonable to assume that the printer of the *Bulletin* would advertise there; and since

Front wrapper of the October 1891 Lawrence High School *Bulletin,* edited by Robert Frost. Compare the uncials in the motto with those on the first page of the commencement program following. *Courtesy of the Clifton Waller Barrett Library of the University of Virginia.*

"Vincit Qui Se Vincit."

———

ORDER OF EXERCISES

FOR THE

FORTY-FIRST ANNIVERSARY

OF THE

—※LAWRENCE HIGH SCHOOL,※—

FRIDAY, JULY 1st,

1892.

Commencement program for the Class of 1892 at the Lawrence High School. Frost wrote the lyrics for the class hymn on p. [3], and he and Ellinor]*sic*] White are listed as events 18 and 19 of the day. Note the uncials in the motto on p. [1]. *From the Clifton Waller Barrett Library of the University of Virginia.*

✳PROGRAMME.✳

Accompanists—Helen Davitt and Annie Barker.

1. CHORUS.—"Praise Ye the Father."   *Gounod*

2. ESSAY, with Salutatory Address.—"The Influence of Home-life on Literature."

   ANNIE H. DESMOND.

3. ESSAY.—"The Power of Music."
   EDITH M. ANDREWS.

4. PART SONG.—"There's Nothing so Gay."   *Holcomb*

5. ESSAY.—"Priceless Things."
   JENNIE A. McMANUS.

6. ESSAY.—"The Progress of Lawrence."
   JOSEPHINE M. SPALDING.

7. ESSAY.—"The Ethics of Good Manners,"
   BEATRICE R. DOE.

8. VOCAL SOLO.—"Across the Dee."   *Coombs*
   ANNIE BARKER.

9. ORIGINAL DECLAMATION.—"The Chinese Question."
   FRANK B. McALLISTER.

10. ESSAY.—"Lights on the Way."
    ELIZABETH G. McINTYRE.

11. PIANO SOLO.—March from Suite, Op 91.   *Raff*
    BEATRICE R. DOE.

12. ESSAY.—"Isabella, the Foster-mother of America."
    ELLEN G. DUNN.

13. ESSAY.—"Footprints on the Sands of Time."
    GEORGIA M. DAME.

14. VOCAL SOLO.—"Good Bye, Sweet Day."   *Vannah*

LILLIAN G. CATE.

15. ESSAY.—"Mary Lyon's Influence in the Education of Women."

HATTIE W. CARTER.

16. CLASS HISTORY.

AMY G. WILLAN.

17. CHORUS.—"Columbia's Jubilee."   *Trowbridge*

18. ESSAY, (of Valedictory Rank.) — "Conversation as a Force in Life."

ELLINOR M. WHITE.

19. ORIGINAL DECLAMATION, with Valedictory Address.—

"A Monument to Afterthought Unveiled,"

ROBERT L. FROST.

20. AWARDING OF HOOD, VALPEY AND BULLETIN PRIZES

BY SUPERINTENDENT W. C. BATES.

21. CLASS HYMN.

WORDS BY ROBERT L. FROST.

Music by Beethoven.

There is a nook among the alders
Still sleeping to the cat-bird's "Hush";
 Below, a long stone-bridge is bending
Above a runnel's silent rush.

A dreamer hither often wanders
And gathers many a snow-white stone;
 He weighs them, poised upon his fingers,
Divining each one's silvery tone.

He drops them! When the stream makes music.
Fair visions with its vault-voice swell:
 And so, for us, the future rises,
As thought-stones stir our heart's "Farewell!"

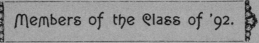

Members of the Class of '92.

Edith Mabel Andrews,
Harold Virgil Andrews,
Annie Barker,
Ella Cynthia Blood.
Harriet Wilson Carter,
Lillian Gertrude Cate,
Mary Elizabeth Anastasia Curtin,
Josephine Louise Dacy,
Timothy Joseph Daly,
Georgia May Dame,
Annie Helena Desmond,
Helen Devitt,
Beatrice Russell Doe,
Caroline Gertrude Donovan,
Ellen Genevieve Dunn,
Ellen Agnes Ford,
Robert Lee Frost,
Lueva Sargent Herrick,
Ellen Josephine Hogan,
Margaret Anastasia Lane,
Ruby Steere Littlefield,
Frank Barr McAllister,
Grace McFarlin,
Elizabeth Colbraith McIntyre,
Jennie Agnes McManus,
Catherine Gertrude O'Leary,
Charlotte Isabelle Pratt,
Thomas Joseph Shanahan,
Josephine Mabel Spaulding,
Thomas Lee Sullivan,
Harriet Reeves Warren
Ellinor Miriam White,
Mary Lillian Whittredge,
Amy Gertrude Willan,
Harriet Florence Wilson.

the American Printing House is the only printer to advertise in the *Bulletin* during Frost's editorship, it also is reasonable to assume that the American Printing House printed the *Bulletin* at that time.

Evidence supporting this conclusion is another job done for the Lawrence High School during the same period of time. An unusual stylized uncial type font appears on the front cover of the commencement exercise program for the graduating class of 1892. (Frost was co-valedictorian with Elinor M. White.) The identical font appears in the *Bulletin* advertisement for the American Printing House. And the very same font is used in the Latin motto on the front of the October 1891 issue of the *Bulletin* itself.

As editor of the Lawrence High School *Bulletin*, Robert Frost had frequent dealings with its printer. When he decided to have *Twilight* printed in an edition of only two copies, he is likely to have gone to a printer he knew well — one who would have been likely to accept such an eccentric and (to the printer) unprofitable order as a friendly favor. There are fourteen job printers listed in the Lawrence city directory for 1894; evidence points strongly to the American Printing House as the one which printed *Twilight*. The book they presumably produced may be described as follows:

Collation: 146 x 97 mm.; [1]^6; [1–12].

Contents: [1], half-title; [2], blank; [3–4], blank? [see *Note*]; [5], 'TWILIGHT'; [6–8], 'MY BUTTERFLY'; [9], 'SUMMERING'; [10], 'THE FALLS'; [11], 'AN UNHISTORIC SPOT.'; [12], blank.

Paper: Heavy, wove, antique vellum.

Binding: Red-brown (55.s.Br) pebble-grained calf. Front: Within a blind-stamped double-rule border (rule endings intersect and extend to the edges) one line gilt-stamped 'TWILIGHT'. Back: A blind-stamped double-rule border as on the front. All edges trimmed; sheets center-sewn at [1]$_{3^v.4^r}$. Wrapped around the printed gathering is a gathering of six binder's leaves — three at front, three at back — with the first and last leaves of this gathering as pastedown endpapers. The paper of this gathering is lighter, wove, vellum, watermarked with a shield containing the date '1850' over a Gothic **G**, surmounted by an arm-and-scimitar crest; and countermarked 'LINEN'.

Note: (1) Frost said that excised leaf [1]$_2$ contained a contemporary inscription from him to Elinor White.

(2) Frost inscriptions appear on the binder's leaves as follows:
    (a) Recto first front flyleaf: to Earle J. Bernheimer;
    (b) Recto second front flyleaf: to R. V. Thornton;
    (c) Verso second rear flyleaf: two lines (not in a concordance to Frost's poetry).

Although *Twilight* has gone unpublished until now, there are other elements in its bibliographical history. 'My Butterfly' was published subtitled 'An Elegy' in *The Independent* (Lawrence, Mass.), 8 November 1894. It later was collected in *A Boy's Will* (London, 1913; New York, 1915, 1934); *Collected Poems* (New York, 1930, 1939); *Complete Poems* (New York, 1949; London, 1951); *Selected Poems* (London, 1955); and in Edward Connery Lathem, ed., *The Poetry of Robert Frost* (Barre, Mass., 1971). Aside from quotations in Lawrance Thompson's *Robert Frost: The Early Years* (New York, 1966), pp. 173–74, the other poems in *Twilight* have not been published individually.

One poem and the entire book (without Frost's inscriptions) were printed subsequently. In 1947 Earle J. Bernheimer had a facsimile of 'The Falls' printed by the Ward Ritchie Press in sixty copies as a Christmas card. In 1966 a facsimile of the text of *Twilight* was printed in 170 copies by the Reynolds Company of Charlottesville, Va.: twenty copies on handmade Maidstone paper for special presentation; 150 copies for distribution to guests at a meeting of the Poetry Society of Virginia as a memento of a Frost exhibition in the Barrett Library. The title poem will be reproduced in facsimile in *Robert Frost: A Descriptive Cataglogue of Books and Manuscripts in the Clifton Waller Barrett Library.* (Charlottesville: The Associates of the University of Virginia Library, 1974).

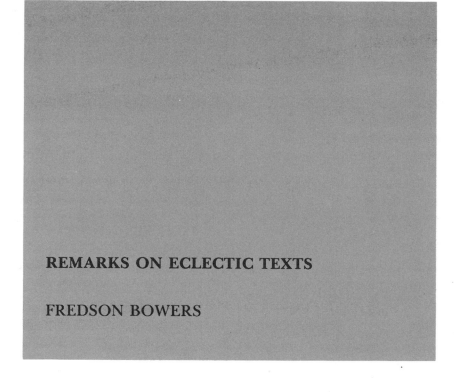

REMARKS ON ECLECTIC TEXTS

FREDSON BOWERS

AS WITH SO MANY COMMONLY-USED BUT LITTLE-ANALYZED CONCEPTS, one must grope for a definition of eclecticism in editing among popular commonplaces and general scholarly usage — not always in a technical or an informed sense — instead of appealing to a logically shaped thesis agreed upon by textual critics.* Properly, an eclectic text should be any text in which readings different from those of the document serving as the basis for the edition have selectively been admitted from other sources as substitutes for originals that, conjecturally, have been transmitted in error. This is a lengthy way of saying that any text admitting emendation of error is necessarily eclectic in the purest sense, for the principle of choice has been invoked. If we were to rest here, however, we should not be much forwarder. On the one hand

* An abridged form of this paper was read at a Conference on Editorial Problems held under the directorship of Dr. Hans Walter Gabler at the Villa Serbelloni Study and Conference Center, Bellagio, Italy, 20–25 September 1973.

we should have photographic or type facsimiles of documents, and we should also admit to this group diplomatic reprints,[1] in which no choice is given the editor to substitute readings from other documents or from editorial tradition. His function is to make available to scholars in completely trustworthy form the exact details of the text of a particular document, errors and all, to serve as a substitute in one's own study for the manuscript or book that may be preserved in some distant or inaccessible library.[2] Such reprint and facsimile editions are scholarly

[1] A diplomatic reprint may be defined as an exact transcript of a document but the text run on without consideration for the original line and page endings, whereas a type facsimile is a line-for-line and page-for-page reproduction of the original. No strict rules for such diplomatic reprints have been laid down, in fact, except for the requirement of absolute fidelity to the transcription of the substantives and accidentals of the document without anything that could properly be called emendation of the text itself as distinguished from some few of its formal typographical details. Offhand, it seems to me that a diplomatic reprint of a printed text may normalize the typography by ignoring, for example, the reproduction of display and ornamental capitals, variant spacing, and such irregularities as wrong-font types, whereas these must be reproduced in a type facsimile. The diplomatic text, of course, will not reproduce running-titles and paginal numbering or signature and catchword notation in the original, also required in a type facsimile. However, both forms of reproduction should be as responsible as a photographic facsimile for providing records of press-variation during the course of printing, for which see note 2, below.

[2] The emphasis should be on the trustworthiness of the form, which in turn is as much the product of the facsimile process as of the editor. Fine-screen offset, which has now displaced collotype for all practical scholarly purposes, is not susceptible of retouching that will alter negatives of the photographed document. On the other hand, the cheaper lithographic process that produced the inaccurate Praetorius facsimiles of Shakespeare quartos was peculiarly liable to retouching that altered the text, and a general suspicion has attached itself to the similarly produced Methuen Shakespeare Folios because of a few identified examples of manipulation. An editor, of course, in collotype or fine-screen offset may substitute leaves without warning from another copy to procure more sightly examples (as in the Lee Folio facsimile) and thus create bibliographical monstrosities because of clashing results among textual states of press-variation. Even when editors of lithographic reproductions are themselves guiltless but are negligent in supervision, serious faults may occur. The facsimile of the Yale First Folio was consistently retouched by a series of ignorant underlings, it would seem. For the extraordinary details of this modern venture, see my review in *Modern Philology*, 53 (1955): 50–57. Consistent principles for the treatment of press-variant formes must also be expected in a photographic facsimile, as well as in a type facsimile and diplomatic reprint. On this point one may consult my 'The Problem of the Variant Forme

tools but they have little or no appeal to the usual literary critic, historian, or general reader, who ordinarily will want to work with a closer approximation of what the author intended, at least verbally, than such exact reprints furnish — paradoxical as such a statement may sound, for what can be more authoritative than authority? If we hold to McKerrow's necessarily strict and narrow definition of authority, the answer is necessarily, 'nothing'. McKerrow rightly points out that authority can reside only in authoritative documents, that is, in texts that descend in some direct line from the author and do not, as a whole,[3] derive from other texts without the infusion of independent authorial alteration whether directly or through some intermediary. If this is so — and I think textual critics are unwise if they write of authority in any other terms — it follows, as McKerrow points out, that even obvious

---

in Facsimile Editions,' *The Library,* 5th ser., 7 (1952): 262–72, although C. J. K. Hinman's procedures in his Norton facsimile of the Shakespeare First Folio (1968) call for serious consideration as dealing successfully with the problems found in that document, less acute than may be encountered elsewhere.

[3] 'As a whole' is inserted here to take account of the common authorial practice of annotating an already printed edition to form the printer's copy for a revision instead of furnishing the printer with the manuscript from which the annotation was being drawn. Such a revised text is, of course, of mixed authority since part of it is derived and part of it is authoritative, consisting of the author's alterations — at least as reflected in the manuscript being used for the purpose. Thus mixed texts are susceptible of considerable variety. A scribe may copy a holograph manuscript and the author then look it over with greater or lesser care to make what corrections and revisions occur to him. This situation is also created when an author's copy is given to a professional typist. Marked copies of any non-holographic derived form, in short, having passed through another hand in a vital part of the transmission from holograph (or author's own typescript, its equivalent) are only rarely exact reproductions of the original. Moreover, the corrections and revisions an author may make in such a document are not likely to restore in every detail the exactness of the original from the styling of the transcriber, or even all of his significant verbal departures from copy. When a non-authorial hand annotates the document by reference to some source of authority, the situation is exacerbated. Indeed, unless the author furnished the document on which annotation is to be based, it is possible that inferior readings may enter the text under the guise of revision. That is, the scribe may take as his authority what is actually a document early in the history of the text and therefore in a state that the author has rejected. Hence a non-authorial intermediary in the revision of a text is always subject to suspicion not alone on questions of his accuracy but also because the authority of the documents used may be in doubt.

errors are authoritative and their corrections, no matter how judicious, are without authority according to the definition.[4]

The tribe of editors has grown up to fulfill the requirements of the majority of scholarly purchasers of texts for general purposes, those who find more useful to their needs a text soundly corrected by editorial expertise than one of pure documentary authority with all its errors. Depending upon the nature and extent of the apparatus, it may not be a misnomer to state on the title page that the scholar who has supervised the production of a photographic or type facsimile has 'edited' it, but the strict view of an editor is one who edits, that is, one who does his best to restore the purity of the author's text from the imperfection of the preserved transmissional documents even when these may include the author's holograph.[5] In the simplest cases this restriction of meaning may require no more than enlightened emendation of established errors in the original. In the most complex, when more than one authoritative document is preserved, editing may involve highly sophisticated critical and bibliographical choices among the various authorities not only to weed out error in the basic document chosen to represent the text, in the main, but also to ensure that the latest — if possible the final — readings representing the author's most comprehensive intentions have been introduced.

The aim of a critical edition, remarks McKerrow, is to reconstruct as nearly as is possible from the preserved documents what would have been an author's careful fair copy of his work.[6] One must comment that this ideal edition envisages a careful fair copy of the latest and most comprehensive form and in any case is a theoretical concept although a generally useful one even in cases where an author has revised proof after submitting a careful fair copy to the printer. In most examples the deficiencies of the preserved documents (especially if printed) will prevent a reconstruction as minute as the recovery of every detail of the accidentals of an author's lost holograph; neverthe-

---

[4] R. B. McKerrow, *Prolegomena to the Oxford Shakespeare* (Clarendon Press, 1939), p. 12.

[5] The more useful meanings of 'edit' are often obscured in these days of commercial scholarship by the misapplication of the term on titlepages of paperback reprints, stated to be 'Edited by Professor X.' It is rare that this 'editing' consists in more than the writing of a popular introduction and the furnishing the printer with some previous edition out of copyright, without investigation of its readings and usually with no alterations. Most readers of these paperbacks do not understand the distinction and believe the text has a value that it does not possess.

[6] *Prolegomena*, p. 6.

less, a fully worth-while result may usually be obtained for the substantives and enough progress made with the accidentals to justify the effort.[7] For instance, when Henry Fielding's publisher gave him a copy of the third edition of *Tom Jones* to annotate as printer's copy for the revised fourth edition, the decision to choose the third edition was made on practical grounds, for the fourth was to be a general paginal reprint of the third, which in its turn had been a typographically condensed version in four volumes of the six volumes of the first and second editions. It was fortunate that the third was a reprint of the first, not of the second, edition, but even so it had created fresh errors of its own which Fielding failed to correct so that these unauthoritative variants became inextricably mixed in the fourth edition with Fielding's own revisions. Not quite inextricably, of course, when the work is properly edited, for these errors can be isolated and removed by a scholar who can exercise more care than did Fielding in surveying the text. Moreover, since Fielding did not read proof on the fourth edition, apparently, new mistakes by the compositors were added to the existing underlay of error. It follows that the first step in the process of clarifying the text is for the editor to reconstruct as best he can the annotated copy of the third edition as it left Fielding's hands for the printer. But he may not stop there, for he must then do what the author did not do, which is to remove the third-edition errors that Fielding had perpetuated by passing them over without knowing that these were indeed printer's variants from his original manuscript as represented by the first edition.

For substantives, therefore, an editor in effect creates a text that would have resulted if Fielding had annotated a copy of the purer first instead of the more corrupt third edition. If he then follows Sir Walter Greg's principles of copy-text,[8] as he should for this book, he will reject all the accidentals in the fourth edition that in his opinion vary

---

[7] *Substantives* are the words of a text as meaningful units. The *accidents* of a text — or its *accidentals* — are the spellings, capitalizations, punctuation, word-division, contractions, and emphases in which these substantives are clothed. Of course, on occasion an accidental can have a vital effect on the transmission of meaning, even changing white to black, in which case it is convenient to distinguish it as a *semi-substantive.*

[8] 'The Rationale of Copy-Text,' *Studies in Bibliography,* 3 (1950–51): 19–36, reprinted in W. W. Greg, *Collected Papers,* ed. J. C. Maxwell (Clarendon Press, 1966), pp. 374–91. This classic and definitive statement for early texts is resurveyed, principally for its pertinence to modern conditions, in Bowers, 'Multiple Authority: New Problems and Concepts of Copy-Text,' *The Library,* 5 ser., 27 (1972): 81–115.

from the first by reason of annotation,[9] and thus he will end by substituting the revised fourth-edition variant substantives for those of the
first but incorporating them in the texture of the spelling, punctuation,
capitalization, word division, contraction, and emphasis of the most
authoritative document for these, the first edition set directly from
holograph. Behind this edition he cannot go in respect to these accidentals, but experience suggests that they will retain a number of
personal characteristics of the author that are worn away by the successive restylings of later editions. Finally, the editor must attack the
problem of printer's errors in the first edition passed on to the third
and unaltered in the fourth; having emended these and conservatively
clarified the first-edition accidental texture when faulty according to
its own standards, he can offer an ideal text of Fielding's last recorded
intentions. This will not be an exact reconstruction of what a careful
fair-copy holograph would have been like (for the original holograph
is lost that would have furnished the basis for such a detailed recovery),
but instead the closest reconstitution that the preserved documents
permit of what would have been its major features, generally comprehensive for the substantives and at least approximate for the accidentals. When the intermediate step of reconstructing the annotated third
edition has progressed to the final transfer of the identified revisions
to make up a hypothetical reconstruction of the similar annotation of
a first edition, the modern critical edition enters the realm of the ideal
and leaves the evidential world of the material in which such a document never existed. But since McKerrow's definition of a critical edition is itself an ideal and even in the simplest cases of single-text
authority requires that process of reconstruction furnished by emendation, the difference is one only of degree and not of kind. If one
swallows the gnat, one might as well swallow the camel.

It is obvious that a critical text of *Tom Jones* is at a far remove from
any text that a type or photographic facsimile could present. If one
reproduced the first edition, not alone its compositorial errors would
be embalmed but also all of Fielding's desired later revisions would
be omitted. If one reproduced the fourth edition, the reader would
unwittingly accept scores of plausible third-edition corruptions as part

[9] Less, of course, all necessary corrections made either in the terminal second or in the derived third edition, regardless of their source when they are
of a nature as to be made in normal course and independently in any careful
scholarly edition of the work.

of the authorial intention,[10] as well as fresh compositorial errors, and in addition a texture of accidentals at three removes from those of the holograph. Also, a part of the Man of the Hill episode that by an accident was unrevised would be presented in the midst of a revised edition.[11] A reprint edition, or a facsimile, of the first edition, then, would give a reasonably but not fully accurate picture of Fielding's original intentions (provided the errata list variants were substituted in the first five volumes for the original misprints or rejected readings) but would be silent on his more sophisticated stylistic and artistic second thoughts. A reprint of the only fully revised edition, the fourth, would provide these final intentions (except for the Man of the Hill) but so intermixed with an accumulation of transmissional error as to be an untrustworthy witness for critical study. Some critics — especially among the amateur explorers of the jungles of textual criticism of American literature, but also in England — would adopt the aesthetic attitude that each of the two editions is an artistic entity in itself that must be preserved without the intermingling of eclectic editing that joins the best features of both.[12] *Tom Jones* is a long novel. One may grant that there could be a pleasure in reading both versions separately for whatever flavor and general impressions an aesthetic critic might absorb on an overall basis for each text. (Precious little,

[10] That these errors would have been approved by Fielding since he passed them (although in ignorance) is a textual concept sometimes advanced in other connections but one that logically dwells in cloud-cuckoo-land. The case is quite different from Pound's conscious and expressed preference (whether or not perverse) in one of the *Cantos* for a printer's error over what he had written and his incorporation in later editions of this originally unauthoritative variant now given authority.

[11] The complex history of *Tom Jones,* and its implications, will be found in the Wesleyan Edition of Fielding, edited by F. Bowers with Critical Introduction and Commentary by Martin C. Battestin (Wesleyan University Press and Clarendon, 1974).

[12] This extreme view about works of American Literature is adopted by Donald Pizer in 'On the Editing of Modern American Texts,' *Bulletin of the New York Public Library,* 75 (March 1971): 149–50. For answers to this rejection of eclectic texts as scholarly tools, see Norman Grabo, 'Pizer on Copy-Text,' *NYPBL,* 75 (April 1971): 171–73; Hershel Parker, 'In Defense of Copy-Text Editing,' *NYPBL,* 75 (October 1971): 337–44; and Bowers, 'Multiple Authority,' *op. cit.,* pp. 86–87, n. 11. See also note 28, below. For other anti-eclectic arguments, see Pizer in *Fifteen American Authors Before 1900,* ed. R. A. Rees and E. N. Harbert (University of Wisconsin Press, 1971), p. 100, and *MP,* 68 (1970): 212–14.

in fact.) *Roderick Hudson* or *The Portrait of a Lady* and the revisions of its fourth edition have quite other purposes than the thorough reworking of concept and texture that Henry James performed on his early work for the New York Edition. There is no argument that some of these James novels require parallel texts or separate editions; but neither a text of the first nor of the fourth edition of *Tom Jones* (without a table of variants that for the accidentals would be impossible) would be suitable for detailed study of the work as a whole. Thus it is probable that ordinary mortals will continue to prefer McKerrow's concept of an ideal edition that attempts to offer a composite text of *Tom Jones* that is closest to what the author would have secured if the printer had produced an exact corrected reprint of the first edition that incorporated his later revisions. This is not the equivalent in all its details of an authorial fair copy, but it is the farthest reach in the pursuit of this ideal that the preserved documents permit. Literary or other works so different in their forms in different editions as to represent quite distinctive artistic concepts are not here in question,[13] and textual theories based on their unique status merely serve to muddy the waters.

Not all texts by any means require the eclectic treatment suggested here as necessary for *Tom Jones*. The question then arises whether every text to which the McKerrow doctrine of ideal edition can be applied is necessarily eclectic. I suggest that such application creates too broad a criterion to be useful. It is true that viewed with extreme narrowness any text that admits emendation is eclectic in comparison with the rigorously non-emending principle applied to facsimile or diplomatic-reprint texts. But the spectrum of edited texts is too broad in its variety for any one point of view to be valid, even though it can be argued, and I think successfully, that it is proper to apply the McKerrow definition of ideal edition to the most limited textual situation of all, that

---

[13] Not in question here or elsewhere in the present study is the special problem of modern plays and the manner in which the original text accepted by the producer will be substantially rewritten in a communal manner on the battlefield of rehearsals, so much so indeed that a dramatist may feel impelled to publish his own 'literary' version of the play in competition with that of the final acting script. For a discussion of the problems and some illustrations, see L. A. Beaurline, '*The Glass Menagerie:* From Story to Play,' *Modern Drama*, 8 (1965): 142–49; but especially 'The Director, the Script, and Author's Revisions: A Critical Problem,' *Papers in Dramatic Theory and Criticism*, edited by D. M. Knauf (1969), pp. 78–91.

in which only a single edition (or document) exists, for any editorial alteration of the copy-text here would certainly represent an attempt to restore readings that the editor believed were correct and therefore would have appeared in a careful authorial fair copy.

We may start with the general proposition that an eclectic text should be defined more narrowly than the admission of alteration from some external source. The first step in the process of definition is to look into the varieties of emendation made in single-text works — that is, material that has been found to exist in no more than a single authoritative document. If only one early edition of the text has been published, emendations will necessarily come from the editorial tradition. Those who mistrust eclecticism are not ordinarily perturbed by such emendation,[14] but it might be possible to regard as an eclectic operation an editorial choice of variants drawn from other early editions although these are reprints without authority. Here we ought to be clearsighted enough to admit that, *au fond,* no real distinction holds between an editor's own emendations not found in some documentary source and those that are present in early though unauthoritative forms of the text, as, for instance, in Shakespeare's Second, Third, and Fourth Folios. The notion that early forms of a text, even though mere reprints, have some vague 'secondary authority' was prevalent in eighteenth-century Shakespearean textual criticism when the derivation of the printed texts one from another was not really understood and had not been established. But authority is authority. Authority can derive only from the author. Since neither Shakespeare himself nor independently derived forms of his papers had anything to do with the Second Folio text of *All's Well That Ends Well,* it makes no basic difference for the value or the rightness of the emendation whether the First Folio error *there was never Virgin goe, till virginitie was first lost* (TLN 133–134) is corrected to *never Virgin got* by some editor's own estimate of the sense or else by that of the Second Folio compositor's. Since I have a respect for the historical details of the transmission of a text, I should myself always record the Second Folio as the originator of the corrected reading — one, incidentally, which has never been chal-

---

[14] In fact, it is interesting to contemplate how much eclectic editing of Shakespeare (where it is the normal method) is swallowed without comment by the most rigid adherents of faithful reprints of one authority in American literature and among English scholars in relation to nineteenth-century works. *Hamlet* and *King Lear* are excellent examples of eclectic texts constructed from multiple authority.

lenged — but in no sense should such a notation be taken to imply that the Second Folio gives the emendation any more weight in the conjectural recovery of the word in Shakespeare's manuscript than, for instance, Theobald's unchallenged *loneliness* for the reading of the first four Folios, *now I see | The mistris of your louelinesse* [i.e., *lovelinesse*], *and find your salt teares head* (TLN 497–499). In either case one must apply McKerrow's strict definition of authority as limited to what an authoritative document reads, whether sense or nonsense. In this light whether the Second Folio or an eighteenth-century editor conjectures that *got* and *loneliness* are the right readings has no bearing whatever on the question of their correctness, for in such a case correctness and demonstrable authority are not synonymous.

If simple substantive emendation of a single-text authority is not to be taken as producing eclecticism except in the very limited sense that the strict reprint pattern has been broken, then of course the correction of faulty accidentals in a similar manner must come under the same head. Most editors of old-spelling editions content themselves with the correction of what appear to be errors and of serious ambiguities that might puzzle even an informed reader. In some texts, however, another kind of correction is possible. McKerrow once speculated on the possiblity of normalizing Shakespearean accidentals not by modernizing but by a system that would bring them into agreement according to their own standard; but he concluded that such a feat was impossible because of our lack of sufficient linguistic or philological knowledge to perform the task. This passage is one of several in the *Prolegomena* that exhibit what may be some basic confusion of idea or else an insufficiently worked-out though defensible notion.

I have long been interested in the problem of the limits of normalization possible both in early and in late texts and my sympathies lie in this direction. But in the Elizabethan period the lack of uniformity of spelling found in almost every author makes desperate any attempt, at least in a single-text work, to penetrate the screen of possible scribal transcription and then of the styling of perhaps several compositors working on the same text.[15] Even a project to normalize the accidental

---

[15] Actually, the presence of several compositors offers evidence not otherwise available to penetrate to some degree the characteristics of the underlying copy if one makes the assumption that common characteristics result from common copy, at least when these characteristics are normally variable according to compositors. For example, in Shakespeare's *Measure for Measure* in the First Folio, set by compositors from idiosyncratic copy transcribed by Ralph

characteristics of a single compositor would be defeated by the hard fact that most compositors in the sixteenth and early seventeenth centuries in England had relatively few invariable spellings when options were open, although they used a number of more or less preferential forms, and their punctuation system was on occasion so much affected by the relative quantity of sorts in the type cases as to make the distinction, say, between a semicolon and a colon sometimes as much a matter of mechanical supply as of rhetorical convention. If Compositor B in the First Folio *Julius Caesar* sets an apostrophe in *'tis* with relative consistency but omits perhaps two or three, I see no harm in supplying the few missing ones by recorded emendation, although I would see harm in an old-spelling text if he had had no conviction in the matter or had had even just a general preference for the apostrophe. We have no means, of course, of knowing whether or not the apostrophe in *'tis* was customary in the manuscript of *Julius Caesar* from which Compositor B was setting. Even if we did we should be no wiser about Shakespeare's own practice, for the printer's-copy manuscript was almost certainly a scribal one except, just possibly, for one or two hundred or so lines of holograph in two revised sections. Thus if one added an apostrophe or two to make B consistent, in no sense could one believe in the recovery of the lost holograph, as one does in substituting *got* for *goe* in *All's Well*. Instead, one is merely normalizing a minor feature of the accidentals to make it accord with the usual compositorial pattern. An editor's ability to do anything significant in this direction in a Shakespearean text is at present strictly limited.[16]

Crane, each compositor exhibits the frequent use of parentheses and the occasional Jonsonian apostrophus known to be characteristic of Crane. Thus the case is stronger for an underlying Crane manuscript than if only one compositor had set the play, for it would then have to be demonstrated that these were not this particular compositor's own characteristics that he had imposed on the copy.

[16] As another example of fruitless attempt at normalizing an Elizabethan text one may take the problem of the capitalization of titles in Q1 of *Richard II*. Here one compositor normally capitalizes such titles of *King, Liege, Sovereign, Duke,* and so on, whereas the second compositor is mixed in his habits and often leaves them uncapitalized. If an old-spelling editor were to emend all non-capitalization in the work of this compositor in order to make him correspond with the other, he would be violating a compositorial characteristic (not firmly established as the result of type shortage) in only one matter while neglecting dozens of others. Nor could the restoration of the characteristics of the underlying copy be adduced as a reason for this isolated attempt, for

As for the possibilities of true reconstruction, few early authors have left us sufficient holograph material to serve as a proper basis for selection of their accidental characteristics from the conflicting evidence presented in the prints. McKerrow, however, seems to have been thinking less of an authentic reconstruction of authorial characteristics than of the possibility of adopting a kind of standard Elizabethan that could be applied to any author, somewhat in the manner that editors may normalize Middle English texts. The virtues of such normalization are arguable, and McKerrow never took the subject seriously enough to move beyond his speculative remark. (The edition of Samuel Johnson published by the Yale University Press has drifted unsystematically in this direction with deleterious results, although it is evident that the editors have in fact been concerned with partially modernizing the text and not with standardizing it according to eighteenth-century practices.

On the contrary, once the language and its accidentals have become relatively standardized by the nineteenth century, certain forms of normalization may be contemplated in 'old-spelling'[17] texts when enough manuscripts of the author close to the date are preserved to give an editor confidence that in at least some features (although by no means in all) he can recover the characteristics of an underlying lost holograph. I am not suggesting that an editor rewrite the text in respect to its accidentals as he fancies the author would have written them if a manuscript had been preserved. But some small though significantly useful normalizing of consistent authorial characteristics can be managed in certain circumstances if an editor is prepared to agree to a few key rules to ensure some appeal always to authority in the copy-text, or another authoritative document of the same text, to back up the nature of the alterations, as the recent editions of Nathaniel Hawthorne and of Stephen Crane will illustrate.[18]

---

we have no means of knowing what the manuscript read. It is just as possible that the one compositor imposed capitals on his uncapitalized copy more frequently than the other as that the other compositor reduced from time to time his capitalized copy.

[17] One wishes that another phrase could be found to apply to the editions of books from the nineteenth century that conform in their accidentals to the original copy-texts. Perhaps *copy-text form editions* would do — better certainly than *author-form editions* — although a superior phrase is no doubt suspended in someone else's consciousness.

[18] References throughout this paper to Stephen Crane's texts are to the *Works,* published by the University Press of Virginia; Hawthorne's texts are

I doubt very much that normalizing of this kind produces a true eclectic text even if the emendations — although they restore conjectural departures of a compositor from his copy — can scarcely be said to repair errors in the sense that Theobald's *loneliness* corrects the error *lovelinesse*. Ultimately, the full control of an editor over the accidentals, as in a modernized Shakespeare — or a modernized Hawthorne that imposes present day standards of light punctuation on an author who preferred intricate parenthetical comma constructions — seems to me also to have nothing basic to do with eclecticism. The original has been vastly altered, and choices have been made of what does and what does not need modernizing, but no suggestion can hold that the resulting selection is likely to restore the accidentals that the author himself would have written. On the contrary. Accordingly, in the last analysis the selective process of modernization is as arbitrary as an emendation of whatever kind when it is made in a single-text work. Nothing that is done in this textual situation can have authority; hence I query whether eclecticism is possible under these circumstances. As for normalization of accidentals according to the author's own system, in a single-text situation the authority comes from analogy with preferred characteristics elsewhere within the same document. Thus no conflation with another authoritative document is taking place, and no eclecticism results. It should be possible, then, to exclude single-authority texts from consideration. They cannot be edited in an eclectic manner because no combination with another authority is possible.

I am not an historian of textual criticism, but my understanding is

---

cited in the Centenary Edition published by the Ohio State University Press. Briefly, the important rule is that the document itself being edited must be variant so that one form of the variant is recognizably authorial and the other, then, presumably compositorial in origin. It is obvious that spelling and word-division can often be normalized in this manner, but questions of enforcing uniformity on punctuation habits is far trickier owing to the fact that most authors are not themselves invariably consistent, and also their habits may change with the years. Author will differ from author in all these respects. However, some occasional characteristics like Crane's use of a colon to introduce dialogue may prove to be practically invariable in the manuscripts, and in general his punctuation (or rather non-punctuation) of adjectives in a series can be forecast, as well as his lack of a comma before the *and* of the final element in a series. Hyphenated compounds versus unhyphenated are usually a solvable problem. It seems to me improper to normalize a text in respect of these characteristics when they are not present in variant form in the document being edited and hence no evidence can be offered other than opinion that they existed in its copy.

that in the early days of scholarship the recovery of texts was often an eclectic process. In biblical and in classical scholarship one is often confronted by a large group of manuscripts of uncertain origin, inter-connection, and date, manuscripts that can seldom be totally excluded from authority the way in which the Shakespeare Second Folio can be excluded. Even in a bad and generally corrupt manuscript, or even in an almost totally derived one, if contamination — or cross relationship with another line — is suspected as present, the theoretical and some-times the practical possibility always exists that some one reading may have been transmitted in its purity although corrupted in other docu-ments. For many years, thus, all documents were thought, in essence, to be of substantial authority; and even if some were distinguished as of primary and others of secondary authority, the difference was a vague one and in any isolated crux an editor could pick and choose among variants according to his personal taste with small regard for the often unsolved questions of derivation, date, and evidence of au-thority. The process was greatly aided, also, by the custom of modern-izing the accidentals of the texts, or at least of normalizing them according to some arbitrarily selected document. It was to counteract the lack of principle inherent in this essentially subjective form of editing that, as I understand it, Lachmann became the proponent of the most-authoritative-manuscript hypothesis, from which divergence was to be accepted only with what may be described as extraordinary reluctance. In this manner the most important effort of the editor was diverted to the selection of a text to reprint and away from the treat-ment of that text after its selection. Again as I understand it, the classical scholar A. E. Housman so devastatingly criticized the results of a rigid adherence to this principle as markedly to reduce its value as a scholarly panacea. I am not here concerned with biblical, classical, or medieval vernacular manuscript texts to which these theories apply, and so I wish to avoid the editorial quicksands of a form of editorial problem with which I have had no practical experience. My point even in raising it is to suggest two particular considerations: (1) The distrust of eclecticism in editing has an historical basis in the treatment of material that is not really in question with us since it is not, in general, subject to what can properly be called bibliographical analysis as are most textual problems from the Renaissance to the present day that involve the printing process. Thus it is worth emancipating ourselves from prejudices about eclectic texts inherited from a past inapplicable to our present concerns, which are devoted to texts that are printed, or are mixed manuscript and printed, dating roughly from the sixteenth century to the present. (2) In retrospect it seems clear that the controversy about this earlier eclectic editing proved to be less about its principle than about the abuses in its practice which had been confused with its principle.

The principle was clear enough: it was no more than an attempt to recover a lost original by reconciling the evidence of multiple authorities. When joined in old-spelling texts with the important theory governing copy-texts, this early principle is perfectly operative today in controlled bibliographical situations. The treatment of multiple authority, I suggest, is the operative key to all questions of eclectic texts and their formation. It is proper, then, to examine some standard situations in which multiple authority evolves. A text may be said to exist in multiple authorities when more than one document is preserved that derives ultimately from the author's holograph and not in its entirety — immediately or with lost antecedents — from some other preserved document. In the period with which we are concerned the standard examples involve two central situations: first, the recovery of the author's intentions from more than one authoritative document when variants in the different witnesses result exclusively from the transmissional process and not from authorial revision; second, the recovery of an author's intentions when one or more of the preserved multiple documents represents a revised or variant text — that is, some other authorial form of the text than that contained within a single holograph not thereafter altered by the author in itself or in some derived (or, earlier, in some antecedent) form.

The examples of the first situation may serve to illustrate those texts in which the problem centers on the recovery of the author's original intentions only. The limbs of the family tree that can be drawn are likely to radiate from the X, the lost archetype, in as many independent lines as there are preserved documents. The simplest illustration may be drawn from the newspaper syndication of an author's work. Here the customary process (when it is not sent out in boilerplate) is to typeset X, the author's manuscript or a derived typescript, and to mail proofs pulled from this master typesetting to subscribing newspapers which in turn use these identical proofs as copy for their own compositors. When the proofs are indeed identical,[19] each newspaper is at an

[19] This is the normal assumption. That a few anomalies in Crane's newspaper syndication may go back to proof somewhat altered between pulls is only a suspicion. One or two cases exist, however, in which the Nebraska *State Journal* set up the master proof, mailed it out, and then printed the article in its own columns from the same typesetting but slightly edited. Of course, this

equal distance from the same master copy and thus of precisely equal authority. It follows that the central problem is one of recovering the lost proofs by stripping away the unauthoritative variation in the different newspaper texts and arriving at what general consensus should establish was the form of the common copy, the proofs. Given even relatively few witnesses, something close to one hundred percent accuracy in establishing the substantives is certainly possible. The accidentals are more difficult to recover than the substantives, and the difficulty is increased if enough holographic material to guide the editor to a knowledge of the author's characteristics has not been preserved. Stephen Crane's 'An Impression of the Concert' (1897) about the fleet of the allied powers at Crete during the Greco-Turkish War is an example. Eight newspaper versions are known, all stemming from an identical set of proofs syndicated from New York by the S. S. McClure Co. With only a handful of doubtful accidental readings, it is possible to reconstruct these proofs from the variable evidence of the witnesses with almost absolute and demonstrable accuracy. The result is certainly eclectic in that on sufficient evidence the readings of some authorities are rejected and others accepted and the final result is a composite text that in all its details reproduces no single one of the authorities. However, one may remark that no logical reason exists to favor any one of these eight authorities over the others, for all are at the same transmissional distance from their common source. Obviously some of these newspapers reproduce the basic proof more faithfully than others. Nevertheless, no bibliographically determinable reason can be found for this diversity save for the care or carelessness of a number of unknown compositors, and the fact itself cannot be determined until the collation of variants has been analyzed and a composite text arrived at from its evidence. Hence under usual circumstances the generally determined superior fidelity of one newspaper to its source has no bearing on the editor's reconstruction of the text, for in this process one authority is not ordinarily matched against another on a qualitative basis. In this sense, the final composite text can scarcely be said to be based on any one of the documents except

---

represents a very special situation. In another special situation, the newspaper syndication of Crane's *The Red Badge of Courage* came from identical proofs, but one late reprinter — the San Francisco *Examiner* — somehow got hold of a copy of the more complete book proofs and in part conflated the two versions.

arbitrarily. Given the opportunity to print his reconstructed text of the basic proof, at one nearer remove to holograph than any preserved witness, an editor would be singularly narrow-minded to select, instead, the most generally correct of the newspapers and to reprint that as it stood, in the name of pedantry.

A more elementary but essentially similar situation occurs — especially in international publication — when an author's typescript may be set in one country from the ribbon copy and in another country from the exact duplicate represented by the carbon copy of the typescript, or in these days from electroprints. The example of Crane's short story 'The Price of the Harness' (1898) may be cited. Crane wrote the manuscript in October 1898, when he was living in Havana immediately after the end of the Spanish-American war. He mailed the manuscript to his agent Paul Reynolds in New York, who had a typescript and a carbon made up. One copy he sold to the *Cosmopolitan* magazine in the United States and the other to *Blackwood's* in England, both of which printed the story in December. This is close to a laboratory case in its purity, for Crane's isolation prevented him from correcting the typescript or reading proof. Variants between the two magazine texts are exclusively transmissional, therefore, with no possibility of authorial revision to disturb an editor's choice. Since each magazine text is of equal authority with the other, the typescript text may be substantially recovered from the common readings supplemented in cases of variation by editorial selection from either document of what critical and philological evidence suggests were the typescript words and their forms. At least for substantives, ordinarily the reading of one or the other magazine will represent the typescript except in cases of double sophistication.[20] From this process emerges an elementary eclectic text that for the author's original intentions is superior to either of the imperfect forms of the magazines.

An example from earlier literature introduces more troublesome pre-publication problems and a lost intermediate stage in one branch of the family tree, but the principle is the same as in the illustrations from Crane — that is, essentially direct radiation in two branches from a lost archetype without authorial revision in either branch. The play *Beggars Bush* by Beaumont, Fletcher, and Massinger was first published

[20] Double sophistication may occur in theory even in texts set from an authorial manuscript, for these are not necessarily impeccable. But it usually occurs in an attempt to repair some blunder in a transmitted form of the text being used as copy, like a typescript or a syndicated proof.

in the 1647 Beaumont and Fletcher Folio but it also exists in the form of a presentation or favor manuscript. Analysis of the readings reveals the following textual history. The underlying manuscript seems to have been the fair copy sold by the dramatists to the King's Men. From this lost manuscript the book-keeper of the company (probably Edward Knight) made a prompt-book, now lost, and from this prompt-book was transcribed the preserved Lambarde manuscript, now in the Folger Shakespeare Library. On the other hand, the 1647 Folio was set directly from the fair copy, which had been preserved in the theatre. In this case the Folio branch of the family tree derives directly, without intermediary, from X, the Massinger fair copy, but the Lambarde manuscript is at two removes from the same document since the lost prompt-book intervenes. Only transmissional error appears in the Folio text except for some censorship cuts in the printing-house and the accidental loss from the manuscript of a song, probably written on a separate sheet of paper, as well as a similarly written part of an amplified scene. On the other hand, the book-holder Knight introduced a few (although a surprisingly few) attempts at reordering the impossible time scheme of the play, and these unauthoritative modifications of the original must be added to the partly inadvertent, partly sophisticating corruptions natural to the double copying, although on the whole the manuscript substantives are in better shape than those transmitted through the incompetent Compositor B of this section of the Folio. At least for the accidentals, however, and sometimes for the substantives, the unequal distance from X of the 1647 Folio and the Lambarde manuscript makes for a greater presumption of authority in the Folio; but the two Folio compositors were of unequal carefulness in their typesetting and in their ability to read the handwriting of the manuscript, and the physical deficiencies of the Folio printer's copy after the passage of years created lacunae that must be filled from the manuscript. Thus an editor concerned with recovering the authorial intentions must make eclectic use of both documents and sometimes choose readings from the more distant source both in substantives and in accidentals, since in all its readings the genetically superior Folio is by no means invariably superior to the manuscript at one farther remove.[21]

At this point it is legitimate to stop for a moment to enquire how

[21] This textually significant play in its period is printed in *The Dramatic Works in the Beaumont and Fletcher Canon*, ed. Bowers, 3 (1975). For an account of the investigation and evidence, see '*Beggars Bush:* A Reconstructed Prompt-Book and Its Copy,' *Studies in Bibliography*, 27 (1974): 113–36.

these examples of non-revised texts differ in respect to eclecticism of treatment from the texts of single authority admitting alterations from other early editions that are unauthoritative reprints as well as from editorial tradition. Both are similar in that the editorial attempt is entirely one of *correction* to recover the lost source (in whatever form that was) from which the documents immediately derive. That is, when by emendation in a single-text situation an editor alters a reading, he is correcting what must be regarded as a transmissional error and therefore conjecturally restoring the pure original. But the document or other source for the correction can have no authority, and the correction is thus basically undemonstrable even though universal approval may canonize it.[22] On the other hand, when two or more documents have equal authority, or even a relative authority stemming from their unequal distance from the archetype, multiple witnesses exist to the readings of this common source. In general one variant will be wrong and the other right (in a bibliographical situation when revision has not entered); but only in cases of relative authority is there possible even a presumption of superior rightness in one document over another, and such a presumption is often proved false in any specific application to an individual reading. When in single-text authority an emendation is made, no demonstration is possible that it actually recovers the pure source that has been corrupted. But when multiple authority exists, something close to demonstration *is* possible in ordinary cases that one variant is presumably right and the other wrong. No unauthoritative document can be a witness to the archetypal form of a work, but each independent or partly independent multiple authority can constitute such an authoritative witness since its comparison with similar witnesses serves to reconstruct its own and their immediate common source. In simple radiation no one multiple text is technically more authoritative than another; thus a true merging or conflation of witnesses results from the editorial selection of variants. Indeed, when one document has been selected as the basis for an edition and is being emended or amplified by the others, the process is often only an editorial convenience and not an inherent methodical principle. The selection from among any variation, which is the root of eclectic editing, is made almost exclusively from

---

[22] 'Universal approval' may have its temporal aspects, of course. A reading that is given common consent by one generation may two hundred years later seem in positive error or at the least of doubtful validity. However, one does what one can, and it is scarcely news that all truth is relative. Methuselah should have added editing to his other accomplishments.

variants of presumptive authority in one or other of their forms.

Further differences characterizing the two editorial situations have some bearing on eclecticism, also. For instance, the conservative editor of a single-authority text is likely to retain almost any plausible reading in the original from which sense can be made, for no demonstration may be possible that the text reading is wrong or — if wrong — that the most favored emendation is any closer to the original than the assumed error. In *All's Well That Ends Well,* for instance, the well-known crux *I see that men make rope's in such a scarre | That wee'l forsake our selves* (TLN 2063–64) is retained by most editors less on the ground that it is correct in some obscure manner than that they despair of recovering what the original read. If double authority had been present (and if the error had not originated in some post-holographic scribal copy from which both documents radiated), an editor finding, say, *take hopes in such a scare* in one of these two texts would be strongly tempted to view it as authoritative in origin and to accept it with little question, even though conscious of the possibility that it was a printer's sophistication. Demonstration that it was sophisticated could not be made, in fact, unless of three independently radiating documents from the same source two read *make rope's* and one *take hopes.*[23] It must also be remarked that, by presenting equally authoritative alternatives, variation in multiple-authority texts reveals error where it might not be suspected as present in single authorities. For example, if *Hamlet* had come down to us in only one authoritative textual line, any editor would have reprinted without hesitation either the *pitch and moment* phrase as now found in the Second Quarto, or *pith and moment* (TLN 1740) in the Folio, with no suspicion that he was perpetuating error, for each reading is plausible. Moreover, if the Folio *Hamlet,* say, had been wholly derived from the Second Quarto as a mere reprint, it is doubtful that any editor (perhaps after the mid-nineteenth century) would believe he had sufficient grounds to emend Quarto 'pitch' to Folio 'pith'.

Thus the reconstruction of a lost original by the identification and then the eclectic selection of readings among multiple authorities is ordinarily more complete than is possible for single-texts where emen-

---

[23] Of course, if the radiation were not fully independent, as from one source, but the two documents reading 'make rope's' radiated from one source and the text reading 'take hopes' from another, then 'take hopes' could be re-established as a possible authoritative reading. I may remark that I hold no brief for 'take hopes': I use it only as a convenient example.

dation alone can be the corrective agent for emendation, strictly, is always unauthoritative. This greater comprehensiveness arises partly in that multiple-text authorities will ordinarily contain the correct reading in one for the corruption in the other[24] in a form not necessarily occurring to an emender, or if so in a form so undemonstrably the correct one as to persuade him that he might as well retain the original as make what could be only sophisticated sense. For example, when Hamlet in the Quarto addresses Gertrude as *cold mother* (TLN 258), a modern editor might be uneasy about the reading but it is not certain that he would risk *good mother* if it were not that this Folio reading has independent authority. Nevertheless, the essential difference, as I see it, still remains this: In texts existing with only single authority, alteration can constitute nothing but emendation. To emend one must have some basic text to alter, a text that in this situation is automatically provided by the only available authority. On the contrary, in the purest form of multiple authority — independently radiating texts from the same lost document — it is really improper to think in terms of emendation instead of selection, for no standard exists to emend, not even a copy-text in the classic manner of single authority. All texts being equally authoritative, one cannot be 'emended' by the other. Instead, only a composite text can be constructed by the selection of variants. So far as I can reason, this is a difference that constitutes a distinction in the two textual situations.

That not all multiple-authority texts are so pure, and that some — like *Beggars Bush* — exist with one document farther removed from authority than the other, does not, I take it, alter the principle. If the arm nearer to authority — the Folio text of *Beggars Bush* — is selected as the basic text, it would be only because the principle of copy-text (which operates for accidentals when distances are unequal) dictates the choice, or else simple convenience. The substantives of the more distant document might, in fact, have been more faithfully transmitted than those of the nearer one, all depending upon the standards of fidelity maintained by the respective agents. Even the selection of a

[24] This is likely to be absolutely true only when both documents radiate from a holograph. Radiation from a typescript derived from the holograph may produce authority and lack of authority, but also two different attempts to patch manifest error. And derivation from two different sources may produce the same situation. However, even under the worst of conditions a general presumption of authority in one or other form of a variant reading will normally be justified.

copy-text from the nearer document may not always guarantee what are actually the most authoritative accidentals. In Stephen Crane's novel *The Third Violet* (1897) the accidentals of the book form are immediately derived from the professional typescript that was the printer's copy, whereas any one of the newspaper versions derives from the carbon of this typescript only through a lost intermediate syndicate proof. Yet because of the heavy house styling given the book text in comparison with the relatively naive following of copy in the lost proof, an editor familiar with Crane's characteristics will recognize that on an overall basis any one of the newspapers radiating from this proof is likely to be closer in its accidentals to the typescript version of the lost holograph than is the nearer book.[25] But to return to the central thesis — an editor constructs a single-authority text by emending the only standard he has, which is the earliest version. In contrast, an editor confronted with multiple authorities usually has no standard on which he can rely from the start (except presumptively), even in ordinary cases of unequal distance from the archetype in the several branches of the family tree. If he finally comes to estimate one document as more reliable than another, it is only after the facts, and his text, have been decided upon by the eclectic process and he has distinguished the relative faithfulness of each document to his ideal composite. Under these circumstances it is a misconception to think in terms of emending one text by another. Even when a copy-text is finally chosen, the document so selected is only a peg on which to hang the apparatus of variation;[26] under no circumstances can this document

[25] Ordinarily the substantives of the book form of *The Third Violet* reflect the considerable revision that Crane gave its typescript copy after he had sent off the carbon to the newspapers. However, the choice of the book form from among variant substantives is not an inevitable one. The book has its share of compositorial errors not caught in proof. In addition, mixed in with Crane's own authoritative revision of the typescript is a layer of editorial and compositorial alteration of his more strikingly odd idiom and syntax which an editor can detect by comparison with the characteristic forms of the newspapers.

[26] This view is elaborated in my 'Multiple Authority,' *op. cit.,* p. 101 ff. More recently, G. T. Tanselle has put forward an interesting proposal for a form of apparatus to deal with such multiple-authority texts. Here instead of one list of alterations made by the editor in the copy-text and a separate historical collation of rejected readings from the collated authorities, Dr. Tanselle proposes only one amalgamated list without reference to any copy-text but showing the variation of all authorities from the edited text alone. See his 'Editorial Apparatus for Radiating Texts,' forthcoming in the *Library.* The theory seems logically planned. I have not had the opportunity to test it in practice.

be taken as the standard, in a single-authority sense, which is to be emended to produce the final text. Copy-texts are chosen for the authority of their accidentals — not for the authority of their substantives.

An author's revision of his work, the two or more stages preserved by multiple authorities, provokes the most serious editorial problems. The manner in which revision may be accomplished takes a number of forms and is seldom pure since it is often mixed with correction, but the two main situations that affect editorial method may be identified as pre-publication and post-publication.

In post-publication revision two or more documents showing the original and the revised shapes of the text are likely to be in linear relationship. The examples must be few and far between (save for such thorough recasting as took place in the manuscripts of Wordsworth's *Prelude*) in which an author so heavily revises an already published work of any length as to require an entirely new holograph manuscript as an independent act of creation. Ordinarily he annotates and interleaves an earlier printed form, not always the best edition by modern standards of authority, as Fielding worked over a set of the third edition of *Tom Jones* to make up printer's copy for the revised fourth edition. Since the basic copy revised was the third, the fourth edition is in linear relationship to it, for it derives immediately from the third except for the specific authorial revisions. In linear relationships like this, the agent for the fresh authority entering the text may not be the author himself. Instead, a copy of an early printed edition may be brought into general conformity with some example of an authorial manuscript (or a copy thereof at any remove) by a scribe. It seems firmly established, for instance, that when Jaggard found copyright problems had arisen about a simple reprint of the Quarto text of *Troilus and Cressida* for the Folio, he had a quarto annotated by reference to a manuscript preserved in the theater that was in a different stage of composition or revision from that underlying the Quarto. The theater's manuscript itself was not set by Jaggard but instead this marked-up printed copy was prepared, which his compositors preferred. As a consequence, the nature of the Folio *Troilus and Cressida* is mixed. In some part it derives linearly from the Quarto, which was its physical copy. In some part its variants from the Quarto reflect the annotation from the theater manuscript plus scribal error. In some part, like the fourth edition of *Tom Jones,* a proportion of the variants are unauthoritative because they originated with the later compositors.

Once these unauthoritative variants are identified and removed from the *Tom Jones* text, and once the third-edition departures from first-edition copy are removed from the fourth edition, the fourth-edition substantives may be said to represent Fielding's final intentions save for first-edition errors that he did not notice and correct. On the other hand, when some agent other than the author is the corrector, the situation changes and the authority of the revised edition is materially reduced. The scribe's collation of printed edition with manuscript will almost inevitably be imperfect so that not every authorial variant is transferred to the printer's copy. It seems reasonably evident in *Hamlet* that the repetition in the Folio of the Second Quarto reading *a good kissing carrion* (TLN 1219) — universally corrected to Warburton's *a god kissing carrion* — resulted from the scribe's error in passing over a variant, granting the hypothesis that the Folio printer's copy was an annotated Second Quarto. Sins of commission will be found as well, as when a scribe mistakes an author's handwriting or his intention and with his best will either alters a correct reading in the print to a corrupt one, or inadvertently makes a faulty correction that does not reproduce the original in the manuscript. Then there is always the question of the faithful transfer of corruptions from the manuscript being compared if it is a derived one, or even if it happens to be in an earlier state than the manuscript behind the copy being annotated, as has been suggested may be true for *Troilus and Cressida*. Moreover, as happened in *Doctor Faustus,* a scribe may take it upon himself to 'improve' the copy. When an author is not personally involved in the preparation of revised printer's copy, massive corruption can follow an attempt at revision if a document at some remove from the author and thus itself corrupt and sophisticated is used as the correcting agent. The sophistication of the Folio text of Shakespeare's *2 Henry IV* in comparison to the Quarto is so extensive as to lead to queries whether an annotated quarto or a fresh manuscript were the Folio printer's copy; and it is moot how much of the Folio variant text is composed of sophisticating attempts at correction (probably in the manuscript being utilized), how much of purer readings transmitted correctly in the Folio underlying copy, and how much of authorial variants that hypothetically could have been present in this copy. Thus when an agent other than the author is charged with annotating a printed edition to prepare copy for a new edition, a mixture of authority results owing in some part to the non-authority of the agent's departures from copy but also to the superimposition in a post-publication stage of readings from a source that originated in the pre-publication stage and may or may not be superior as a whole or in some of its parts to the source of the original printed edition.

When an author is the revising agent as in *Tom Jones* or in *Joseph Andrews,* or as in the philosopher William James's revision of earlier journal articles for book collection, a reprint of the revised form will on the whole be roughly satisfactory for the substantives; and in this respect it may seem to be only a semantic distinction whether in *Tom Jones* an eclectic text is being constructed by merging the selected revised readings from the fourth with the first-edition substantives, or whether the fourth-edition substantives are being corrected (in a non-eclectic manner) by reference to the first edition and to the transmissional history of the substantives in the third edition. Perhaps in such an example a considerable part of the case for eclectic versus non-eclectic editing — at least in the popular sense — could be argued as resting on the question of the copy-text chosen. If *contra* Greg's principles the fourth edition of *Tom Jones* or the Folio edition of *Hamlet* were selected as copy-text, then at first sight it would seem more logical to take it that variants introduced from the first edition and from the Second Quarto are corrections of transmissional error (including a stage of pre-publication transmission for *Hamlet*) than that they create an eclectic composite of two texts. On the other hand, if Greg's theory of copy-text is observed and the selected revised and corrected substantives of the fourth edition and of the Folio are merged with the accidentals of the earlier editions, then even in a popular sense the fact of eclectic editing cannot be avoided. However, that the question of copy-text cannot truly affect the situation should be apparent when it is considered that the choice of copy-text affects accidentals but not substantives and it is the substantives that must be in question. Thus if my definition of eclectic editing as the selection of variants between two or more authoritative texts is valid, the revision of an earlier publication to produce a linear-derived document serving as printer's copy must always represent the merging of authority with authority. The authority of the earliest edition may be strong owing to its immediate relation to a holograph as is true for *Tom Jones* and very likely for the Second Quarto of *Hamlet,* or it may be weak as in the case of Elizabethan bad quartos ranging from *The Merry Wives of Windsor* to *Richard III* and *King Lear;* but even a memorially transmitted text like a bad quarto has *some* relation to authority just as do the mutilated and much altered newspaper versions of *The Red Badge of Courage.* And we know from the example of *King Lear,* as well as *Doctor Faustus,* that not every variant from the source behind the more authoritative later edition is superior in its authority to that of the bad: a memorial transmission may preserve truth and a scribe or a non-holograph manuscript used for revision may import error.

Common as are the examples of post-publication revision, as in nineteenth-century English novelists like Dickens between periodical and book forms and even between successive book editions, a wider variety and often a more serious set of editorial problems is found in pre-publication changes reflected in a revised document. The simplest cases, again, are those that are linear, for the limitation imposed by their transmission controls or at least exposes error more forthrightly than radiating documents. In its most elementary form we may see linear pre-publication authorial revision in Nathaniel Hawthorne's *The Blithedale Romance* (1852) or *The House of the Seven Gables* (1851). The printer's-copy holograph has been preserved for each of these novels as well as the first edition. Missing are the proofsheets that Hawthorne corrected and that account for the actual revision and correction of the original typesetting made from the preserved manuscript. If these proofs were available, especially in their entirety, they would also serve to isolate the printer's departures from copy that Hawthorne over-looked from those that he recognized and corrected. An example of post-publication revision of a substantially similar nature is found in the twelve leaves of cancels that Fielding ordered for the first edition of *Tom Jones* to supplement the extensive errata list. The originals of only four of these leaves have been preserved but in each case they give occasion for an editor to distinguish between the revisions and the corruptions found in the substitute leaves, a process impossible when only the cancellans are present. A more complicated but still linear problem occurs with Stephen Crane's *The Red Badge of Courage.* Here we have preserved the final holograph manuscript (and portions of an antecedent draft) but this manuscript was not the printer's copy. Instead, a lost professional typescript was made from it, which Crane worked over for a few days in New Orleans, making numerous small revisions, before returning it to New York for typesetting. Thereafter he read proof on the pages with no great care before the sheets were printed. The authoritative revisions in the book that derived from the annotated copy of the lost typescript are thoroughly mixed with an unauthoritative restyling by the publisher and by the compositors that affected Crane's syntax and occasionally his idiom and grammar. To these may be added the undetected range of printer's errors as well as the overlooked defects of the typescript ranging from the misreading of words to the omission of parts of several passages through a misconstruction of markings in the manuscript. Correspondingly, a major excision of a whole battle scene in the manuscript was restored in the typescript, perhaps from the original manuscript leaves but more likely, perhaps, from a lost secondary source, a discarded earlier typescript made from the manuscript before the manuscript itself had been revised for its present state. Because of the gaps in the documentary transmission in this linear situation an editor must recover the purity of the authorial text while yet doing justice to Crane's intended revisions. This necessary selection of readings from two authorities (manuscript and first edition) in order to reconstruct the substantives of a third (the missing typescript and proofs), and then to purify it, creates an eclectic text if any attempt is to be made to recover the author's final intentions other than as found in the first edition with its numerous and sometimes serious corruptions.[27] There is nothing purist in reprinting this faulty first edition in the name of scholarship instead of making an eclectic attempt to restore Crane's true authority from the preserved documents, including the all-important manuscript.[28]

[27] This account for the sake of brevity neglects the influence upon the editing of this work of a radiating authority produced when a considerably abridged and unauthoritatively adjusted version was typeset from the unrevised (or very likely separately and differently revised) carbon of the book typescript and the resulting syndicate proof was reprinted in various newspapers. Distant as these newspaper texts are, and fragmentary, they have a form of authority and in a few places can testify to the state of the typescript before the New Orleans authorial revision as well as the Appleton editorial revisions.

[28] Such a position will be unacceptable to those who maintain that multiple-authority texts should be edited only in their discrete single-authority forms without reference to each other for corrections of error or for revisions. In this matter two particular confusions seem to have arisen. In the first, it is evident that a certain kind of critic dislikes eclectic texts because he wants editions in which he can sense the distinctive quality of each form without the hard work of studying the development of the text by the use of the apparatus. (This is to quote Donald Pizer; see above, note 12.) It is, of course, important for critics to have general impressions of works and to describe these impressions in appropriate terms for their readers to share. It is also important, however, for critics (and their readers) to know the *why* of their impressions, which can be arrived at only by hard work and the analysis of concrete and often minute evidence, a process that requires an exact knowledge of the verbal differences between two texts in full detail. A critic who wants parallel texts for general impressions and sensing distinctive qualities is unlikely to put in the labor necessary to collate these texts thoroughly for himself in order to isolate and then understand the facts that have triggered his impressions,

Pre-publication radiation of authority is likely to develop more variation, and more editorial difficulty in assessing its nature and extent,
than strictly linear revision. *Beggars Bush*, already described, exhibits
just this pre-publication radiation when the prompt-book was tran-

---

and it is probable that he will remain content with his generalities. These may
be valuable but chiefly on a subjective basis, a different matter from moving
men's minds by evidence. Thus it is a narrow critical point of view — basically
more impressionistic than analytical — to object to the necessity to use the
apparatus of a definitive edition in order to reconstruct the history of the text.
(Once more, all questions of texts like *Roderick Hudson* and others that cannot
be conflated according to Greg's rationale of copy-text are not in question.)
So far as I can determine the intellectual basis for objections to final-intention
texts arrived at by eclectic methods, it appears to be aesthetic. Secondly,
objections seem triggered by an uneasy suspicion of the alteration of any
authority by reference to another, seconded by little practical knowledge of
the sifting of evidence, both bibliographical and critical, that is part of the
modern editor's peculiar responsibility. For instance, there is a general exag-
geration of the difficulty of assessing the relation of authorial proof-correction
to compositorial departures from copy as between a printer's-copy manuscript
and the text printed from it. In this connection, Bowers, 'Current Theories
of Copy-Text with an Illustration from Dryden,' *Modern Philology*, 48 (1950):
12–20, may still be useful. Thirdly, the objectors still do not understand Greg's
basic doctrine that copy-texts are chosen on the authority of the accidentals
and not of the substantives, and thus that the copy-text substantives may be
inferior to those of some other authoritative edition and should be replaced
when they can be shown to be errors or readings that were later revised.
Because of this confusion Pizer finds himself in the odd position of arguing
that he would prefer to read the misprint *flashed* in Crane's 'The Monster'
instead of the correct *flushed* since *flushed* comes from the manuscript being
used as copy-text in this part of the text and he wants the copy-text to remain
the first edition. The point of the selected reading is not one of copy-text at
all, for that *flashed* is a typist or compositorial misreading of the manuscript
flushed is perfectly clear from parallel passages. Thus *flushed* was printed in the
Virginia edition of Crane not because it appeared in the manuscript (which
had no copy-text bearing on the case) but because it was demonstrably the
reading that Crane had first written and no evidence could be brought forward
to suggest that he had altered it in proof. Like *pitch* and *pith* in *Hamlet* this is
obviously a case of one reading being right and the other wrong. If the situation had been reversed, the manuscript could still have remained the copy-text
for this passage because of its authoritative accidentals, but the correct *flushed*
would have been inserted from the first edition for the inadvertent mis-inscrip-
tion *flashed* of the manuscript which, after all, was not here the printer's copy.
One would wish that the old Lachmann-Housman debate could have been
revived at the present day among students of American literature with more
historical awareness and with less confusion about the issues involved.

scribed from Massinger's fair copy and then itself became the source for the Lambarde manuscript, whereas the fair copy was preserved to become the printer's copy for the 1647 Folio. In this case, however, the only revision that took place between the fair copy and the prompt-book was unauthoritative and thus outside the present discussion. More to the point, if textual theorists are right the quarto edition of Shakespeare's *Othello* in 1622 was printed from a manuscript representing an early state of the composition whereas the copy behind the First Folio was a later authorially revised manuscript. If this situation had existed in a pure state, in which each manuscript directly behind the printed copies was holograph and unworked-over by any other hand than the author's, each text would have equal basic authority and an eclectic choice of readings would have been required in order to remove the compositorial errors of each print and effectively to isolate the authentic revised readings. As it is, the errors behind the Quarto are perhaps no more than the compositor's, at a minimum, providing the manuscript actually were a holograph. But the copy behind the Folio offers more difficulties. It may be scribal, not holograph, and thus it may exhibit sophistication by another hand as well as the normal double layer of error resulting from two transmissions. This murky pre-publication history ensures that neither preserved document is adequate to represent the author's intentions. Moreover, it has been established that although a revised manuscript of some sort lies behind the Folio, the Folio printer's copy was a scribally annotated example of the Quarto, brought into general conformity with a manuscript from the theater. The usual errors of omission as well as commission may be expected as a consequence of this additional stage of transmission and its peculiar nature. It is generally believed that the wording of the Folio *Othello* represents a form of the text closer on the whole to Shakespeare's ultimate intentions than the Quarto. But however true this estimate may be on an overall basis, it can scarcely operate as a decisive factor for individual readings, given the farther distance from the holograph source (even a revised one) from which the Folio suffers. A conservatively emended reprint of neither authority would be satisfactory for Shakespearean critics: what is needed is a critical eclectic text that attempts to weed out errors from both preserved documents by reference to the authority of now one and then the other, with the intent to establish the authority of the original text; and then finally completes the task by identifying and retaining the authoritative revisions found in the Folio, once they have been distinguished from error and sophistication, and conflating these with the established original composition.

In the late nineteenth century a case of mixed authority requiring eclectic treatment occurs in Stephen Crane's *The Third Violet* (1897) which has a complex pre-publication history. When a rural typist failed to make a copy that he thought satisfactory for the printer, Crane expressed the manuscript to his New York publisher for a professional typescript to be prepared. The carbon of this typescript became the copy for syndication in a number of newspapers. Before the book was set some months later, Crane worked over the ribbon copy of the typescript and revised it, and as usual the Appleton editor took a hand with eliminating some idiosyncracies of usage and syntax that characterize Crane's writing. Any individual newspaper is at three removes from the holograph — the unrevised typescript carbon, the syndicate proof, and the newspaper setting. However, from the various newspaper witnesses something approximating the syndicate proofs can be recovered for the accidentals as well as an exact reconstitution of the substantives. By comparison with the book a very close reproduction of the original typescript substantives of the original can then be put together, a text that has its historical interest but is scarcely worth reprinting in its entirety for the study of scholars. Critics concerned with other than textual matters will want to use Crane's final intentions as the evidential basis for their conclusions about such matters as Crane's powers of characterization, his ordering of scenes, his humor, sentimentality, language, and whatever else interests them. If they are wise enough to evaluate these matters by studying the early state of the text from the security of the final, the apparatus of variants to a critical text can record for them the precise verbal forms of either. A reprint of the book text would not, of course, provide a scholar with Crane's intentions in their exact form since it would leave untouched the compositorial and editorial sophistications of Crane's style, the original authorial readings for which can be recovered only from the composite reconstruction of the syndicate proof, with due allowance for its share of error and sophistication. Only an eclectic text contrived in this manner can bring to a critical reader what he must have: a reconstruction as close as textual scholarship can manage of Crane's share of the revised typescript that served as printer's copy for the book. This is the ideal, and it includes even the hypothetical (and probably very few) corrections and revisions that Crane may have made in the book proofs, since these alterations cannot be distinguished on the evidence from his alterations of the typescript. The documentary evidence does not permit us to penetrate farther back into the text than this to link it with the antecedent manuscript: the original of any plausible departures from copy by the typist can never be known unless by chance they were altered in the revision of the typescript.

Two final examples of mixed texts requiring eclectic treatment can only be mentioned, since a full account of them may be found elsewhere.[29] In Crane's short story 'The Revenge of the *Adolphus*' a typescript and its carbon were made from the manuscript. The carbon, say, was sold in the United States and published there in a magazine without Crane seeing proof or concerning himself with the text beyond what may be a change or two (not transferred to the ribbon copy) that he made before mailing. The ribbon copy was very considerably revised after criticism of its technical naval details had been given Crane by the United States Naval Attaché stationed in London, and in this form it appeared in an English magazine. Later when Crane was collecting his Spanish-American War stories for the book *Wounds in the Rain* he discovered that he had no typescript, nor did he have a copy of the revisions he had made for the English magazine. By returning to the manuscript he seems to have made up a new typescript in which he included some true literary revision as well as what he could remember of the Attaché's technical criticism. This version, accidentally less its final page or two, was sent to the book publisher, who set it up only to find that the missing end had to be supplied from a copy of the English magazine that he was able to procure in New York. However, in order to make room for an illustration this magazine had, unfortunately, cut the original ending that may be found only in the American magazine, and so the book of course follows the unauthoritatively reduced conclusion. If anything less than an eclectic text can do justice to this extraordinary textual situation, it would be a miracle.

The second example is less one of revision, since this seems to be very slight in the texts, but instead one in which eclectic editing can succeed in recovering a text that in even small details of accidentals is substantially that of the lost manuscript. This is Crane's short story 'Death and the Child', which radiates from one typescript and its carbon in an English magazine and book collection, and, made from the same manuscript, exists in an independent typescript and carbon

[29] See 'Multiple Authority,' *op. cit.,* p. 108 ff.

radiating in an American magazine and book collection. Briefly, the common features of all four, or even any three, of these printed forms must represent the common consent of the two typescripts and therefore the features of the manuscript.[30] A reprint of any one of these four authorities would provide only an imperfect text for critical study, and its imperfections could scarcely be ameliorated by an apparatus that would enable the reader to reconstruct the features of the other three, since he would still lack the expertise to evaluate these and recover Crane's actual text. The Variorum principle applied to literary, not to textual, study is of very little use and may even be a positive danger to a critic since it puts the business of determining bibliographical and textual authority on inexperienced shoulders. A literary critic would have notable difficulty, for example, in knowing what words of *Hamlet* he should be writing about if he had been furnished only the Variorum volume containing a reprint of the First Folio, with all Second Quarto variants, all other early editions, all editors' emendations from 1709 both apt and foolish, everything jumbled together in the collation at the foot of the page.

I conclude with a general categorizing of the main kinds of single and of multiple authority, and a brief analysis of the eclectic or non-eclectic editorial treatment appropriate for the different categories.

Single authority exists in its simplest state in an unpublished manuscript representing the only textual authority available. More commonly, it is found in the first edition with or without the printer's copy, and with or without subsequent editions so long as these are simple reprints lacking the intervention in any manner of fresh and independent authority. Stephen Crane's novel *George's Mother* (1896) exists in only one edition, the first, although with a scrap of an early draft for part of a page. Except for the accidentals of the brief draft fragment, the only recovery of antecedent authority that is possible is contained within the printed text itself; hence a faithful reprint, corrected as necessary, is all that an editor can manage save perhaps for the normal-

[30] The principles governing the reconstruction from radiating witnesses of a lost document so that one can always penetrate one step farther back towards authority than any single preserved document are remarked in 'Multiple Authority,' p. 101 ff. It follows that when, as in 'Death and the Child,' two lost radiating typescripts can be reconstructed, by comparing them one can then reconstruct in turn the document from which they radiated, in this case the holograph manuscript at two removes from any preserved document.

izing of some of Crane's accidentals to agree with Crane's known characteristics when there is variance in the text itself. The first edition of Shakespeare's *Measure for Measure* appeared in the First Folio of 1623, which was thereupon reprinted in 1632, 1664, and 1685. In none of the later Folios did authority enter. The pre-publication history that can be recovered for *Measure for Measure* suggests that the manuscript given the printer was a transcript of Shakespeare's 'foul papers' made by the professional scribe Ralph Crane. The recovery of this information assists an editor materially in his conjectural emendation, because he can expect error not only from Compositors B, C, D, and F who worked on the play but also from the scribe's manipulation. Thus he may be emboldened to more and certainly to different kinds of emendation from what may seem appropriate for *All's Well That Ends Well,* also a Folio play, that was almost certainly set directly from Shakespeare's own working papers. However, in either case the appearance of later unauthoritative Folio editions has no bearing on the recovery of antecedent authorial text. The First Folio print is the only authority we have, and a conjecturally emended reprint of this is the best any editor can manage to present Shakespeare's work in a scholarly manner. The only evidence of its immediate antecedent is locked in the witness itself and cannot usually be disengaged to recover the details of the manuscript that Ralph Crane copied, or even Ralph Crane's own transcript except here and there when recognizable idiosyncracies peer through the compositorial overlay.

On some occasions pre-publication forms of a text may be preserved without interfering with the concept of single authority so long as the relationship is linear and the different forms derive one from another without fresh authority entering into the chain of transmission. One curious case is Stephen Crane's short story 'A Little Pilgrim'. The manuscript of this was sold to Harper's and was set for the firm's magazine in such a hurry to get it out before the book, already close to completion, that one compositor set the magazine text from the first half of the manuscript (cast off for the book) while the book compositor was setting from the latter half. When each came to the end of his stint he exchanged not the manuscript copy but instead the proofs pulled from his setting: hence the book proof became the printer's copy for the latter part of the story in the magazine, and the magazine proof for the first part of the book. Since in this mixed manner each witness is one-half original and one-half derived, an eclectic editor chooses from each the primary and non-reprint typesetting as his copy-text.

Another interesting case comes in Crane's article 'The Scotch Express'. This was set up in England in 1898 by *Cassell's* magazine from manuscript. Proofs were pulled and immediately mailed to *McClure's* magazine in the United States, which set up its own version of the article from this copy. However, between the two witnesses, one authoritative and one derived, two differences appear beyond normal compositorial variation. First, *Cassell's* cut some of the article for publication, so that the *McClure's* text for such excisions (derived from the lost *Cassell's* proofs before cutting) is the only printed form to preserve the original text. Secondly, the editor of *Cassell's* proceeded to make what he regarded as judicious changes in the proofs of Crane's article before publication so that the *Cassell's* version here and there differs from the original state of the proofs as reproduced by *McClure's*. This situation might be thought of as verging on multiple authority, and in a sense it does; but in a more important sense no new authority ever entered the printed transmission of the text not present in its original typesetting from the manuscript, which was not again consulted or made the source of another transcript. If this manuscript had not, fortunately, been preserved so that an editor would have been forced to work only with the printed results, it could be said (lacking the manuscript) that the *Cassell's* copy-text, the only document set from manuscript, must be *corrected* (not *revised*) from the evidence of the derived reproduction in *McClure's* in order to restore as nearly as possible the state of its original proofs before editorial alteration. In point of fact although the manuscript is preserved, and must become the copy-text, the evidence of *McClure's* settles for an editor any question he might have had about the authority of the variants between *Cassell's* and *McClure's* as resulting in *Cassell's* from Crane's own intervention. The only editorial problem that remains is to assess the authority of the variants between the early state of the *Cassell's* proof (as preserved by the *McClure's* text) and the manuscript.

The question of derivation also puts Crane's romance *The O'Ruddy* (1903) into the single-authority category despite its complicated history. Crane's part of the novel exists in a holograph manuscript from which a lost typescript with carbons was made. One carbon went to a magazine, which began serializing the story, whereas the ribbon copy went to the London publisher Heinemann where typesetting of the book started. After several installments of the magazine, the book setting had caught up with the magazine text, and thereafter the magazine became a simple reprint of the book proofs, with some added cuts and censorship. If the manuscript had not survived, the textual problem would certainly have involved the double authority of book and magazine set independently, in the early part, from typescript and carbon although reverting to single authority once the book proofs became the magazine copy. But since the typescript was, apparently, never revised by Crane except perhaps for one or two insignificant readings of doubtful validity, it is utterly derived from the manuscript and thus unauthoritative; hence a reconstruction of the typescript from the evidence of magazine and book in the early part of the romance, which otherwise would have been of crucial textual importance, has now only an historical significance owing to the preservation of the manuscript, the only possible copy-text especially considering the fact that publication was posthumous.

When only drafts are preserved of a work and the printed version stems from a rewritten but lost later holograph, we enter a gray area between single and multiple authority. In respect of its substantives, no question holds but that the single newspaper version of Crane's Sullivan County sketch 'The Octopush' has ultimate authority since it was set from a now lost manuscript that had thoroughly rewritten and revised the state of the text in an untitled draft generally called 'The Fishermen', which is known only in the form of a posthumous typescript made by Cora. On the other hand, if we assume that when the two texts are closely parallel Crane's rewritten arrangement would in manuscript have reproduced, on the whole, the accidentals of the draft, these accidentals would be of superior authority in a relatively naive typescript to those of the printed version which has been strongly compositor-styled. But the texts are by no means always parallel except in scattered patches; hence when the substantives markedly diverge, the printed text's accidentals join them in general authority in their new and changed form. I would not say that an editor would be wrong to treat this problem as if it did not exist and to reprint 'The Octopush' from the New York *Tribune* (10 July 1892) as a single-text authority without regard for the shifting authority of the accidentals of the draft manuscript. One hopes, of course, such an editor would then add the text of the typescript draft in an appendix, a sop to the scholar in a definitive edition but of little use in truly attempting to establish the best overall text of 'The Octopush' for reading. Nevertheless, in the parallel portions the textual problem may seem partly to approach that of *Hamlet;* and an editor may certainly be tempted to try emending the printed accidentals whenever the authority of the draft accidentals could be applied without creating a real mishmash of texture clothing the basically single-text authority of the substantives.

Another inhabitant of this gray area is a book like Hawthorne's *The House of the Seven Gables,* preserved in the printer's-copy holograph manuscript and in the first edition set immediately from this copy. The missing link is the lost corrected proofs. But since these are of the same typesetting as the first edition, it is only the variants between book and manuscript assessable as Hawthorne's revisions in proof, and not as compositorial departures from copy, that can be given any authority. If the proofs had been marked by another hand without reference to the author there could be no question of anything but single authority resident exclusively in the manuscript. However, authorial proof-corrections do insert fresh and independent authority and to that extent they introduce problems of multiple text into what is essentially a single-authority textual situation. But the setting of the derived book text remains the same after proof-correction except for the specific corrections, and thus the proportion of conflation of two stages of authority is so small that no comparison can be made with a situation in which a book has been set up from the lost authorial fair copy of a preserved earlier holograph, where multiple authority would certainly be present. At any rate, the copy-text situation for *The House of the Seven Gables* is perfectly clear, in that the manuscript remains the sole authority for the accidentals, and indeed for the substantives, also, when an editor feels convincing evidence is present that a variant book substantive was not the result of authorial proof-correction. It may be assumed for Hawthorne, and the case is nearly demonstrable, that he concerned himself little if at all with revisions in proof of the forms of the manuscript accidentals; thus all book accidental forms can ordinarily be taken as derived and unauthoritative. With an author like Whitman, who consistently revised accidentals as well as substantives, no such assumption could be made and the choice of copy-text would necessarily shift to the printed edition that had most lately come from his hands, with a minimum of necessary *correction* from earlier editions.

Fortunately such scrupulous revising authors in the proof stage are less common than authors whose main purpose in reading proof is to correct printer's error; but when such authors appear, as in William James's *Pragmatism* (1907), the identifiable alterations can be treated on their merits as special exceptions. One cannot build a principle upon them. The ideal copy-text will ordinarily remain any preserved holograph manuscript close to the print derived from it. This is an application of Greg's principles — devised for Elizabethan conditions — to modern times, and generally (although not invariably) they are quite pertinent and will produce the best text.

Obviously exceptions will exist, and obviously an editor cannot apply Greg's principles rigidly unless he knows that they are, in fact, applicable to the material. An example about halfway between Hawthorne and Whitman exists in the book *Pragmatism* (1907) by the American philosopher William James. Some part of the text is known only from the book; some was set from annotated clippings of journal articles; but the last two chapters were set from holograph used as the direct printer's copy and preserved. In addition, James's own copy is known containing seventy-four small variants marked in his hand, only six of which are represented among the nine changes made in the plates for the second and third printings. The marked revisions indicate that here and there he was as concerned with eliminating such accidentals as parenthetical commas as he was to correct misprints or mistakes in names and occasionally to touch up his idiom. When one compares the text of the book with the seventh and eighth chapters set from holograph, one sees that James made numerous substantive changes in the galley proofs; and the alteration of a number of the accidentals seems to be attributable to him as well, although it is also clear that a number represent the printer's styling and are unauthoritative. On the whole, the evidence of the last section suggests that the printed text represents his final intentions more faithfully on the whole than the printer's-copy manuscript, which was his first draft but which he heavily revised before sending it to the press. The special circumstances that the holograph printer's copy was not really a finally approved fair transcript but from the start seems to have been intended for further revision in proof, the evidence that perhaps more of the significant accidental differences are due to authorial proof-correction (or to positively necessary compositorial styling) than to unauthoritative house-styling one would wish removed to restore the purity of the manuscript's intention — this situation makes possible a choice of the first edition as copy-text to be corrected by reference back to the manuscript, instead of the manuscript as copy-text to be revised by those book variants thought to be authoritative.

Actually, if the editing were scrupulously performed, the resulting text would in theory be identical since by whichever process it was arrived at it should reproduce only ascertained authority. Two caveats may be mentioned, however. First, despite the best efforts of an editor to seek evidence for his decisions, not all necessary choices have an equally evidential basis and for some no evidence whatever as to their origin is available. In such conditions it is almost inevitable that an editor will find it more convenient to accept the general authority of his copy-text even though that authority may be split between substantives and accidentals and of lesser weight in the category in which the decision lies. Thus on practical grounds it is most unlikely that two identical texts would be produced by the same editor working on the one hand from the manuscript as copy-text and on the other from the first edition. Second, the mundane question arises of the form of the apparatus. If the copy-text is the manuscript, all changes made in the print that are accepted will be recorded among the emendations so that the exact form of the manuscript will be recoverable from the apparatus, but not the exact form of the book text when its accidentals are rejected: its rejected substantives would of course be recorded. On the other hand, if the book is the copy-text, only the corrections of its accidentals from the manuscript would be noted in the emendations list and thus the reader would have no chance whatever of reconstructing from this the form of the authorial manuscript (which may ordinarily be taken as holding more interest for close students of a writer than the form of the readily available printed book) unless the editor were to obligate himself to give in his Historical Collation a list of the rejected manuscript accidentals as well as of the rejected substantives that would automatically be recorded. (Of course, with the the manuscript as copy-text an editor could provide a list of rejected book-text accidentals, but in some cases this listing could get out of hand and the scrupulous recording of non-authority would be ridiculous to perpetuate.) The balance governing an editor's decision about copy-text in examples like *Pragmatism* is so delicate that each case must certainly be judged on its merits. Any rigid following of a principle not really applicable to the special circumstances would be mere pedantry. On the other hand, when an editor violates the sound and usually operative principles enunciated by Sir Walter Greg, it should be treated as an exception and the decision made on that basis, not on the false basis that Greg's principles do not apply to modern texts, or the false hypothesis that since some authors give no evidence that they cared about the form their accidentals took in print, the editor can safely ignore what they wrote in manuscript and happily plump for house-styling as the ideal for an edited definitive text. Moreover, when such exceptions are made, one would always like to hear a reasoned account by the editor of the causes that moved him to depart from a generally sound principle.

Multiple authority, it has been remarked, exists both in linear and in radiating documents or in some combination of the two. This authority may exhibit itself either in simple or in complex relationship among the textual documents. I take simple relationships to consist of linear or of radiating authorities from which the same antecedent document immediately behind each can be reconstructed in whole or in part. Put another way, the preserved documents are immediate witnesses to the source behind them, and this source is identical in cases of radiation. Whenever a work is printed in two or more different typesettings from the same document (whether a typescript and its carbons, or photographic reproductions) simple radiating multiple authority results. As remarked, even the principle of copy-text vanishes except perhaps for the purposes of the apparatus (in cases where Professor Tanselle's proposals are not adopted), and with reference to quantitative and qualitative evidence the editor reconstructs the lost common source so far as the documentary evidence permits. Crane's short story 'Three Miraculous Soldiers' (1896) is known in eight newspaper texts set independently from a common proof. It is clear that when all eight agree, the exact reading of the proof has been recovered. Statistically, considerable weight can be placed on a seven-to-one or on a six-to-two agreement. Qualitative evidence — the nature of the variant as compared with Crane's known habits — may begin to enter with a five-to-three and certainly with a four-to-four split, and even when an editor may select a variant supported by a reasonable number of witnesses although it is in the minority, provided he conjectures that some marked characteristic of Crane has been subject to standard restyling by the majority of the compositors. Obviously the use of qualitative evidence is based on the conjecture that in the particular reading the proof reflected faithfully the manuscript copy so that an idiosyncratic feature was transferred to it though rejected by a majority of the compositors who set from the proof.

Experience with trial reconstructions of Crane's newspaper articles against a few examples of surviving proofs confirms the hypothesis that the agreement of more than one compositor in an idiosyncratic accidental will often reflect the actual proof. For example, in an article called 'Nebraska's Bitter Fight for Life', syndicated on 24 February 1895, and known in nine newspapers, the tenth — the Nebraska *State*

69

Journal typesetting — having served as the common proof, the misspelling *phenominal* in the proof was followed by one newspaper although corrected in the remaining eight, and the proof's variant spelling *meagrely* was followed in two. The proof was erratic, and often wrong, in reproducing what must have been the manuscript's lack of capitalization in *East* and *West,* but, even so, two or three compositors would usually agree. In no case of substantive variation from the proof did more than one newspaper differ from the other eight and the proof except for one highly ambiguous reported piece of dialogue where several compositors thought they were correcting the original and sophisticated it in the same manner. In the whole article of about 4500 words, the comma punctuation of the proof was rejected by a majority of the newspapers only nine times, and then usually by a five-to-four split.

One must never forget, of course, that in simple multiple authority only the document immediately behind the preserved witnesses can be recovered. Obviously, the syndicate master proof for Crane's newspaper articles and sketches is not the full equivalent of the holograph from which it was set; nevertheless, even though the proof will normally differ from the manuscript in some respects, except for the conjectural correction of positive error in the proof an editor cannot go in back of its characteristics to the holograph on any form of documentary evidence.[31] It may be that in the recovered proof an editor of Crane will find accidental characteristics violating Crane's consistent practice that must have differed in the holograph. In such a situation, when the recovered document is not the holograph itself I suggest that an editor should be satisfied with the progress he has made

---

[31] That is, if the simple-radiating documents are all that are preserved, as is usual in newspaper syndication. In complex cases something more must be done. Crane's sketch 'The Snake' (1896) shows that the syndicate proof was set from a holograph and that this identical manuscript was thereupon employed as printer's copy for an associated magazine publication in different format. Here the features of the proof can be recovered from the newspapers, and insofar as this reconstruction is complete one has a text to compare with that of the magazine, both radiating directly at one remove from the same manuscript. Thus many of the features of the holograph can be recovered in an eclectic text based on the common readings of reconstructed proof and printed magazine. Variants can then be analyzed on an informed basis according to the estimate of their respective authority in each specific case, since technically the magazine and the reconstructed proof are in general of equal authority.

back toward ultimate authority, and without further documentary evidence in the work he should not arbitrarily emend what he finds in the proof to what he believes would have been holograph characteristics when the evidence of the witnesses does not permit the assumption. Documentary evidence bearing on this matter may be viewed in two ways. First, literally, the evidence for the reading under examination. That is, in all his holographs with the rarest of exceptions Crane introduced dialogue or reported speech with a colon (or occasionally no punctuation) and only a handful of times in the whole body of manuscripts with a comma. If of eight newspaper witnesses to a text every one prints a comma before a certain speech, the assumption must be that the common copy read a comma there, without regard for what was the punctuation of the holograph one step farther back. Hence it would be improper, because without documentary evidence, to emend by a colon even though an editor could, of course, be morally certain that a colon had been inscribed in the holograph. However, if — secondly — the editor accepts the principle of selective normalization on documentary evidence, he can conjecturally emend to a colon here if elsewhere in the document being edited the colon introducing speech is found. This is a form of documentary evidence, not for the reading in question but for the document as a whole, indicating that the compositor(s) were not consistent in following the characteristics of the holograph when they set introductory commas. Thus since known idiosyncratic characteristics appear, although not consistently, an editor may assume that they were present throughout the basic copy but were erratically transmitted. If he is prepared on this form of evidence to emend to a consistent texture such accidentals known to be strongly authorial that appear in inconsistent form, then discreet normalization (always with record) may be a useful editorial intervention even though not justified on the normal basis of the positive evidence for a specific reading.

The fewer the witnesses the more reliance must be placed on qualitative over quantitative evidence until one arrives at the irreducible split of 'The Price of the Harness', printed in two magazines in different countries from a ribbon and carbon copy made from Crane's manuscript. On the evidence that the American magazine restyled certain of Crane's accidentals — like his spelling — less than the English compositorial adaptations, an editor with perfect freedom to use his critical judgment about the authority of variant substantive readings from either magazine may extend this freedom and although preferring in general the texture of the American typesetting yet admit other accidentals from the English for their specific characteristic features. A reprint of neither witness for this story would be as satisfactory for substantives or for accidentals as an eclectic text.

Simple linear authority would seem to be classified in the same relationship as simple multiple whenever the same criterion is possible: the recovery of the immediate antecedent of a revised derived document. As has been illustrated for *Tom Jones,* the fourth edition was revised by Fielding marking a copy of the third; thus there is no problem in substantially recovering the fourth's antecedent, the annotated example of the third. More conveniently, when Fielding revised the second edition of *Joseph Andrews* by marking a copy of the first, then the third by marking a copy of the second, and the fourth by marking a copy of the third, the linear relationship remains simple despite the layers of revision.

Linear relationship becomes complex when the derived revised edition may be reconstructed but the source of the revisions is not immediately authorial since it has been transmitted to the printer's copy not by the author but by a scribal intermediary and thus is at one or more stages of remove from the holograph, corresponding to the author himself. *Hamlet* is perhaps the classic case. Here, if the reconstructed textual history is accurate, we have a copy of the Second Quarto (supposedly set from Shakespeare's own working manuscript) brought by scribal annotation into general substantive conformity with a late prompt-book which would have been a modified scribal transcript either of the working manuscript or (more likely) of an intermediate copy of that manuscript, or else of an earlier prompt-book based on such a copy. Here the Second Quarto stands as the immediate witness to its manuscript copy, but the annotated example cannot be reconstructed with the precision of *Tom Jones*'s authorial revisions nor can the manuscript that was the basis of the scribal annotation be perfectly reconstructed even in its substantives from the Folio variants since at best the annotation was inaccurate and incomplete. That the perfect authority of the readings in the manuscript that underlies the Folio variants may also be questioned is a part of the problem as well.

With authorial annotation, on the other hand, one can be sure of the author's full intentions at that particular time (attested by the changes he chose to make) even though these may in fact fail completely to correct or revise imperfections in the text that he might alter on a later occasion. When William James annotated a few journal articles to serve as printer's copy for chapters in his book *Pragmatism* (1907), he missed various desirable if not necessary alterations that he subsequently marked in his privately corrected example of the first printing, some few of these then being incorporated into the text by changes in the plates of the second and third printings. These annotations in the journal texts (as demonstrated by some preserved printer's copy) preceded still another layer of revision made before publication when he considerably modified the text in the galley proofs where it had not been marked in the copy; as a result, the first-edition text, by this further revision, does not always conform to the revised printer's copy that had been prepared. A still more complex case occurs when an author makes separate revisions of the same copy. Samuel Johnson in revising the second edition of the Preface to his *Dictionary* annotated a copy of the first; but when he came to revise the text for the fourth he inadvertently chose another copy of the first so that the two layers of revisions do not reflect each other.[32] In more modern times precisely the same situation arises in the works of William James. When he was working just before his death on the posthumously published *Some Problems in Philosophy,* he had a family typescript made from his manuscript, and while in England worked over one copy of this typescript but — without reference to the English revisions — he later revised the other typescript copy in America. Since he died before he could put the two stages of revision together, his mixed intentions are known well enough from these two marked typescripts, but not necessarily his final intentions.

Whatever the completeness of the author's own attempts at revision and correction, therefore, the total evidence at each stage is almost wholly recoverable and is fully authoritative even though some of the final intentions may need critical analysis. On the contrary, no critic can guarantee that the readings of the Folio replacing those of the Second Quarto *Hamlet* are either a complete record of substantive variation in the manuscript behind the Folio annotations or fully authoritative for the changes that were made: the readings may have become corrupted in their transmission through stages up to the document itself, and authoritative readings that survived transmissional error may have been incorrectly (and incompletely) transmitted by

---

[32] W. R. Keast, 'The Preface to *A Dictionary of the English Language:* Johnson's Revision and the Establishment of the Text,' *Studies in Bibliography,* 5 (1952): 129–46; 'Some Emendations in Johnson's Preface to the *Dictionary,'* *R.E.S.,* n.s., 4 (1953): 52–57.

scribal annotation. Even James's careful proofreading passed various errors, and Stephen Crane — a reluctant and careless proofreader — seems to have made only token changes in the proofs for *The Red Badge of Courage* and 'approved' a thoroughly anomalous and often corrupt text. Since Fielding did not himself (apparently) read proof for the fourth edition of *Tom Jones,* a fair number of errors made by the printer in setting from Fielding's revised copy for the edition went unnoticed. It follows that in cases like the Folio *Hamlet* where the author neither prepared the revised copy nor read the resulting proof, departures from authority will be frequent.

In the most clearcut cases a complex relationship is established between radiating documents when the immediate physical antecedent of each form of the text differs (authorial annotations aside) regardless of its origin. If the Folio *Hamlet* had been set from the identical manuscript behind the Second Quarto (whether or not further revised), simple radiation would have resulted. But because the manuscript that provided the source for the scribal annotation of a copy of the Second Quarto (the purpose being to bring that Quarto into such general conformity with the source manuscript that it was considered to be the equivalent of sending that manuscript to the printer) was a later derivative of the working-papers manuscript behind the Quarto, a complex relationship develops, one that would obtain even if this other derived manuscript had itself been the Folio printer's copy. the situation, indeed, is substantially the same in this mixed linear relationship as it would be if in complex radiation the Folio *2 Henry IV* had been set from a scribal copy at least one remove from the working-papers manuscript behind the Quarto edition. In complex radiation, of course, neither antecedent document in the two lines can be recovered as fully as, for example, even 'The Price of the Harness' typescript from its two simple radiating witnesses. In simple radiating documents, of two variant readings one is almost certainly bound to be right and the other wrong except in the special cases of independent sophistication of an error or ambiguity in the copy. On the other hand, in complex radiation the impossibility of reconstructing at least one of the documents that has affected the transmission makes for concealment of error, and a distortion of authority that cannot always be documented. The superior authority of some readings in the Folio *Hamlet* is manifest, and they must be adopted in preference to the authority of the Second Quarto, but these seemingly pure and authoritative words are sometimes embedded in a tissue of scribal and compositorial error. That an editor should follow Greg's precepts and select the Second Quarto as copy-text on the basis of its closeness to the holograph is incontestable. That no critical text of *Hamlet* has ever been attempted that did not blend together in various proportions the readings of Quarto and of Folio is equally incontestable. There can scarcely be an argument here about the necessity for eclecticism.

Finally, we come to a practical consideration that I think cannot be ignored. The more 'scientific' the editor the more likely he is to brush aside suggestions that his main job should be to establish not merely a simple form of a text, such as a manuscript in one particular line but not in another, or the Folio form of the *Hamlet* text, or the revised edition of Crane's *Maggie,* or the unedited manuscript form of William James's *A Pluralistic Universe,* except as a part of the necessary preparation of textual documents for the final editing process. Nevertheless, except for the narrowest investigations, ones usually quite satisfied by facsimiles or diplomatic reprints plus apparatus (as in the German manner), the main scholarly demand is for an established critical text embodying the author's full intentions (not merely one segment of them in an inevitably imperfect form) insofar as these can be ascertained by an expert who has had available all documentary sources and has devoted time and study to their transmissional history and authority. It is then important, I believe, to put this expertise not exclusively to the determination of the best documentary form of a text to reprint, in the Lachmannian manner, but instead to the eclectic reconstruction of the author's intentions in as full a sense as they can be realized from the multiple authorities, as Housman advocated, but with the application of controlled bibliographical as well as critical reasoning behind the selection of readings such as he could not have envisaged. With the accompanying apparatus that a definitive edition should offer, a reader who needs to trace the evidence for the eclectic results can be provided with substantially all of his legitimate needs for the purpose. There is neither need nor market for two texts of *Tom Jones,* the first and the fourth editions, when the fourth-edition revisions can be incorporated in the first-edition accidentals (the third-edition corruptions having been weeded out) and from the apparatus the reader can isolate every change in the first-edition substantives and accidentals from whatever source, and every rejected substantive from the second, third, and fourth editions. If he wants to know what were the rejected unauthoritative accidentals of the fourth edition, he is making an unreasonable request, and it would be proper to refer such specialized enquiry to a set of electroprints. It is only the textual scholar who is concerned with the exact forms of Quarto and Folio *Hamlet, Othello, 2 Henry IV, Troilus and Cressida, King Lear,* and the like, beyond what can be made readily available in collations. That such textual scholars provide the editions should not blind them to the essential fact that the rest of scholarship does not share their specialized interests, which in fact require photographic facsimiles, and that the basic demand — by no means entirely a popular one — is for the concentration of textual expertise on producing a single text that reflects as far as the evidence permits what Shakespeare would have liked to see published.

Literary critics, historians, general scholars, students of all kinds — these need as authoritative a reconstruction of a full text as the documents allow, not editions of the separate documents, except when the distance is so great as to make eclectic reconstruction impossible, as with Henry James's *Roderick Hudson* or Wordsworth's *Prelude.* When this aim should constitute the finest flower of textual scholarship, what Galsworthy in another connection calls 'the spire of meaning', and when our increasing knowledge and expertise can constantly be stimulated to assist the validity of our recovery of an author's true text in its most authoritative form, to distrust the eclectic methodology that in some cases can alone assist in this process of recovery is to thrust one's head with the ostrich under the sand. The difficulty and expense of producing definitive editions these days are so acute that a good edition cannot shortly supersede an imperfect one as a good textbook can drive out a bad. An edition is likely to preempt the field for several generations or more. Under these circumstances it ought to be the most authoritative and comprehensive that can be contrived for its time and place in the history of scholarship.

THE AUTHORSHIP OF 'TO GOVERNOR M'DUFFIE', A UNIONIST'S DIATRIBE AGAINST THE GOVERNOR OF SOUTH CAROLINA

LILLIAN B. GILKES

AMERICANS WHO KNOW THEIR HISTORY SHOULD NEED NO INTRODUCtion to George McDuffie. A distinguished member of the bar, he served his country as well as his state in the Congress from 1821 to 1834. Then he was elected governor of South Carolina and publicly declared for it over country. The trouble started almost immediately. There was background to it, of course. In 1832 South Carolina had responded to an unwise and unjust tariff with the Ordinance of Nullification, which affirmed the superiority of the individual state over the Union. McDuffie was a prominent Nullifier, a leader in the enactment of the ordinance and a defender of its right.

Not everyone in South Carolina agreed with him. Among those demurring was William Gilmore Simms, owner of the Charleston *City Gazette* and a prominent Unionist. To his literary agent, James Lawson of New York City, Simms wrote his strong feelings over McDuffie's impending visit to the coastal city a short time after the Nullification Ordinance was passed:

We are, at this moment in a state of excitement little short of phrensy, and do not suffer surprise to hear of collision and bloodshed in our streets. You will readily understand the occasion, if you have read the villainous ordinance of our convention, embodying tests the most dishonorable to honest men, and the most degrading to free men. The union men of our city will take none of them — and the imprisonment or punishment of one of them will put the whole of them in arms. They speak but one language — action, action, action! — On Thursday next, McDuffie arrives in the city and they give him an entertainment of course![1]

McDuffie did not come that Thursday, so Simms's anticipation of violence did not happen to be realized. But tension continued to build.

Nullification and McDuffie loosed some lighter manifestations than the dramatic thunderbolts Simms promised. Park Benjamin records an occurrence during a voyage he undertook as a business trip to Demerara (British Guiana), the seat of his family holdings, in 1833. It shows a side instinctive to the folklore propensity of a race which delights in turning fatality into sport, song, and jokes conceived in the idiom of the common man. Yankee Doodle, in the person of 'our captain', made ready for the ceremony of 'speaking' between ships at sea with a roar 'to the careless sailor, who, in his haste to set the flag, has entangled it in the rigging. . . . "Mind your eye, my fine fellow . . . if you tear asunder those stars and stripes, I'll nullify you, you lubber!" '[2] The lightness does nothing but reveal the depths at which the controversy was striking the public mind.

It struck violently when McDuffie was elected governor of his state and gave his inaugural address in 1834. According to the epigraph of an anonymous poem published in the *New-England Magazine* for February 1835, he disavowed ' "That miserable mockery of blurred and obliterated parchment — the Constitution of the United States." ' He pledged, instead, ' "*undivided* ALLEGIANCE to the State of South Carolina." '[3] More than two decades would pass before McDuffie's position spread and firmed into the basis of civil war; almost immediately, however, there was a reaction.

[1] Simms to Lawson, 25 November [1832]; in Mary C. Simms Oliphant, Alfred Taylor Odell, and T. C. Duncan Eaves, eds., *The Letters of William Gilmore Simms* (Columbia: University of South Carolina Press, 1952), 1: 46–47.

[2] Benjamin, 'A Voyager's Common-Place-Book', *New-England Magazine*, 8 (March 1835): 262.

[3] 'To Governor M'Duffie', *New-England Magazine*, 8 (February 1835): 138–41.

One of its more notable phenomena in a literary way was the poem in the *New-England Magazine* almost immediately after the speech. 'To Governor M'Duffie' was nationalistic and caustic, thirteen octets attacking the man and the divisive position he represented. There can be little doubt that the editors of the magazine made it still more fiery: it was they who put *'undivided'* in italics and 'ALLEGIANCE' in capitals; and it was they who supplied the long footnote on the significance of McDuffie's use of the term 'allegiance' in connection with a government of freemen. It may even have been only one editor who did all of those things. In February 1835, the *New-England Magazine* was in the hands of three young Bostonians — John O. Sargent, Samuel Gridley Howe, and Park Benjamin — but the next month Benjamin's fellow proprietors went about their own professions and gave him full control of the venture.[4] If it was Benjamin who intended to increase the anonymous poet's heat against the governor of South Carolina, he succeeded admirably. 'To Governor M'Duffie' was reprinted in the *Essex Gazette* for 9 July 1836 and further inflamed the people of Massachusetts.

It was not a direct cause of the Civil War, nor was it even a very good poem, but it has come down through the years coupled with McDuffie's inaugural. Part of the reason must be that it made an impact at the time. A more important part of the reason, however, certainly is that when the *Essex Gazette* repeated the poem it attributed it to John Greenleaf Whittier. The fierce Quaker Abolitionist seemed its natural author. In 1937, more than one hundred years afterwards, Whittier's bibliographer, Thomas Franklin Currier, said he was; over a decade later, C. S. Wilson and David A. Randall thought they had proof of the point; and today the attribution is generally accepted.[5] It seems right. It is not.

Around the time of McDuffie's inauguration, Dr. Samuel Gridley Howe wrote to Robert Montgomery Bird soliciting a contribution to

---

[4] Details on Benjamin's acquisition of the *New-England Magazine* are in my 'Park Benjamin, Literary Agent, *Et Cetera*', *Proof*, 1 (1971): 38–39; and my 'Hawthorne, Park Benjamin, and S. G. Goodrich: A Three-Cornered Imbroglio', *Nathaniel Hawthorne Journal*, 1 (1971): 83–85.

[5] Currier, *A Bibliography of John Greenleaf Whittier* (Cambridge: Harvard University Press, 1937), p. 363; Carroll A. Wilson, *Thirteen Author Collections of the Nineteenth Century and Five Centuries of Familiar Quotations*, ed. Jean C. S. Wilson and David A. Randall (New York: Privately printed for Charles Scribner's Sons, 1950), 2:711.

the *New-England Magazine*.[6] Bird, like Howe, was a physician turned literary man. By today's standards his novels are diffuse, wordy, and loosely-structured, but in his own time he was ranked as a novelist with Simms, just below James Fenimore Cooper. His best novel, *Nick of the Woods*, was a couple of years away when Bird received his invitation from Howe. Still, he had a developing reputation as a playwrite as well as a writer of fiction. Arthur Hobson Quinn judged that 'Before he was thirty years old' Bird 'had lifted romantic tragedy to a level higher than it had reached in English since Congreve and had written plays which even to-day can be placed on the stage with effect.'[7] When Howe wrote Bird, he offered a minimum payment of $1 a page for prose, $2 for poetry, and held out the promise of more money for 'articles of more than common ability.' He and his fellow editors, Howe stressed, 'would be glad to receive some dramatic scenes from your pen; they fix no price, but suggest to you 10.cts per line'.

Bird responded almost immediately with — not a play nor an article, although Howe refers to his contribution as an 'article' in the sense of an 'item' — but a poem. It was the poem 'To Governor M'Duffie' that has so long been misattributed to Whittier. The proof is Howe's letter of acceptance:

Dr Bird.,
Dear Sir,
I thank you as editor of the N.E Magazine for your spirited article; I thank you as an individual for the courteous manner in which you communicated it; and I thank you most heartily as an American for the expression of indignation, which every patriot must feel toward the author of the "Inaugural Address."
It is a melancholy subject; but when the first feelings of indignation with which we repel the thought of dis-union have subsided, we cannot but give a melancholy assent to the fact that the bonds of our Union are fast withering away. It is not that there is no patriotism in the country; it is not that American hearts cannot be made to thrill by appeals to national feeling and national pride; it is not that the bosoms of men cannot be made to swell with patriotism; but alas! — these swellings and thrillings are but momentary — while interest — dear self interest is the eternal locum tenens of the heart.

[6] Howe to Bird, 29 December 1834; in the R. M. Bird Collection, Pattee Library, PU. Howe's letters to Bird are published in this article with the consent of Dr. Neda M. Westlake for the library.
[7] Quinn, *A History of American Drama From the Beginning to the Civil War* (New York: Harper & Brothers, 1923), p. 248.

But politics are not my forte, and the subject of dis-union is too melancholy an one for me to dwell upon. . . .

I beg you will favor us from time to time with more communications for the Mag. Your injunction of secrecy shall be regarded and your *incognito* preserved, unless as we hope, you remove it yourself.

Yours truly
Sam Gdly Howe

Boston Jan. 26 1834 [1835]

P.S.   I rate your article at 10$. I send you enclosed
5$, and the Magazine for the yr. 5-5-10.

— S.G.H.

Howe, Sargent, and Benjamin behaved honorably and did preserve Bird's incognito as author of 'To Governor M'Duffie'. Bird himself never removed it. Until today the veil of secrecy he enjoined on his editors remained unpierced.

THE FIRST EDITIONS OF JOSEPH CONRAD'S *ALMAYER'S FOLLY*

FLOYD EUGENE EDDLEMAN, DAVID LEON HIGDON, and ROBERT W. HOBSON

WRITING IN 1922 FOR THE *Smart Set*, H. L. MENCKEN PRONOUNCED Joseph Conrad's *Almayer's Folly* 'a work of absolute genius' and challenged 'the nobility and gentry of Christendom to point to another Opus 1 as magnificently planned and turned out.'[1] In all fairness, Mencken should have stipulated whether his judgment was based on the text of the first American edition or that of the first English edition. The distinction is crucial because there are 306 variants — ninety-five of them substantives — between the two texts. The American reader could praise Conrad's psychological perception and subtlety in having the unarmed Dain, after facing the armed Almayer, admit ' "I was

[1] 'Conrad Revisited', *Smart Set*, 69 (December 1922): 141–44.

We wish to thank Dean J. Knox Jones, Jr., of the Graduate School, and Dean Lawrence Graves, of the College of Arts and Sciences, Texas Tech University, for their generous support of this project.

Quotations from the work of Joseph Conrad are made with the permission of the Estate of Joseph Conrad, J. M. Dent & Sons literary executors.

much afraid"' (M233.22).[2] The English reader, on the other hand, encountered the more conventional bravado and heroics of ' "I was not afraid"' (U232.3).[3] In the English edition, the corpse pulled from the river by Mahmat is a 'formless mass' (U131.22); the American edition uses the rare, almost archaic, word 'inform' (M129.7) to describe the 'mass'. The American edition contains melodramatic 'violent' flames (M266.18), an 'unmoved' Nina (M133.1), and a 'sound of' wild pigs (M220.14); the English edition has impressionistic 'violet' flames (U262.21), an 'attentive' Nina (U135.11), and a 'sounder of' wild pigs (U219.12). Finally, the Malays in the English edition say 'bourrouh' (U122.24) but 'Courrouh' (M119.23) in the American edition. Inadvertent errors and non-authoritative compositorial interventions account for several of the 306 variants; but most of the substantive differences result from Conrad's revision of his novel in proof. The American edition, set from unrevised, uncorrected advance sheets of the English edition, preserves a state of text much closer to that written with what Conrad declared 'the serene audacity of an unsophisticated fool',[4] whereas the British edition, printed after Conrad had revised and corrected proof, is the sophisticated product of an author to whom *every* word is an object to be considered anxiously with heart searchings and in a spirit of severe resolution.'[5]

Jocelyn Baines and John D. Gordan have traced the history of *Almayer's Folly* from its tentative beginning in September 1889 to the completion of its manuscript on 24 April 1894,[6] and Conrad himself chronicled the manuscript's peregrinations from England to Australia, the Congo, the Ukraine, and Switzerland.[7] However, tantalizingly little is known for certain about the history of the text from the time it was accepted by T. Fisher Unwin on 3 or 4 October 1894 to the time it was published in England (29 April 1895) and in America (3 May

[2] *Almayer's Folly* (New York: Macmillan, 1895). All references to this edition are by the siglum 'M' followed by page and line numbers.

[3] *Almayer's Folly* (London: T. Fisher Unwin, 1895). All references to this edition are by the siglum 'U' followed by page and line numbers.

[4] Conrad to E. L. Sanderson, 21 November 1896; in G. Jean-Aubry, *Joseph Conrad: Life and Letters* (Garden City: Doubleday, Doran, 1927), 1:196.

[5] Conrad to John Galsworthy, 17 April 1899; in *Life and Letters,* 1:276.

[6] Baines, *Joseph Conrad: A Biography* (London: Weidenfeld and Nicolson, 1960), pp. 103–38; Gordan, *Joseph Conrad: The Making of a Novelist* (Cambridge, Mass.: Harvard University Press, 1940), pp. 177–86.

[7] *A Personal Record* (New York: Harper and Brothers, 1912), especially chapters 1 and 4, pp. 17–50, 114–46.

1895).[8] It is evident, though, that three men had a hand in shaping the text during that little-explored period: Conrad, through revisions; W. H. Chesson (Unwin's editor), through suggestions concerning idioms and grammar; and the anonymous editor we call the 'Macmillan grammarian', through editorial impositions.

Although his initial interview with Unwin in October led Conrad to expect proof sheets within a month, they did not reach him until 24 December 1894.[9] Conrad's characteristic reaction that 'Je n'ai rien a corriger en fait de style ou composition et quand aux fautes d'imprimerie les correcteur de la maison en prendrant bon soin' (14 or 21 November 1894)[10] did not anticipate what he actually did aboard G. F. W. Hope's cutter *Ildegonde*, on Chesson's advice, once proof began to arrive. Suddenly, the proofs which were to need little correction became 'la chose imprimée qui a l'air si bête — pire — vide de sens.'[11] Even before proof sheets were struck, Chesson had edited the typescript.[12]

Delays continued; the proposed March 1895 publication was pushed to early April, then mid-April, and finally late April. Although he affected indifference later, Conrad most eagerly anticipated the novel's appearance, so eagerly that on 12 March 1895 he wrote Unwin:

> I return to town next week — for the 18th. Isn't the 18th the date for the appearance of a certain Immortal work?!
>
> I warn you that if I am disappointed I shall surely have some kind of a fit; and if I die on your office carpet the Conservative papers will have big head lines: "Horrible cruelty of a well-known Publisher'. . . .
>
> The above frivolity of expression disguises very deep feeling. In common mercy to a suffering fellow creature let it be the 18th, without fail.[13]

[8] Theodore G. Ehrsam, *A Bibliography of Joseph Conrad* (Metuchen: Scarecrow Press, 1969), pp. 259–60. See also T. J. Wise, *A Bibliography of the Writings of Joseph Conrad (1895–1921)*, 2nd ed. (London: Privately published, 1921), p. 5.

[9] Gordan, p. 187.

[10] Conrad to Marguerite Poradowska, 14 or 21 November 1894; in Gordan, p. 187.

[11] *Ibid.*

[12] Ugo Mursia, 'The True "Discoverer" of Joseph Conrad's Literary Talent and Other Notes on Conradian Biography: With Three Unpublished Letters', *Conradiana*, 4 (1972): 10.

[13] Conrad to T. Fisher Unwin, 12 March 1895; at CtY-Beinecke; in H. M. Tomlinson, *'Almayer's Folly:* The Prelude', *A Conrad Memorial Library* (Garden City: Doubleday, Doran, 1929), p. 9.

With much the same playful spirit disguising 'very deep feeling,' he wrote again, probably in early April:

I do not want to make myself a nuisance — at least not very much, but since I have been staying with my friends here I became aware that the expectation of Almayer's Folly is unsettling this glorious and free country. All the people that have been told to look out for the book in March are writing letters full of anxiety and tears to know when — Oh! When! they will get the immortal work. Letters by every post. They come from North and West and South and East — they are as numerous as the raindrops — as persistent and loud as the wild west wind. . . . You will ruin my career at its very outset by a too prolonged delay. Can you? Will you? give me a date so that I can appease the universal thirst for information — and be called blessed by anxious and enthusiastic crowds of respectable and intelligent people.[14]

The delay was created by the American edition. To Marguerite Poradowska he wrote, 'On ne peut pas me donner la date definite encore. La maison Macmillan de New York se charge de la publication en Amerique et a cause de la loi sur le Copyright il faut attendre qu'il soient prete la-bas.'[15]

Conrad was referring to the Chace Act of 1891, which stipulated that a foreign work could be copyright in the United States only if it was set and printed here, and only if it was published simultaneously here and abroad.[16] The Chace Act had two far-reaching effects on such books, and those effects must be accounted for in any bibliographical and textual study of East-to-West transatlantic transmission. Because of the act's manufacturing clause, a book like *Almayer's Folly* almost had to exist in two separate editions. The American edition collates [A]² B–S⁸ T², has twenty-eight lines to the text page, and is trimmed to 190 x 125 mm.; the English edition collates [1]⁸ 2–17⁸, has thirty lines to the text page (except for pp. 119, 172, 188, and 239,

[14] Conrad to Unwin, 'Thursday' [1895?]; at CtY-Beinecke. Quoted with the consent of the Beinecke Rare Book and Manuscript Library of Yale University.
[15] Conrad to Poradowska, 12 April 1895; in Gordan, p. 188.
[16] Hellmut Lehmann-Haupt, *The Book in America*, 2nd ed. (New York: R. R. Bowker, 1951), p. 203. See also Simon Nowell-Smith, *International Copyright Law and the Publisher in the Reign of Queen Victoria* (London: Oxford University Press, 1968), p. 65: 'the Chace Act . . . required deposit in Washington of an American-printed edition "on or before the day of publication in this or any Foreign country." In other words to conform with both United States and British law a book must be published in both countries simultaneously.'

which have thirty-one), and measures 222± x 125± mm. untrimmed.[17]

But the effects of the Chace Act on such a book were not limited to bibliographical differences only. There were also textual differences, which are the point here. The publication requirement of the act almost guaranteed a relationship between the two editions in which they would share a history up to some point in time (usually at some proof stage), after which their histories would diverge. That kind of relationship is apparent in a few easily recognized features of their texts. The American text records such British spellings as 'colour', 'honour', 'civilise', 'patronise', 'realise', and 'tranquillise', while its pointing is a blend of British punctuation overlayed with house-styling from the American firm. Moreover, the American text repeats two errors from the English ('Sambira' for 'Sambir' [U36.2, M30.6–7]; 'and as' for 'and was' [U63.6, M58.21]) while correcting two others ('grayish' to 'greyish' [U54.23, M49.27]; 'Blando' to 'Blanda' [U36.10, M30.15]). Evidently, some things went wrong during the first printing of the English edition but not during the first printing of the American: extra spacing rather than necessary punctuation appears at U24.30, 161.6, 178.29, 184.5, 184.29, and 265.12; no punctuation and no extra spacing appear at U271.20; 'g nerosity' instead of 'generosity' and 'prestige   his' instead of 'prestige of his' appear at U110.29–30; and the omission of the terminal period in the heading to chapter 4 on U66 breaks a pattern otherwise consistent in the book. Most of these flaws were set right in the second and third printings of the English edition, and none of them appear in the American.[18]

The history of the two editions is easily traced. It begins, for present purposes, with the Leeds Typescript (named for its second owner, W. B. Leeds, and now housed in the Humanities Research Center, University of Texas at Austin).[19] The Leeds Typescript was setting

---

[17] Cf. Ehrsam, p. 259; Wise, p. 5.

[18] The 'Colonial Edition' (the second[?] printing of the first English edition) supplies two letters and one comma omitted from the first printing (U110.29, 110.30, 271.20). The third(?) printing retains those corrections and adds five of its own, supplying one missing period (U161.6) and four missing commas (U184.5, 184.29, 212.30, 265.12), and repairing one badly battered quotation mark (U186.7). It also changes 'if they were suspicious of him' (U114.3) to 'If they were suspicious of them' and 'over, go at once?' (U114.8) to 'over. Go at once?', the latter corresponding with the typescript (L107.22).

[19] All references to the Leeds Typescript are by the siglum 'L' followed by page and line numbers. Quotation from the typescript is with the consent of TxU-Humanities Research Center.

copy for Unwin's printers. Their proofs — presumably galley proofs or the equivalent — served both for correction by Conrad and transmission to Macmillan. Macmillan presumably used those proofs first for editorial marking and then as copy for its printer. This history can be traced easily because, although not all crucial documents survive, those documents that do survive clearly reveal their past. Compositorial stints marked on the Leeds Typescript is among the evidence that it was setting copy for Unwin's printers. The evidence that the American edition was prepared from early proofs of the English takes slightly longer to explain but is no more recondite. First, accidental variants from the English in the American are almost without exception what can be expected in an East-West transatlantic publication of the time. Second, isolated substantive variants from the English in the American usually reproduce readings in the Leeds Typescript. Third, the English edition contains some material in neither the Leeds Typescript nor the American edition. Presumably they are additions made in proof. One of them is five lines long; possibly it was this passage to which Conrad was referring when he wrote Chesson: "In reference to a paragraph (of 2 sentences) left out in the setting of Almayer I must own that the fault is mine entirely. The typescript is in error not the printer."[20] Finally — although this point is purely critical speculation — the ninety-five substantive variants which include the five-line passage just mentioned seem to be revisions that might be made by an author hoping to improve his text.

With that outline as background, it obviously is useful to explore in detail the differences between the English and American editions of *Almayer's Folly.* Such an exploration is obviously useful for three reasons: 1. it is the necessary preliminary to a critical edition of the novel; 2. it focuses on Conrad's methods of composition and revision; 3. it suggests once again the need to come to terms with the specifics of house-styling in a particular house, at a particular time, as related to a particular work of literature.

I

Of first interest, of course, is what the author did. Most striking is Conrad's restoration in the English edition of that five-and-one-half-line sentence (U69.20–24) missing from the Leeds Typescript — and therefore from the American edition — but present in the manuscript.

[20] Conrad to Chesson; quoted in Mursia, p. 9.

In chapter 4, Nina returns home and unexpectedly finds a prosperous-looking brig anchored in the Pantai near her father's house. She cautiously lands her canoe and silently makes her way to the house. The restored sentence, 'Stopping her course by a rapid motion of her paddle, with another swift stroke she sent it whirling away from the wharf and steered for a little rivulet which gave access to the back courtyard of the house', precisely describes her handling of the craft, detailed information missing from the typescript (L62.10) and the American edition (M64.20). Restoration of the sentence bespeaks a master mariner's attention to the step-by-step process in handling any kind of boat. The sentence, however, was not taken over without change from the manuscript, but underwent extensive revision. The manuscript reads 'She stopped her course by a [a *inserted over a caret*] rapid motion of the paddle and by another swift stroke sent it whirling away from the wharf and into a [small *canceled*] narrow rivulet leading at the back of the house' — a total of eleven differences from the English text.

Not all the substantive variants which so markedly distinguish the English edition from the American involve such lengthy additions and revisions. Conrad's revisions, astonishingly diverse and numerous, demonstrate his preoccupation with the problems of repetition and redundancy, idiomatic rephrasing (possibly with the help or at the suggestion of W. H. Chesson or Lancelot Sanderson),[21] more precise images, and grammatical consistency.

In his refinement of sentence structure, Conrad seems to have been concerned with both rhythm and focal precision. A sentence from chapter 1 reads in the typescript: 'And motionless there in the still and oppressing calm of the tropical night she could see at each flash of lightning the forest lining both banks up the river, bending before the furious blast of the coming tempest, she saw the upper reach of the river whipped into white foam by the wind, and the black clouds torn into fantastic shapes trailing low over the swaying trees.' (L 22.4–10.) The English text's excision of 'she saw' brings the direct object-verbal modifier combinations 'forest . . . bending, upper reach . . . whipped, black clouds . . . torn' (U28.20–21) into a more rhythmically parallel relationship. The participial phrase 'lining both banks up the river' is a restrictive element. The American edition retains 'she saw'

21 See Dale B. J. Randell, *Joseph Conrad and Warrington Dawson* (Durham: Duke University Press, 1968), p. 25.

(M23.6) and secures the break by substituting a semi-colon for the comma after 'tempest' (M23.7).

On several occasions Conrad apparently changed verb tense in order to maintain consistency with the verbs in the preceding sentences. The inhabitants of Sambir, curious about Dain's presence, question one another in the American edition about his activities: ' "Had he seen the Sultan? What did the Sultan say? Has he given any presents? What would he sell? What would he buy?" ' In the third question in the English edition, the auxiliary for 'given' is 'had' instead of 'has' (U78.12). The second adjustment occurs in a discussion of Dain's motive for returning to Sambir: 'Yes, he had come back to Sambir for Nina, although aware that the Dutch would look for him there, but he also calculated his chances of safety in Lakamba's hands.' The Unwin addition of 'had' (U112.12) between 'but he' and 'also' is functional in two ways: it obviously makes the independent clauses parallel, and it also clarifies that the calculation took place *before* he returned to the village.

In seven instances, the Leeds Typescript auxiliary verbs also underwent adjustment, with the American edition retaining six typescript readings, while the British changed six, often — apparently — for neither grammatical nor logical reasons. For example, the first, second, and third person uses of 'shall' are changed to 'will' in the English text (U176.13, 194.18, 200.12, 201.21, 243.15), but are retained in the American (M175.23, 194.18, 200.20, 202.3, 246.12). The substitution in the English edition of 'might' (U191.19) for 'may' (M191.25) obviously corrects the sentence ' "I thought you may have been tender" ', which calls for the past active indicative. And the English retention of 'should' (U164.27) in the typescript sentence, ' "The arrest should be effected before dark" ' (L162.7) more readily suggests the sub-lieutenant's dazed uncertainty and lack of control of the situation than does the American 'shall' (M163.27): at this point he has to contend with a drunken Almayer, a hysterical Nina, and the prospect of failure in the mission; for him to say 'shall' smacks of sheer military bluster.

Elimination of repetitive meanings and word sounds seems to have been very much on Conrad's mind as he made proof corrections. In the previously-cited description of Nina's contemplation of the storm, the typescript and the American edition have her standing 'motionless there in the still and oppressing calm of the tropical night' (M23.4). To avoid the redundancy of 'motionless', 'still', and 'calm', the phrase 'still and oppressing' is condensed to the single adjective 'oppressive'

(U28.17). An even more obvious example of Conrad tightening sentence structure occurs in the sentence 'He remembered the narrow and slanting deck of the brig, the silent and sleeping coast, the smooth and black surface of the sea' (M17.29–18.1). For the English edition, he eliminated the 'and's (U12.8–10), thus turning attention from the adjectives to the nouns modified, compacting the rhythm, and emphasizing the alliteration. Later in the novel, when Nina, Almayer, Dain, and Ali leave the canoe which has taken them to the islet where they are to be met by another boat, the reader of the American edition is told that 'after carefully laying Nina down in the shade of the bushes growing in the middle of the islet, Dain threw himself down beside her' (M247.21–23). The second 'down' (U244.25) of the sentence was removed, presumably to eliminate repetition. To avoid further redundancy, Conrad also rephrased 'Almayer, steering in the stern,' (M246.14) to read 'Almayer, who was steering' (U243.16). Since the canoe Almayer is in cannot be steered from any other position but the stern, the word is obviously repetitious.

Inverted or unidiomatic word order is an obvious characteristic of Conrad's English, even in his later novels. In *Almayer's Folly*, one often finds sentences with inverted adjective or adverbial phrases and clauses: 'she pushed gently her daughter towards the canoes' (M198. 19–20). Some of his sentences contain misplaced phrases: 'There again Dain met in Almayer with unexpected resistance' (M107.23–24). That Conrad was conscious of these faults in his first novel is demonstrated by the adjustments he makes to idiomatic usage in the English text: Nina's 'black, long hair' (M20.7–8) becomes 'long black hair' (U25.22–23); Mrs. Almayer warns Nina 'not to make a noise' (U70.27), rather than 'not to make noise' (M65.24–25). Conrad often effects more idiomatic positioning of prepositional and adverbial modifiers. In both the typescript and the American edition, Almayer 'paused in his endeavours to make for himself a passage' (M123.24). The English edition relocates the object to its more conventional position immediately following the infinitive: 'to make a passage for himself' (U126.18). Similarly, 'carrying in his arms Nina' (M247.12–13) becomes 'carrying Nina in his arms' (U244.14); and 'laying down Nina' (M247.23) is altered to 'laying Nina down' (U244.23). Conrad's English edition distinguished between 'into', denoting motion from the outside to the inside, and 'in', denoting location inside. Lakamba's desire that Dain not 'fall in the hands' of the Dutch (M169.12) becomes a desire that he not 'fall into the hands' (U170.10). Mrs. Almayer is portrayed as having jumped 'into the river' (U38.18), rather than 'in the river' (M32.25). And the corpse is tossed 'into a hole' (U204.21), instead of 'in a hole' (M205.7). In both the typescript and the American edition, the preposition 'in' originally followed the verb 'insisted' (L105.13, M108.12). Idiomatic phrasing is, of course, 'insisted on', a reading followed in the English edition (U111.28). That 'to insist' comes from the Latin verb which means 'to persist in' may account for the error. Revisions such as these were probably made at the suggestion of W. H. Chesson. For example, a Conrad letter to Chesson gracefully acquiesces to his judgment: 'As to that preface (which I have shown you) I trust it may be dispensed with, but if it must appear you are quite right — *Aversion from* not "aversion for" as I wrote — and stuck to like a lunatic. You will correct?'[22] The preface mentioned in the letter is the 'Author's Note' written in 1895 but not published until 1920.

The crippled sentence 'You have trodden the poor fellows — whoever he is — hand' (kept intact in the American edition, except for the addition of a possessive 's' after 'fellow' [M127.27–28]) is made less awkward in the English edition by transposing the interpolated element to the beginning of the sentence: ' "Whoever he is, you have trodden the poor fellow's hand." ' (U130.16–17.)

In the description of Dain's forest hideout, where the ultimate fate of trees was strangulation by parasitic vines, the narrator had originally observed that 'only the parasites seemed to live there in a sinuous rush upwards into the air and sunshine, feeding on the dead and the living alike' (M220.4–5). The emended passage, however, shows the creepers 'feeding on the dead and the dying alike' (U219.3). One sentence earlier, it was observed that 'entombed and rotting' trees lay 'where their successors stood as if mourning, in dark green foliage immense and helpless, waiting their turn.' To maintain this notion of inevitability, the substitution of 'dying' for 'living' removes from the image its only suggestion of hope.

A third of the significant emendations involve Conrad's attempts to change, refocus, or sharpen images. Here indeed we can glimpse Conrad and his craft of the word and can understand why he was later to claim, 'Give me the right word and the right accent and I will move

---

[22] Conrad to Chesson; quoted in Mursia, p. 10. There were further revisions: the phrase 'aversion from' eventually was changed to 'disapproved'. The ribbon copy and a carbon with revisions in Conrad's hand are in the Philip H. and A. S. W. Rosenbach Foundation Museum.

the world.'[23] Much of his attention focuses on Nina, particularly in his use of descriptive words to accentuate her ability to conceal her emotions in the interest of fulfilling her desires. The intensity of her efforts to maintain an 'unmoved' exterior indicates the power of her feeling — a point Conrad wished his readers to comprehend.

The first significant emendations relating to Nina occur in her confrontation with Almayer immediately following Babalatchi's intentionally false identification of the dead man as Dain. Throughout this scene, Conrad strives to maintain the irony of Almayer's misunderstanding of Nina's apparent indifference to the defeat of her father's plans. She knows that Dain is alive, but, until Almayer's indignant outburst, had been unaware of her father's concern for her well-being and his intense despair following the collapse of his planned expedition for gold. As the initially calm Almayer sat on the table, 'Nina stood quietly, her hand resting lightly on her father's shoulder, her face unmoved, but every line of her features, the attitude of her whole body expressing the most keen and anxious attention.' (M131.28–132.4.) Nina's outward composure contrasts with her inward anxiety. The complexity of the image arises from Conrad's insistence that Nina's features would betray her deep concern to one who had eyes to see it.

But the unaware Almayer accuses Nina of indifferently observing his desperate quest for riches: ' "You never cared; you saw me struggle, and work, and strive, unmoved; and my suffering you could never see." ' (M132.13–15.) The paragraph immediately following reads: 'He looked at his daughter's unmoved face and jumped to his feet upsetting the chair.' (M133.1–2.) Conrad substitutes 'attentive' for 'unmoved' (U135.11), thus reminding the reader of Nina's involvement. Nina, who has assumed a pose to protect Dain, cannot genuinely express her feelings without endangering his life. Ironically, Almayer fails to notice her attentive face, though the reader is meant to. Almayer's pitiful confidences and demands for sympathy weaken Nina's ability to maintain the pose: 'With her heart deeply moved by the sight of Almayer's misery, knowing it in her power to end it with a word, longing to bring peace to that troubled heart, she heard with terror the voice of her overpowering love commanding her to be silent.' (M134.25–135.1.) In the American text, Nina 'had listened to Almayer's appeal for sympathy, for one word of comfort, apparently unmoved' (M134.20–22). This painfully maintained exterior made her

[23] 'A Familiar Preface', *A Personal Record,* p. 2.

appear inwardly unresponsive to Almayer. 'Apparently indifferent' (U137.1) emphasizes Almayer's misunderstanding of her emotions at this moment.

Nina also conceals her thoughts on the evening of Almayer's ghoulishly comic presentation of the corpse to the Dutch officers. Her furious response to the lieutenant's questioning acts as a kind of emotional smokescreen against any suspicion on the officer's part that either she or Almayer is engaged in duplicity. When the lieutenant agrees that he and his men will leave when 'the scoundrel' is captured, Nina replies, ' "Then I would get him for you if I had to seek him in a burning fire." ' (M184.23.) The typescript and the American edition have Nina speaking these words 'with passionage energy' (M184.23). By substituting 'intense' for 'passionate' in the English edition (U185. 3–4), Conrad avoids the implication that Nina's passion dominates her consciousness of purpose. Though her hatred of white men is real, her tirade is at least partially feigned. She is anxious to precipitate the officers' departure, but more for Dain's sake than for the reason she gives — that she hates white men. The phrase 'intense energy' reflects Nina's 'paroxysm of nervous restlessness' and her succeeding anxious appeal for Almayer to show the officers the corpse.

Later in the novel, Conrad twice revised sentences pertaining to Nina's relationship with Dain and her father. The lovers' attitude towards each other during their reunion in Bulangi's clearing is given a note of ambiguity. Nina's smile during their embrace is inscrutable: 'It might have been a smile of triumph, or of conscious power, or of tender pity, or perhaps of love.' (M227.26–27.) By emending the following sentence, 'She spoke tenderly to him' (M227.27), to 'She spoke softly to him' (U226.17), Conrad may have wished to avoid repetition but, more importantly, to leave her inscrutability unresolved. However, if he only wished to avoid repetition, why, in the same scene, does he leave unchanged the sentences 'she felt a great pitying tenderness for that man' (M227.5–6), 'the murmur of tender words lingered' (M228.18), and 'Their voices rose and fell tender or animated' (M229.1).

During Nina's final conversation with her father, she rebukes him for his insensitivity to her feelings after her return from schooling in Singapore to a hoped-for peaceful refuge in Sambir. She tells Almayer that she found only doubt and uncertainty: ' "But, when he [Dain] came, all doubt disappeared" ' (U250.9). With Dain's appearance, Nina's life acquires purpose, and she rejects white civilization with no further uncertainty. Both the typescript and the American edition introduce her explanation with the adverb 'Then' (M253.17); however, Nina clearly intends to contrast her former miserable state with her newly awakened one. The conjunction communicates her meaning more precisely than the adverb, which indicates only a difference in time. Moreover, the phrase 'when he came' renders any other time reference superfluous.

The other emendations, though equally complex in their effects, seldom reveal new insights into characterization. For example, when the Dutch lieutenant admonishes Almayer to produce Dain so that he can be arrested, Almayer responds, ' "You can do nothing without me, and I, knowing the man well, am to help you in catching him." ' (M163.3–5.) Conrad emends 'catching' (M163.5) to 'finding' (U164.5), possibly to avoid repetition, but possibly to underline Almayer's drunken jest in his plans to give the Dutch a headless corpse. The Dutch officers are originally shown standing side by side and 'looking curiously' (M185.25) as they listen to Nina berate them and watch Almayer receive her elaborate sympathy. The change to 'looking on curiously' (U186.3–4) rescues the officers from caricature by detaching them from the scene they are witnessing. Elsewhere, in the description of Babalatchi and Mrs. Almayer, holding their tête-à-tête on the verandah of Almayer's house, Conrad tries to intensify rather than subdue caricature: and 'at every louder shout they nodded at each other with a ludicrous assumption of scandalised propriety' (M179.24–26). A substitution of 'ridiculous affectation' (U180.9) for 'ludicrous assumption' (M179.25) more clearly depicts their comic postures of moral indignation.

In another scene, when Dain confirms Lakamba's worst suspicions as to the fate of the brig, the sultan responds with 'a short and malevolent glance' (M103.20–21). The English edition is emended to 'a short and hostile glance' (U107.14). 'Hostile' provides a stronger sense of overt and active antagonism. Later in the scene, Dain leaves Lakamba's stockade during a heavy rainstorm. In the American edition he calls to his boatmen, 'who responded with a unanimous "Ada! Tuan!" while they looked apprehensively at the river.' (M111.25–27.) In the English edition, they 'looked uneasily' (U115.13). 'Uneasily' does perhaps convey more of a sense of constraint than 'apprehensively', which suggests fear. However, it is quite difficult to justify the use of one word over the other. The emendation is simply an example of inexplicable authorial tinkering.

A similar emendation occurs when Reshid attempts to gain information about Dain from Taminah, a slave girl who secretly loves Dain and who knows that he is alive. Reshid stops her on a path, and 'when near Reshid Taminah waited with downcast eyes' (M143.28–144.1). Conrad changed 'waited' (M143.28) to 'stood' (U145.28), possibly to avoid repeating the verb of the preceding sentence or possibly to suggest greater passivity. Indeed, Reshid views her now as nothing more than an object and treats her with haughty disdain.

Two groups of word changes emphatically concern attention to detail and vividness of imagery. Representative of Conrad's attention to detail is his change of 'barrel' (M233.6) to 'chamber' (U231.17) in the clause 'during which one barrel of the revolver went off harmlessly' (M233.6–7). Revolvers, as Conrad must have recalled, simply do not have multiple barrels. Similarly, Conrad revised the sentence, 'Men and things shook off the torpor of the noontide heat and stirred into life under the first breath of the sea breeze.' (M173.14–16.) By changing 'torpor of the noontide heat' (M173.15) to 'torpor of the hot afternoon' (U174.7), Conrad more reasonably assigns 'torpor' to the 'afternoon' rather than to the 'heat'. Also, by making 'afternoon' the object of the preposition and by modifying it with 'hot', Conrad implies some passage of time, while retaining the heat causing the torpor of the Sambir natives. The preceding paragraphs, with their mention of 'declining sunlight' (M173.11) and 'the afternoon breeze' (M172.18), establish that it is afternoon, thus necessitating a change from 'noontide'.

Conrad's desire for specificity led him to make numerous seemingly minor changes. The imagery of Almayer sagaciously 'putting his finger to the side of his nose' (M183.7) acquires digital specificity in the British text, in which Almayer is seen 'putting his forefinger to the side of his nose' (U183.18). At the beginning of chapter 12 in the American text, Dain points to an islet 'about a mile ahead of the canoe' (M246.9–10) and twice exclaims, ' "This is the place' (M246.8, 246.10). To allow for the distance which the boat has yet to travel, 'this' is altered to 'that' in both instances (U243.10, 243.12). Mrs. Almayer's reference to her 'people' (U178.2) in the English edition is preferable to the American allusion to her 'race' (M178.6), because it suggests the closeness of more primitive tribal or communal relationships. In the American text, Babalatchi tells Captain Ford that the islanders had lived in felicity 'before a white Rajah ruled in Kuching.' (M273.28.) The English edition adds political detail by substituting 'English' (U269.23) for 'white'. Each of these changes vests the sentence with a concreteness absent in the typescript and the American text.

Often, Conrad animates certain images. For example, Almayer tells Nina that he will never forgive her for deceiving him: ' "When you were caressing my cheek you were counting the hours to the sunset that was the signal for your meeting with that man — there!' (M251. 1–4.) Conrad revised 'hours' (M251.2) to 'minutes' (U247.28), thus intensifying Almayer's conception of Nina's eagerness to meet Dain. In describing Almayer's facial expression in this same scene, the narrator remarks in the English text that 'All passion, regret, grief, hope, or anger' had been 'erased by the hand of fate, as if after this last stroke everything was over' (U248.11, 13). The American reading, 'life was over' (M251.17), simply cannot achieve the image of inclusiveness and bleak finality implicit in 'everything was over' (U248.13).

A similar emendation strengthens a major theme of the novel: the hostility of Almayer's environment. By personifying the natural forces, often in lengthy examples of pathetic fallacy, Conrad stresses nature's playful unconcern and, at times, her outright indifference to man. For example, in the American edition, the breeze played 'capriciously for a time around' (M173.6) the Dutch flag flying over Lakamba's campong. In revision, the breeze plays directly 'with' (U173.28) the flag, thus turning this emblem of power into a toy of the wind.

When he read the proofs, Conrad must have become aware that he had overused the word 'suddenly', because he paid special attention to it. Of the seven substitutions of various other words for 'sudden' and 'suddenly', all but one change is made, at least in part, to avoid repetition of the word within the space of a page or two. For example, within eight lines of one another, the prau 'suddenly' (M258.16) disappears and the crested wavelets 'suddenly' (M258.24) die. Conrad revised these to read 'all at once' (U255.1) and 'quickly' (U255.9). In addition, to avoid frequent repetition of the word, the first emendation also changes the image from immediate disappearance to gradual but rapid disappearance. Two other substitutions concern character reaction. When Dain sees Nina for the first time, Almayer is struck 'by the sudden change in the expression of his guest's countenance' (M69. 17–18). Unaware that Nina has entered the room, Almayer assumes that Dain's response is to something he has said or done. Hence, Conrad's use of 'unexpected' (U74.12–13) in place of 'sudden' focuses attention on Almayer's reaction rather than on Dain's visage. While preparing to flee with Dain, Nina experiences a 'sudden desire to look again at her father's face' (M198.24–25). By substituting 'passing' (U198.18) for 'sudden' (M198.24), Conrad renders the modifier of 'desire' more consistent with the lack of 'strong affection' mentioned in the same sentence. Possibly, the substitution also makes Nina a less sympathetic character. The only instance of a change not made to avoid repetition involves Almayer's breaking down 'suddenly' (M243.12) when he realizes that Nina has rejected him for Dain. By changing 'suddenly' to 'completely' (U241.5), Conrad emphasizes the extent — even the totality, rather than the unexpectedness — of Almayer's breakdown.

II

The Macmillan grammarian's rage for correctness accounts in part for thirty-three substantive variants as well. In his grammatical nicety, he carefully corrected verb forms, changing 'laid' (U91.12) to 'lay' (M86.20), 'should be' (U164.27) to 'shall be' (M163.27), and 'lay still' (U222.7, 223.9) to 'lie still' (M223.12, 224.15). He also corrected several obvious errors in the proofs sent him, errors which unfortunately neither Conrad nor the Unwin readers caught. He perceptively caught an error in the Malay word 'Blanda' (M30.15) which was typed 'Blando' (L30.3) in the Leeds Typescript, although both he and the English manuscript editor failed to catch on the same page an analogous misspelling, 'Sambira' (M30.6–7, U36.2), which should be 'Sambir'. Elsewhere, he corrected the absurdity of 'He [Mahmat] put the palms of his hand' (U123.20) by pluralizing 'hand' (M120.21). His other changes often involve niceties of usage — for example, distinguishing between 'awhile' and 'a while' (U145.29, 189.17; M144.1, 189.19), 'around' (U149.5) and 'round' (M147.2), 'upon' (U244.12) and 'up on' (M247.11), and the inversion of 'she had' (U205.16) to 'had she' (M207.2) required by the sentence's peculiar negative construction. But this grammatical acumen dulled considerably in many attempts at substantive revision. Several of these well-intentioned efforts significantly obfuscated meaning.

In at least ten instances, the Macmillan grammarian undertook to 'correct' the text when indeed no correction was called for. A few moments with any dictionary would have demonstrated that 'sounder' is the correct collective noun for a herd of wild pig. In the typescript and the English edition, Dain hears a 'sounder of wild pig' (L224.10, U219.12), which the Macmillan compositor changes to 'sound of wild pig' (M220.14). In another instance, his substitution of 'violent gleams' (M266.18) for 'violet gleams' (U262.21) to describe the flames of Almayer's burning house as they appeared flashing 'in the strong sunshine' (M266.18) renders the description obtrusively melodramatic and destroys the color progression from 'brick-red' (M266.17) to 'violet' (M266.18) to 'clear blue' (M266.20). The noun 'gleams' and the adjective 'violent' are incompatible: one suggests brief glints of subdued light, while the other connotes fury and intensity.

Macmillan's alteration of the present participle 'decaying' (U44.20) to the past participle 'decayed' (M39.6) in an early description of the house Lingard had originally built for Almayer and his wife wrongly conveys a notion of conclusiveness, rather than gradual but continuous deterioration. For even this first house is associated with the folly which, in the course of the novel, leads to Almayer's decline. Use of the past participle here prematurely fixes the image of decay and thus damages its vital symbolic relationship to the central character. That the other participles in this passage are in the past tense may have misled the compositor.

Somewhat similarly, hyphenation of the word 'misfortune' (U122. 4–5) at the end of a line in the English text and presumably in the advance sheets may be responsible for the American text dropping the first syllable — an unfortunate omission perhaps, because it allows Almayer briefly to anticipate 'some new fortune' (M119.4) in a life that has come to expect only disappointment. In the same paragraph, phrases such as 'unwonted solitude' (M118.27), 'frightened fancy' (M119.3), and 'oppressive stillness' (M119.2–3) suggest no hope for fortune. Not even hyphenation, however, can explain the American 'almost audible' (M66.3) in place of the typescript and English 'almost inaudible' (L63.19, U71.3). In responding to Nina's question about Dain's arrival, Mrs. Almayer, who clearly intends Nina to hear her reply, but who also does not wish to draw any attention from the men in the house, *should* speak almost inaudibly.

Perhaps the most significant substantive emendation calls into question Dain's bravery by changing his response to Almayer (following a brief scuffle with him for a revolver) from ' "Your hand shook much; for myself I was not afraid" ' (U232.3) to ' "Your hand shook much; for myself I was much afraid" ' (M233.22). The American version presents a strikingly-modern hero willing to admit fear and thus quite unlike Conrad's later protagonists who cling to illusions of their self-sufficiency. Unwin's Dain is a more conventional nineteenth-century protagonist whose adventure-story ancestry shows clearly through his boast.

Two insignificant but interesting errors that probably are compositorial involve the word 'ho'. In the English text, during her final conversation with Nina, Mrs. Almayer recalls her husband's refusal to allow her a last look at her daughter prior to the child's being taken to Singapore. Mrs. Almayer angrily remarks, ' "I wanted to look at your face again. He said no!" ' (U197.1–2). The American text's substitution of 'ho' (M197.5) for 'no' as Almayer's reply is probably explained by the cluster of cancellations at this point in the typescript (L201.4). The American compositor may simply have replicated an error present in the proof sheets. But elsewhere Almayer's drunken laughter, 'Ha! ha! ha!' (U187.7–8) inexplicably becomes 'Ha! ho! ha!' (M187.4–5). Another American variant that may be the result of compositorial error occurs in the description of Bulangi's clearing, in which Dain is to meet Nina. The clearing is surrounded by large, majestic trees 'lashed together with manifold bands by a mass of tangled creepers' (M217.17–18). Although consistent with the 'cable-like coils' of the description, 'bands' does not so strongly suggest — as does the English 'bonds' (U216.19) — the idea of captivity and enslavement inherent in such phrases as 'merciless creepers' (M217.21), 'their victims' (M217.26), and 'silent destruction' (M217.26).

But the Macmillan grammarian is clearly responsible for approximately 150 accidental variants. In preparing the proof sheets for resetting in accord with the manufacture clause of the 1891 Chace Act, he took the opportunity to correct numerous obvious errors in spelling and errors in punctuation created by loose type in the English setting. Unfortunately, however, he erroneously 'corrected' the text in several instances when the reading was accurate. He did not Americanize the spelling, possibly because Macmillan at this time was still a branch office of the English firm.[24] For the most part, his changes concern punctuation. He repunctuated numerous sentences for clarity, especially where lack of commas — either before or after nonrestrictive clauses and phrases and after introductory phrases — created ambiguity or awkwardness. In accordance with American usage, he added

---

[24] Macmillan's American operation remained a branch office until 1896 (see Charles Morgan, *The House of Macmillan* [*1843–1943*] [London: Macmillan, 1943], p. 163). The phenomenon of American editions retaining English orthography seems more common than is generally assumed: see J. A. Lavin, 'The First Editions of Virginia Woolf's *To the Lighthouse*', *Proof*, 2 (1972): 189.

hyphens and repunctuated series, vocatives, rhetorical questions, and so on. Occasionally, he repunctuated simply because his interpretation of the context or logical consistency required other punctuation. His interventions become a significant part of the textual history of *Almayer's Folly,* because later Macmillan issues and several Doubleday reprints before 1922 used his revised text for their copy.[25] Consideration of the major types of variants for which he must be held responsible — hyphenation, repunctuation of various kinds of phrases and clauses, and other changes not readily categorized — demonstrates the extent of his intervention.

Of the thirty variants created by hyphenation, at least twenty-three may be attributed to house regularization. The American edition consistently hyphenates 'thunder-storm',[26] whereas the English edition (in accord with the typescript and English usage) prints it as one word. On the other hand, the English edition treats 'hiding-place', 'armchair', and 'cooking-shed' as compound nominatives, while the American considers them nominatives with accompanying adjectives.[27] Not all the variants, however, can be so easily explained by reference to usage and the *OED* but instead suggest that the Macmillan editor strove for logical consistency. The American edition hyphenates 'Rajah-Laut' in every instance, but the English edition, which hyphenates it for the first thirty-one pages of text, treats it as two words thereafter.[28] Other such inconsistencies include 'roof-sticks' (M18. 17–18) in the American edition, given in the English as 'roof sticks' (U24.4) and 'roof-stick' (U258.3). On a single page, the English edition has 'salt water diplomat' (U50.8) and 'salt-water jests' (U50.26); the American logically hyphenates both of these identically-structured adjectival phrases (M45.8, 45.26). Later, the American edition correctly changes 'bird's' (U78.27) to 'birds' ' (M74.9), but in an excess of punctuation adds a hyphen to give the reading 'birds'-nests' (M74.9). All possible combinations of 'goodbye' are present through the various

[25] Our collation of later editions reveals that the Doubleday, Doran reprintings in 1919 and 1921 are of the first American edition.

[26] M22.7/U27.22, M95.9/U99.22, M96.12/U100.23, M97.6/U101.16, M111.13/U114.29, M230.27/U229.12, M244.12/U242.2.

[27] 'Hiding-place': M152.19/U154.4, M155.10/U156.21, M157.12/U158.20, M168.21/U169.20, M172.2/U172.26, M219.8/U218.8, M219.19–20/U218. 19. 'Armchair': M99.9/U103.10, M100.18/U104.17, M116.3/U119.14, M131. 2/U133.14. 'Cooking-shed': M176.14–15/U177.3–4, M203.23/U203.9–10, M261.26/U257.9.

[28] M27.2/U32.29, M34.3/U39.22, M48.25/U53.22.

texts: 'Good bye' (L260.14) in the typescript; 'Goodbye' (U253.14) in the English edition; and 'Good-bye' (M256.27) in the American. That the hyphenation generally reflects editorial normalization rather than authorial usage is the unmistakable conclusion to be drawn from the evidence. The printed texts disregard hyphenation or lack of it in the typescript. For example, the typescript spellings of 'coal black' (L19.8), 'note book' (L39.21–22), 'water palm' (L61.6), 'high heeled' (L67.5), 'up country' (L140.7), and 'side arms' (L161.20) appear hyphenated in both editions (M20.9, 40.21, 63.12, 69.14–15, 141.13–14, 163.15 and U25.25, 46.3–4, 68.12–13, 74.9–10, 143.14–15, 164.15); 'open-hearted' (L73.3) becomes 'open-hearted' (M75.19, U80.6–7); 'paddy field' (L226.14) 'paddyfield' (M222.19, U221.15–16); and 'water side' (L226.22) is hyphenated in the English edition (U221.26) but printed as one word in the American (M223.2). It is difficult to maintain that hyphenation or lack of it affects the meaning in any of the thirty variants; however, it clearly evinces further intervention — some which Conrad had the opportunity to see, some which he had not seen.

The Macmillan grammarian intervened frequently to add commas after introductory phrases and clauses, before the final items in a series, before vocatives, and between verbs and accompanying adverbs at the ends of sentences. These additions frequently clarify meaning significantly. In several instances, a well-pointed clause salvages an otherwise awkward sentence. For example, in the sentence, 'Shortly after the murmur of many voices reached him across the water' (U21. 21–22), the Macmillan grammarian added a comma between 'after' and 'the' (M16.2); otherwise, a reader could include the 'murmur' or logically even the entire sentence in the introductory clause as object of the preposition. Addition of a comma also avoids the unintentionally comic image possible in the clause 'and as he drank, his teeth chattered against the glass' (M131.17–18). The comma added to 'When she attempted to speak, her first words were lost in a stifled sob' (M195.2–3) is essential for avoiding confusion. Because the introductory clause concludes with a verb form, the subject of the succeeding independent clause can all too easily be mistaken for its object. The same may be said of the vocative punctuation. The addition of the comma changes what was the direct object of the verb into a nominative of direct address — for example, ' "You hear this Dain!" ' (U233.9.) The comma between 'this' and 'Dain' (M235.1) removes any hint of scorn attached to Dain. In the sentence ' "Here is where you may land, white men" ' (M244.17), the comma transforms the landing-place from a segregated pier to a place for general disembarkation. More complex, however, is the sentence, ' "White women have their customs, as you know, Tuan having travelled much, as you say." ' (M71.24–26). 'Tuan', referring to Dain, should be treated as a vocative; but neither text treats it as such. In the English phrasing, 'know Tuan, having' (U76.17), it is the object of 'know', but in the American 'know, Tuan having' (M71.25), 'Tuan' is a nominative absolute. In five instances of terminal verb-adverb construction,[29] the American and English texts use exactly opposite punctuation: for instance, 'said slowly' (M20.18) and 'said, slowly' (U26.4); 'said the officer, impatiently' (M186.24) and 'said the officer impatiently' (U186.29). In a simple series such as 'goods, brass gongs, rifles, and gunpowder' (M7.22), the American text adds a comma before 'and'. However, in a more complex series such as 'over them, under them, in the sleeping water, all around them' (M92.18–19), the English text uses a semicolon before the final item (U97.6), thus incorrectly setting off what follows as well as what precedes. In a somewhat similar series, 'weep over it, laugh at it, scold it, beg of it to go away: curse it' (M268.5–6), the English text again uses a semicolon (U264.7), whereas the American uses a colon (M268.6). The semicolon, almost a full stop in itself, sets 'curse it' off from the series, whereas the colon simply indicates a supplementary climactic addition to the series. Correct though these additions are, and helpful though they may be, they remain interventions with logical but not authorial authority behind them.

Not all of the variants in the American text are improvements, of course. In particular, obviously editorial punctuation of restrictive and nonrestrictive clauses and phrases make one wonder about the qualifications Macmillan required of its American editors. This one uses commas to set off concluding nonrestrictive adjective clauses in ten instances[30] and nonrestrictive adverb clauses in six instances[31] — whereas, in every instance except one (when a dash is used [U97.13]) the English edition uses no mark of punctuation. In another such instance (M98.14), the nonrestrictive adjective clause is compound, and both the American and English editions have commas before the

---

[29] In addition are M22.25/U28.10, M160.23/U161.28, M182.12/U182.24.

[30] M12.25/U18.17, M13.12/U19.2, M98.14/U102.17, M101.9/U105.7, M101.26/U105.24, M118.19/U121.20, M131.18/U134.1, M141.24/U143.25, M163.15/U164.15, M261.13/U257.24.

[31] M81.3/U86.1, M92.26/U97.13, M212.28/U212.2, M261.21/U258.2, M262.3/U258.13, M262.16/U258.25.

'and' which precedes the second subordinating conjunction. In another (M101.26), the nonrestrictive adjective clause comes at the end of the first independent clause in a compound sentence. In one additional instance, the nonrestrictive adverb clause (a clause of manner), preceded by a comma in the American edition only (M110.28), but followed by a comma in both editions, falls between the two elements of a compound verb. Elsewhere, the American edition uses a comma to precede what seems to be a restrictive adjective clause: 'Remember there is that woman, who, being half white, is ungovernable, and would raise a great outcry.' (M169.15–17.) Only two times does the English edition add a comma before a final nonrestrictive adverb clause when the American edition does not. One of these clauses contains a nonrestrictive adverb clause within it (U179.30, M179.16); the other clause is peculiar: 'you can see in the daytime his houses across the river, there, where those fires are burning on the shore.' (U71.30–72.3, cf. M67.2–4.) Of the nine nonrestrictive adverb clauses considered here, four are clauses of manner (three of them elliptical: M92.26, 110.28, 262.16), two are clauses of time (M179.16, 261.21), one is a clause of place (M67.3), one a clause of condition (M212.28), and one, apparently, a clause of cause: 'He hardly took notice of Dain, whose constant presence in the house had become a matter of course to him, now [that — in the sense of 'because'] they were connected by a community of interests.' (M81.1–4.)

On only one occasion does the American edition use a comma at the end of a nonrestrictive prepositional or participial phrase when the English edition does not (M9.7). In four instances (M4.5, 259.16, 263.27–28, 268.12), the American edition treats such phrases inside a sentence nonrestrictively, while the English edition does not. Only one time in the English edition is the punctuation of a nonrestrictive phrase an improvement over the American, having a comma both before and after the phrase 'crowning all' (U16.29), whereas the American edition has only the final comma (M11.8). In twelve instances, the American edition inserts a comma before a nonrestrictive phrase within a sentence.[32] Both editions use commas at the ends of all of these phrases. In fifteen instances, the American edition uses a comma before a nonrestrictive phrase which comes at the end of a

---

[32] M5.14/U11.13, M19.17/U25.3, M76.24/U81.11, M99.19–20/U103.21, M105.21/U109.11, M118.9/U121.10, M130.19/U133.3, M154.21/U156.3, M167.5/U168.5, M190.28/U190.24, M270.7/U266.7, M270.23/U266.22.

sentence.[33] In one, the phrase concludes the first independent clause in a compound sentence (M107.10); in another, the phrase, a prepositional one, contains within it a dependent clause and a nonrestrictive verbal phrase (M161.28); and in still another, the phrase — also prepositional — contains two dependent clauses (M178.5). Of these thirty-three instances of nonrestrictive phrases, seventeen are preopositional phrases, fifteen participial phrases, and one an appositive.

The English editor treats three participial phrases (U91.14–15, 121.5, 179.28–30), one prepositional phrase (U103.8–9), and one adjective phrase (which modifies an adjective-noun combination, U96.10) nonrestrictively within a sentence — i.e., he sets them off with commas; while the American grammarian uses no commas. In three instances — two prepositional phrases (U152.9, 200.25) and one participial phrase (U146.17) — the English edition contains commas before them at the end of a sentence where there are no commas in the American edition. In one instance of a participial phrase within a sentence, the English edition encloses it with commas, whereas the American has only the first comma. In the sentence, 'Their voices rose and fell tender or animated as they spoke of their love and of their future', the English edition inserts a comma between 'fell' and 'tender' (U227.18).

On eleven occasions when Conrad has ended a sentence with a word, phrase, or clause which does not modify the immediately preceding word, the American editor has inserted a comma, apparently for the sake of clarity.[34] Rather than rewrite so many sentences, he apparently felt that the addition of these commas would aid in lessening any awkwardness or ambiguity resulting from the often peculiar placement of the phrases in the sentences. In two instances of a phrase within a sentence which does not modify the immediately preceding word, the American editor precedes the phrase with a comma; the English editor omits them (M19.9, 47.18; U24.26, 52.15). Both editions follow the phrases in question with a comma. On only one occasion does the English edition precede such a phrase with a

---

[33] M11.16/U17.8, M12.10/U18.1, M15.16/U21.7, M16.6/U21.25, M29.6/U35.1, M100.25/U104.25, M107.10/U110.27, M112.28/U116.14, M133.2/U135.12, M143.24/U145.24, M161.28/U163.2, M178.13/U178.29, M189.18/U189.16, M261.24/U258.6, M274.18/U270.11.

[34] M16.7/U21.26, M18.12/U23.28, M47.18/U52.15, M92.6/U96.22, M112.9/U115.25, M115.28/U119.10, M176.14–15/U177.3–4, M183.23/U184.5, M265.19/U261.24, M266.18/U262.21, M269.23/U265.24.

comma when the American edition does not (U28.20, M23.6). This phrase appears at the close of the first independent clause in a compound sentence.

The American editor's predilection for punctuation is equally evident in his handling of independent clauses. Thrice he raised commas to semi-colons to remove unsightly comma splices (M23.7/U28.21, M114.7/U117.19–20, M261.17/U257.28), and he added necessary commas before conjunctions joining coordinate independent and dependent clauses (M14.23, 127.17, 146.23, 156.8, 268.12). However, his habit of separating compound verbs is, at times, annoying, especially when no punctuation is required: for example, 'He studied the crabbed handwriting of its pages, and often grew meditative over it.' (M40.21–22/U46.4–5.) Only twice did he fail to add obviously needed commas — a puzzling oversight since the English edition contains them. The phrase 'very, very' (U245.27/M248.26) and the compound sentence 'The frigate remained anchored outside the mouth of the river, and the boats came up in tow of the steam launch' (U47.24–26/M42.22) are more grammatically punctuated in the English text. In general, however, the American text contains more thorough, and heavier, punctuation throughout.

Occasionally, the American edition does lighten English punctuation, but just as often it reverses the pattern. In the tense confrontation of Dain, Babalatchi, and Lakamba, the scene gradually focuses on what to do with Dain to avoid his capture by the Dutch. In the English edition, Babalatchi deferentially inquires, ' "Will Tuan Dain go to Bulangi's house till the danger is over, go at once?" ' (U114.7–9), but in the Macmillan text, his final three words have a far more imperative tone: ' "Will Tuan Dain go to Bulangi's house till the danger is over? Go at once." ' (M110.21–22.) Affected is one's impression of Babalatchi's diplomatic powers and Dain's relationship to these potentially dangerous men. In a later scene, the distraught Almayer rushes toward his house repeating ' "Not mad, not mad!" ' (M130.22.) Both the typescript and the English text use a period (L128.22, U133.6), but the exclamation mark obviously is more appropriate to the tenor of the scene and the condition of Almayer's mind. In chapter 12, Nina attempts to explain why she has chosen Dain rather than Almayer's illusions: ' "Could you give me happiness without life? Life! . . . Life that means power and love." ' (M252.15–18.) Here the typescript supplied no assistance to the British compositor; its Almayer responds 'That' (L256.1) and points toward Dain. The American 'That,'

(M252.19) simply fails to capture the emotional intensity, contemptuous scorn, and uncomprehending wonder of the English 'That!' (U249.13).

But many times, the American editor's interventions fall into no recognizable pattern; each instance must be considered by itself. He caught the erroneous possessive forms 'bird's' (U78.27) and 'pigs' (U131.5), correcting them to 'birds'' (M74.9) and 'pigs'' (M128.17); rightly turned a declarative sentence into a rhetorical question (U178. 21/M178.5); but somewhat inconsistently turned a rhetorical question into an exclamation (U97.26/M93.10).

Virtually every page of the Leeds Typescript contains revisions, corrections, and additions in black ink, but it is impossible to say at what point in time these were added. Hasty consideration of the numerous black ink changes which later appear in both the English and the American editions might tempt one to think that all of the changes were made before the English compositors set type. However, there are black ink changes which appear in the English text, but not the American; in the American but not the English; and at times in neither. One of the most interesting of these changes involves a Malay word. Originally the typescript read 'Coorrouh', but the first two letters were canceled and 'bu' were inserted above them (L117.16): the English edition reads 'bourrouh' (U122.24); the American, 'Courrouh' (M119.23). The holograph is of little assistance to anyone trying to decipher Conrad's original intention because his majuscule 'C' is virtually identical with his minuscule 'b'. Less interesting, perhaps, but more typical is the cancel of the second letter in 'come' and the insertion of 'a' above it (L141.8): the English edition reads 'came' (U144.16); the American, 'come' (M142.16). So far there seems to be a pattern in which the manuscript changes might presumably be merely records of what Conrad did in proof — or working scripts of what he intended to do and ultimately did. But this apparent pattern is broken by still other instances in which the black ink alterations of the typescript appear in the American text only to disappear in the English. Here is an example. Typewritten 'with' is canceled and 'around' is inserted above it (L172.13): 'around' is in the American edition (M173.6) and 'with' is in the English (U173.28). Or a typescript change appears in both the American and English editions: 'who' inserted above a canceled 'which' (L168.4) is printed in both editions (M169.16/U170.14). Or a typescript change appears in neither the American nor the English edition: a comma added in holograph to the typescript (L110.1–2) does not find its way into either edition (M112. 22/U116.7–8). What is the significance of these changes in the Leeds Typescript? Who knows. The answer to that question might repay further study of them. Here, at least, they can be considered s'mply as background to the two first editions of *Almayer's Folly*.

Those editions themselves are the point here. And the burden of that point is the story of an intermingling of editors on two sides of the Atlantic with a great writer for whom English was not his native language to produce a first novel that deserves praise. It is an old story revealed in a new context: the writer, the English editor, and the American editor each produced a slightly different version of that novel, with the essential job of unraveling those versions being the province of the textual critic — and anyone else who presumes to discuss Joseph Conrad's first novel.

Which first novel?

THE TEXTUAL HISTORY OF
FAULKNER'S *REQUIEM FOR A NUN*

NOEL POLK

Requiem for a Nun IS PERHAPS WILLIAM FAULKNER'S MOST MISUNDER-
stood novel. We have somehow been content, for more than two decades now, to accept the badly mistaken judgments of the book's early
reviewers that it is a slipshod piece of craftsmanship and that, though
Faulkner is obviously in earnest, *Requiem* is a theologically naive morality play in which his interests are more didactic than artistic.[1] And

[1] See, for example, Malcolm Cowley, 'In Which Mr. Faulkner Translates Past
Into Present', New York *Herald Tribune Book Review*, 30 September 1951, pp.
1, 14; and Herbert Poster, 'Faulkner's Folly', *American Mercury*, 73 (December
1951): 106–12. A much shorter version of this paper was read before General
Topics 8 (Bibliographical Evidence) of the 1972 annual meeting of the Modern Language Association.

I wish to acknowledge here my gratitude to Mrs. Jill Faulkner Summers,
William Faulkner's daughter and literary executrix, for permission to quote
from and reproduce unpublished materials from her father's manuscripts.

I would also like to thank Ruth Ford and Joan Williams, who have been very
generous and kind in allowing me access to their Faulkner materials, and in
answering my questions about *Requiem for a Nun,* and to Professor James B.

so we have discussed it, and taught it — if at all — as evidence of what we have come to call Faulkner's 'decline' during the last half of his career.

The reasons for our failure to understand *Requiem* are many, and most of them are connected in one way or another with a whole series of misconceptions about Faulkner's artistic aims and methods in his post-1940 work, myths which were created largely by journalistic reviewers, and which persist even at this stage of Faulkner scholarship. At the center of these misconceptions are two closely-related critical errors: our unwillingness to separate Faulkner the artist from Faulkner the public speaker, and our inability to understand the character of Gavin Stevens, the garrulous and idealistic lawyer who plays such an important role in Faulkner's late fiction. Michael Millgate and Cleanth Brooks have, of course, done much to correct our ideas about Stevens as he appears in *The Town* and *The Mansion;* but even these fine studies, when dealing with *Requiem,* assume like all the others that Stevens is to Faulkner something of a human ideal, a man whose educational background and humanistic sympathies qualify him for the role of moral arbiter in Yoknapatawpha; the corollary of this is that the hyper-educated lawyer is the 'voice' of Faulkner, and that what he says and does carries the full weight of Faulkner's artistic and moral approval.[2] This has a particularly pernicious effect on our reading of *Requiem* since, if we believe what Stevens tells us, we are left with the neat romantic paradox — almost the one about the prostitute with the heart of gold — that Nancy Mannigoe, who murders a helpless infant, is actually a martyred saint; while Temple Drake Stevens, the bereaved and suffering mother, and who is, in *Requiem,* at least, one of Faulkner's most admirable characters, is in fact responsible for the murder of her own baby. Likewise, and not just coincidentally, we are left to conclude that Stevens is himself the hero of the novel, in his valiant efforts to force Temple to admit her guilt, to face up to and conquer her own evil past.[3]

Meriwether, who continues to be extraordinarily generous with his immense knowledge of Faulkner. Joseph Blotner's two-volume *Faulkner: A Biography* (New York, 1974) covers some of the biographical material in this article. Unfortunately, this long awaited and highly useful biography was published too late for me to have used it here.

[2] Millgate, *The Achievement of William Faulkner* (New York, 1966); Brooks, *William Faulkner: The Yoknapatawpha Country* (New Haven, 1963).

[3] The most complete critical reading of *Requiem for a Nun* is my own Ph.D. dissertation, 'A Textual and Critical Study of William Faulkner's *Requiem for a Nun'* (University of South Carolina, 1970).

This is an unhappy interpretation of *Requiem for a Nun,* and, by extension, of all Faulkner's late work, not just because it cuts us off from a body of fiction considerably more powerful than this approach allows, but also because of the simplistic picture it paints of Faulkner the artist during the last half of his career. It is a portrait, however, which is contradicted at every point by the large body of extant Faulkner manuscripts, and by the *Requiem* materials in particular, which provide a dramatic example of just how wrong the picture is. Indeed, extant evidence makes it possible to trace the pre-publication history of *Requiem* in some considerable detail, almost from the moment of its conception, through two extensive revisions of scene iii of Act II which Faulkner made after the galleys for the original version had been set, and which completely changed the meaning of the novel. And though this essay does not treat that history in as extensive a detail as it deserves eventually, it does provide general outlines — the more significant biographical and bibliographical factors which have a direct bearing on the state of the published text — and more fully discusses the revisions, since they argue most persuasively against the novel's detractors.

According to most published accounts — all of them based on interviews with Ruth Ford, the actress who played Temple Stevens in the London and New York productions — Faulkner wrote *Requiem for a Nun* in response to Miss Ford's request that he write a play for her.[4] This may or may not be the case: Faulkner, at any rate, never referred to the incident in any published statement that I am aware of, and consistently placed her after the fact rather than before. For example, in a quasi-interview with Faulkner, published in October 1951, in the *Oxford Eagle,* Phil Mullen reported that 'When [Faulkner] thought of writing this play he thought of Miss Ford'[5]; and in his prefatory note to the 1959 Random House edition of the play, as adapted by Miss Ford, he is even more specific: 'This play was written not to be a play', he wrote, 'but as what seemed to me the best way to tell the story in a novel. It became a play, to me, only after Ruth Ford saw it as a play and believed that only she could do it right.'[6]

This is not, however, in any way an attempt to refute Miss Ford's

---

[4] Nancy Dew Taylor, 'The Dramatic Productions of *Requiem for a Nun*', *Mississippi Quarterly,* 20 (Summer 1967): 124.

[5] Quoted by Taylor, p. 124.

[6] William Faulkner, *Requiem for a Nun: A Play From the Novel,* adapted to the stage by Ruth Ford. (New York, 1959), p. [vii].

story, nor even to suggest that she did not influence Faulkner's decision to revive in dramatic form the characters of *Sanctuary; Requiem* is, after all, a showcase for a virtuoso female lead, and it is a fact that his longstanding friendship with her and his insistence that the play was strictly for her were primarily responsible for its failure to be produced as originally scheduled in the fall of 1951. Even though he had invested an immense amount of time and work in the stage script, he firmly resisted producer Lemuel Ayers' attempt to dissociate her from the production: 'this play is for Ruth,' he wrote Ayers, 'the part, character-part, is hers until she herself refuses it.'[7] He sent a copy of this letter to Harold Ober, his agent, with a short note in which he reaffirmed his admiration of her rather fierce determination to be an actress, and stated that since he had written the play to abet her career he wanted her interests in it to be protected legally.[8]

On the other hand, Faulkner had been interested in drama since the earliest years of his career. While associated with the University of Mississippi he had belonged to a theatrical group, wrote a short one-act play called 'Marionettes', and reviewed, for *The Mississippian,* plays by Edna St. Vincent Millay and Eugene O'Neill.[9] There is evidence that he even considered doing *A Fable,* in one version, as a play,[10] and there is, finally, the interesting possibility that he originally conceived *Intruder in the Dust* as his play-novel; there are, at any rate, many undated holograph leaves at the University of Virginia recording his attempts to dramatise portions of that novel. Numerous significant relationships between these two novels — they have in common the central symbols of jail and courthouse, a concern with historical and judicial processes, and many images, including that of the jailor's daughter who scratches her name in the jailhouse window — and the highly dialectical nature of the relationship between Gavin Stevens and Charles Mallison make it not at all unthinkable that at one time the action of *Intruder* was projected to be the 'play' against which the long narrative prologues

[7] Faulkner to Ober, 29 December 1951; quoted by Taylor, p. 126.

[8] Faulkner to Ober, *ca.* 4 January 1952; information supplied from the files of Harold Ober Associates by Professor James B. Meriwether.

[9] James E. Kibler, Jr., in 'William Faulkner and Provincetown Drama, 1920–1922', *Mississippi Quarterly,* 22 (Summer 1969): 226–36, discusses Faulkner's early interests in drama, and suggests that he was still borrowing from playwrights like Synge and O'Neill as late as 1959, in *The Mansion.* See also Carvel Collins, ed., *William Faulkner: Early Prose and Poetry* (Boston, 1962).

[10] Faulkner to Ober, *ca.* 17 November 1943; information supplied by Professor Meriwether.

were to be juxtaposed. But unless he planned a somewhat different story — unless he planned to lower the age of Miss Habersham, for example — there is hardly a part in *Intruder* for Miss Ford. Whether his idea to do *Requiem* in the form of a play, then, came before or after Miss Ford's 'request', it is a fact that Faulkner's theatrical interests were working very much independently of her.

Whatever the cerebral origins of the book as we know it, however, the title — which Faulkner considered one of his best[11] — and even, perhaps, the basic idea, had been on his mind since the early thirties; in March of 1934 his publishers announced that Faulkner's new novel by that title was being postponed.[12] Michael Millgate, speculating about the subject matter of this early *Requiem,* suggested that it was 'tempting . . . to see in this early mention of the title a confirmation of that intimate relationship between *Sanctuary* and *Requiem* which the later book makes everywhere apparent', and he called attention to Faulkner's letter to Harrison Smith 'in the early 1930's' in which he stated that *Requiem* was about 'a nigger woman.'[13] The discovery, since Millgate wrote, of three manuscript pages of this early *Requiem* among the papers found at Rowanoak, Faulkner's home in Oxford, confirms Millgate's speculations. These pages, representing two different openings for the aborted novel, are dated 17 December 1933 and suggest, in various ways apart from the affinities of title, that Faulkner did indeed intend a relationship between *Sanctuary* and *Requiem,* and that the early *Requiem* was to concern itself with many of the same themes as the later one. The shorter text, for example, like the 1951 book, has a strong historical dimension, and centers around the image of the jail: the third-person narrator begins by remembering when there was a picket fence around the jail building, and goes on to compare the bars in the jailhouse windows to the picket fences around Jefferson homes. The longer, two-page text, with less perhaps of the significance of the jailhouse window–picket fence comparison, but even more interesting, is a scene in which a man named Stevens, apparently a lawyer, quizzes a Negro man and woman, whom he is trying to help, about

[11] Faulkner to Ruth Ford, *ca.* 18 June 1951. Barbara Izard and Clara Hieronymus, *Requiem for a Nun: Onstage and Off* (Nashville, 1970), p. 296, mention that Faulkner wrote this to Miss Ford, but do not identify the letter.

[12] Marian Nancy Dew [Taylor], 'A Study of William Faulkner's *Requiem for a Nun'*, M.A. Thesis (University of North Carolina, 1962), p. 2, calls attention to this notice.

[13] Millgate, pp. 221, 329.

an incident of the day before in which the Negro man's wife had been cut with a razor.

Whether this early *Requiem* would have taken the form of a play, and why Faulkner abandoned it at this time are, of course, impossible to know; it is, however, extremely interesting that less than two months later, according to manuscripts, also preserved in the Rowanoak papers, dated 11 February 1934, he began the writing of *Absalom, Absalom!,* a novel which also has many affinities with *Requiem for a Nun.* And while it is difficult to do more, until the Rowanoak papers are made available for examination, it is worth noting, at least in this general way, that *Absalom* and *Requiem* appear to be products of the same impulses at this point in his career.[14]

Faulkner signed a contract for *Requiem* on 16 July 1948, and by 11 February 1950 had begun the actual writing.[15] On that day he mailed to Joan Williams a three-page holograph outline of the drama's opening scene,[16] and on March 30 he wrote to Ober that he was writing a play.[17] By 12 June he had apparently already written or was writing or at least thinking about scene i of Act II — an inference drawn from the striking similarity between Temple's speech on p. 134 of the published book[18] and Faulkner's letter to the Secretary of the American Academy of Arts and Letters, which he wrote on that date.[19] He sent the first known version of the prologue to Act I, 'A Name for the City', to Ober during the first few days of July as what he called a 'by-product' of his play.[20] Another bit of internal evidence may help to place the

[14] Information about the contents of the Rowanoak papers supplied by Professor Meriwether.

[15] Information supplied from the Random House files by Professor Meriwether.

[16] Envelope postmarked this date, in Joan Williams' possession.

[17] Information supplied from the files of Harold Ober Associates by Professor Meriwether.

[18] New York, 1951. Throughout this essay I will be quoting from a plate-corrected fourth printing of *Requiem for a Nun* which has been further corrected and de-edited by me.

[19] Reprinted in James B. Meriwether, ed., *Essays Speeches & Public Letters of William Faulkner* (New York, 1966), p. 206.

[20] Faulkner's accompanying note was stamped received by Ober's office on 5 June. Information from the Ober files supplied by Professor Meriwether. The typescript of this version of 'A Name for the City' has recently been discovered in the Manuscripts Division of the Library of Congress, in the *Harper's Magazine* files. It was published in *Harper's* for October, 1950. See pp. 73–74 of my dissertation for a discussion of the relationship of this version to the final form of the prologue to Act I.

writing of the prologue to Act II during the latter part of that summer or early fall. During that time, according to Millgate, Faulkner was involved in the 'battle then raging in Oxford for and against the legislation of the sale of beer'; to that battle Faulkner contributed his now famous anti-prohibitionist 'Beer Broadside' in early September.[21] On the final page of the typescript of the prologue to Act II, one of the 'Diversions: acute' was to have been 'Beer' before Faulkner X-ed it out on the typewriter. On 12 September he mailed to Joan Williams a carbon typescript of versions of most of Acts I and II, with prologues (carbon copies in part of the setting copy and in part of the material on the versos of the setting copy).[22] The completed typescript, except for 'The Jail', went to the printer in late April 1951,[23] and was set in galley by 25 May.[24] The typescript of 'The Jail' went to the printer around 1 June[25] and was in proof by 13 June.[26]

In the meantime, on 11 June, and apparently at Faulkner's request, Robert Linscott of Random House sent to Ruth Ford the first two-thirds of the galleys.[27] One week later, about 18 June, Faulkner wrote to Miss Ford, acknowledging her earlier phone call, and promising to come to New York around the first of July to discuss revisions for a production which she and producer Lemuel Ayers were hoping to mount.[28]

Faulkner apparently liked the idea of the production, agreed to help with the rewriting, and spent several weeks during the summer working with Ayers, Miss Ford, and director Albert Marre on a version which would be suitable to the requirements of the stage. Some time during this period Faulkner made the important revisions of Act II; it is certainly these rewriting sessions which produced the 303 pages of typescript which Meriwether, in his handlist of the Faulkner papers, describes briefly as 'miscellaneous pages from several versions, some of them carbons.'[29] A large number of the pages appear to have been

[21] Millgate, p. 48. The 'Beer Broadside' is reprinted in *Essays Speeches & Public Letters,* pp. 207–08.

[22] Envelope so postmarked. In Joan Williams' possession.

[23] Information supplied from Random House files by Professor Meriwether.

[24] The galleys, preserved at the University of Virginia, are so stamped.

[25] Information supplied from Random House files by Professor Meriwether.

[26] The galleys are so stamped.

[27] Linscott to Ruth Ford, 11 June 1951; letter in Miss Ford's possession.

[28] Faulkner to Miss Ford, ca. 18 June 1951; letter in Miss Ford's possession.

[29] James B. Meriwether, *The Literary Career of William Faulkner: A Bibliographical Study* (Princeton, 1961; reissued Columbia, S.C.: University of South Carolina Press, 1971), p. 78.

professionally typed, and carbon copies of these professionally typed pages were used as setting copy for most of the important revisions. The textual difficulties, while very real, are, however, considerably reduced by the fact that it is possible to identify among these 303 pages Faulkner-typed working drafts, with holograph changes, for nearly all of the revisions.

The point is important since at least one commentator, trying to deal with this particular episode in Faulkner's career, has placed undue emphasis on the effect of this collaboration on the published form of the novel: indeed, Mrs. Izard, while lauding Faulkner's willingness and eagerness to cooperate with theater professionals, notes rather glibly that the corrected galleys at the University of Virginia 'leave little doubt that the book was enriched by the summer rewrite preparations for the stage.'[30] Collaboration there undoubtedly was; and though there is no evidence that anybody besides Faulkner actually wrote any of the published text, the question which will bother the textual purist is one of influence. Is *Requiem*, like *Great Expectations*, a completed novel altered at the advice of a well-meaning friend?

There are several things, however, which militate against such a view. In the first place, the summer rewriting was done in at least two major stints: the first, a period of several days in New York during the first of July; the second, 'several weeks' of as yet undetermined date later in the summer in Cambridge, Massachusetts, where the production was scheduled to open at the Brattle Theater in the fall.[31] All revisions in the novel had been made before July 10, when the final batch of revisions were sent to the printer as part of the corrected galley proofs.[32] Therefore they had to have been done sometime between Faulkner's 18 June letter to Miss Ford and 10 July. The format which Faulkner used to type the revisions is more like that of the playscript than that of the novel typescript, and suggests, therefore, that all of the actual writing was done after Faulkner arrived in New York around 1 July and had had a chance to consult with his three collaborators. But certainly he had his own revisions in mind before leaving Mississippi, and maybe even had done some work on them. In that 18 June letter, responding to one of Miss Ford's telephoned suggestions, he wrote: 'I realise the whole second act should be rewrit-

[30] Izard and Hieronymus, p. 8.
[31] Taylor, p. 3.
[32] Date of letter accompanying revised galleys being returned to printer.

116

ten, that the husband should be in it too'. Later in the letter he says, 'I have already thought of how to get the husband into the second act'.

In the second place, even granting him his repeated statement that the artist will steal from anybody, Faulkner was unusually independent about his work, and there is no evidence whatsoever that he either asked or accepted collaboration on anything but the form of the drama which was to be produced on stage. Miss Ford, for example, asked him specifically to write a major scene between Temple and Gowan, to come at the end of Act I, and he did.[33] The scene became part of the production and was printed as part of the play which Random House published in 1959; but he did *not* include it in the novel, though he did bring Gowan into the end of scene iii to set up his participation in Act II. Further, on 11 July, after Faulkner had returned to Oxford, Ayers wrote to him, expressed his appreciation for the time they had spent together in New York, and made several suggestions for revisions.[34] But the only one of his suggestions which turns up in the novel — the appearance of Gowan at the end of Act III — had already been sent to the printer the day before Ayers wrote the letter; the amount of detail Ayers goes into trying to justify his ideas implies that they are for him new ideas, which they had not previously discussed, even though they had spent time together working on the script.[35] Faulkner's changes, then, almost certainly antedate Ayers' letter. Finally, in that 18 June letter to Ruth Ford, Faulkner had written, apparently responding to another of her suggestions, that he had already thought of how to break up the long speeches so as to render them tolerable on stage; in the novel, however, the long speeches are, if anything, longer than he had originally written them.

There is, then, no real reason to doubt that the published text of *Requiem for a Nun* represents in most important respects Faulkner's own, final, intentions. It did undergo, however, the standard trials of editorial procedure in the process of publication; and though editorial tampering is light, especially as compared with Faulkner's earlier Random House novels, *Requiem* is a poorly edited text. That it is not a badly-mangled text is much less an indication of improved editorial expertise at Random House than of Faulkner's changed status there

[33] Telephone interview with Miss Ford, 21 August 1970.

[34] Letter of this date and accompanying pages of suggestions are at ViU-Manuscripts.

[35] Faulkner's manuscript addition of this material to the final galley is reproduced as Figure 22 of Meriwether's *Literary Career*.

after his receipt of the Nobel Prize in December 1950. As his first novel after the Nobel Prize, then, *Requiem* sheds some interesting light on Faulkner's relationship with his publishers and with his editor.

Faulkner's editor from 1936 to 1958 was Saxe Commins, who simply did not, perhaps could not, for various reasons recognise Faulkner's genius, and who seemed to have no sympathy whatsoever with his artistic aims and methods. For example, his editing of *Absalom, Absalom!*, Faulkner's first novel with Random House, can only be called wholesale revision. He and Harrison Smith deleted many passages outright, sometimes as many as ten lines at a time, shifted others around, corrected what they thought were Faulkner's syntactical inadequacies, substituted many proper names for pronouns, added and subtracted parentheses: they made it, in short, the worst- and most-heavily edited text in the Faulkner canon, excluding 'Flags in the Dust'. Further, against Faulkner's angry protest, Commins changed the title of his 1939 novel *If I Forget Thee, Jerusalem* to *The Wild Palms*. 'Bill was furious' about the title change, Commins told Meriwether in the spring of 1957, and then made it clear that he, Commins, 'had insisted on this and other important changes and that Faulkner was powerless to prevent it but quite angry.'[36]

After 1950, however, Faulkner was not quite so powerless, and the pre-publication matter of *Requiem* illustrates both Commins's inadequacies as an editor of Faulkner and his somewhat changed attitude toward him in their post-Nobel Prize relationship. The typescript is sprinkled with the usual quota of punctuation changes and textbook grammar. Commins modernized many of Faulkner's deliberately and consistently used archaisms — 'irreconciliable', for example, instead of Commins' more modern 'irreconcilable' — and he even changed Faulkner's correct form 'bakhshish' to a misspelled 'bakshish'. Further, he changed Faulkner's 'Juneteenth', a portmanteau word referring to 19 June, the date of the celebration of Negro emancipation in Texas, to 'June tenth', which in the novel is a gratuitous and completely meaningless date. Perhaps the most serious error in editorial judgment is in the slight distortion of the visual if not in the thematic relationship between the three acts and their respective prologues. Faulkner originally typed the beginning of Act I on a new page; but before he typed the beginning of Act II, changed his mind, crossed

---

[36] Quoted in Thomas L. McHaney's dissertation, 'William Faulkner's *The Wild Palms:* A Textual and Critical Study' (University of South Carolina, 1968), p. 2n, from his interview with Professor Meriwether 18 July 1968.

out the heading and the first few lines of the Act, and retyped them on the bottom of the final page of the prologue; he continued this practice with Acts II and III. Disregarding Faulkner's specific move to draw attention to the close connections between prologue and drama, Commins directed that each act of the drama begin at the top of a new page.

On the one hand, he made this kind of change without any reference to Faulkner's wishes. On the other hand, some of the patent errors he did not correct, and some of the questions he asked, are very interesting. At one point, for example, Faulkner, intending to type the two words 'that this', inadvertently typed 'this this'. Instead of simply correcting what is plainly a typing error, Commins either overlooked it on the typescript or just let it stand, and on the galley circled it, placing a large question mark in the margin, where Faulkner himself corrected it. Again, in Act II Temple starts to refer to a female character in Hemingway's *For Whom the Bell Tolls* as a 'girl' then changes in mid-word to call her a 'woman'. Faulkner typed 'g——woman'. On the galley Commins queried this; Faulkner changed it to 'gir——woman' and patiently explained: 'Starts to say "girl" then substitutes "woman".' And this final, telling, example: In the prologue to Act III Faulkner refers to the 'peas and grits and side-meat' which the jailor's wife had 'purchased in bargain-lot quantities by shrewd and indefatiguable peditation from store to store.' On the typescript, Commins changed 'peditation' to 'meditation' — though it is difficult to picture that good lady meditating from store to store. On the galley, however, he turned right around, circled 'meditation' as if Faulkner had made the mistake, and in the margin asked, 'Bill — what?' in big letters. Faulkner's irritation shows through his restrained, gentlemanly reply: 'peditation,' he wrote, 'the science or process of walking — on foot, like equitation = horsemanship.'

Aside, then, from numerous irritating but minor particulars, the published text of *Requiem for a Nun* is in most important respects demonstrably faithful to Faulkner's final intentions. Thus the most significant aspect of the typescript from a critical point of view is that it preserves both the original Act II and the two extensive revisions of it which Faulkner made after the original version had been set in galleys. The revisions represent a fundamental change not only in the design but in the execution of *Requiem,* and therefore a discussion of them is appropriate.

The impetus behind the revisions appears to be Faulkner's renewed interest in the character of Gowan, who had originally been allowed, somewhat curiously, to drop out of the play after his large role in Act I, and whose resurrection in Act II and reappearance at the end of Act III by itself alters the meaning of the novel: Temple's problem is *not,* as most critics have suggested, how to live with her past, which she has in fact been doing rather admirably, but how to live with her present, which is symbolized by the demands of her marriage to a weak and childish husband. When the knowledge that Gowan gains in Act II fails to change him in any way, even the bleak hope which the original version offers — the possibility of salvation through suffering — is denied to her. No change in Gowan means, for Temple, no relief from her burden; indeed, because Gowan's new knowledge makes him more volatile and more capricious, Temple is left in an even greater state of uncertainty than before.

Complementing this movement toward darkness are important changes in Stevens and in the Governor which, in effect, actually reverse their roles. Originally, Faulkner actually gave to Stevens some of the compassion and love which he talks so much about; the revision carefully excises all traces of pity in Stevens — makes him harsher, sterner, and much more unrelenting in what he requires of Temple. In the published version his moral idealism rigidifies, his love of Truth becomes a zealous pursuit of justice 'as he sees it' (p. 49) — and it is his insistence on judging a tragic human situation in terms of an abstract absolute Truth that creates and then compounds the absolutely needless suffering which Temple is made to undergo. On the other hand, the Governor, as originally depicted, is the impersonal stern, judicial figure which most critics have found him to be in the published form.[37] In the original version, for example, he is present in his office during all of Temple's confession; it is he himself who hands down the decision not to save Nancy Mannigoe, and, while doing so, even personally reprimands Temple. In the revision, of course, he kindly removes himself from the more humiliating portions of her story, and from her confrontation with her husband — but only after, in scene i, he has tried to warn her that Gowan is present and listening to every word of her confession (p. 138). At one point a desperate Temple pleads with the two of them — though it is primarily Stevens who is guilty — to stop interrupting her, to let her finish telling

[37] Millgate, p. 222.

120

her story: 'If you both would just hush', she says, 'just let me. I seem to be like trying to drive a hen into a barrel. Maybe if you would just try to act like you wanted to keep her out of it, from going into it' (p. 140). In the typescript Stevens reponds to this plea, with a reply that can at least be construed as compassionate: 'It's not a barrel. It's a culvert. A thoroughfare. The other end is open too. Go through it.' (TS p. 137.) In the published book the reply is the Governor's, who says much the same thing: 'Dont call it a barrel. Call it a tunnel. That's a thoroughfare, because the other end is open too.' (Page 140.) His tone, however, is gentler than Stevens', the connotations of 'tunnel' much more civil than those of 'culvert'.

The first version of scene iii of Act II, the most extensively revised portion, is just under half the length of the final version. It is a short, almost doctrinaire summing up by the Governor of the lessons which Temple has learned. Like the other two versions, it opens with Temple on her knees in front of the Governor's desk, where she finishes her story with the moving description of the jail and its relationship to the community, and then hears from the Governor what she both fears and expects, that he cannot save Nancy. His refusal and his ensuing dialogue with Temple are preserved substantially intact in the exchange between Temple and Stevens on pp. 207–12 of the book, though in the published version Temple is given one of the Governor's speeches, and Stevens, as the Governor's vicar, becomes a sterner and even more relentless dispenser of justice.

Two specific passages in the first version are worth looking at. The first occurs right after the Governor has told Temple that he 'cant' save Nancy. He justifies his decision, and Nancy's murder of the child, on supra-judicial grounds:

Yes — cant. We're not talking about law now, anymore than the murdress herself was, than her lawyer was, who could have plead insanity for her at the time and so saved her life without having to bring her victim's mother here at two oclock in the morning to plead for her. We're not even talking about justice. We're talking about a child, a little boy — the same little boy, to hold whose natural and normal home together, the murdress didn't hesitate to cast the last gambit she knew and possessed — her own debased and worthless breathing —

The grief-stricken Temple acquiesces to this, even though she does not really understand why one child should have to be sacrificed in order to preserve the other: 'So now you're telling me that good can come from evil', she says, humbly and penitently, so that the Governor can didactically sum up: 'Granted. And more than that: it not only can, it must.' (TS pp. 200–01.)

Finally forced to confront her past, convinced at last that she is indeed responsible for the murder of her own child, she suggests that the only expiation for her sins, both past and present, is to confess publicly her part in the tragedy. She tells the Governor that she will 'Do all this over again to the judge, the court, the newspapers, that I did to you here tonight. Become an accessory, in other words, in the cell next to hers. And who knows?' she continues, 'maybe in her cell, and she will have the second cell as the mere accessory, since I am the murdress, committed the deed eight years ago when I got off that baseball special train.' But the Governor refuses her this, claiming that in doing so she will be doing the very thing, breaking up the family, that Nancy is dying to prevent. 'No', he tells her, 'you wont do that. Your job is still harder. Nancy has the easy job, not you. She has only to die.' Temple objects that that is a punishment she cannot bear: 'Tomorrow and tomorrow, day after day, month after month, and year after year? Cant you see?' she says, 'That's just suffering.' (TS pp. 202–05.)

Thus suffering, which in the final version is to be seen as the necessary condition of life itself, is here treated as an *ex cathedra* penance for a specific evil deed. Temple's recognition of life, then, as a constant, purgatorial expiation for her sin, amounts to a 'conversion' following her confession: 'So you really do have to suffer', she says, 'just to keep on being alive. You really do——' (TS p. 206.) Her exit in this scene is significant too: 'She turns, a little clumsily, like a blind person. She starts toward the steps, stumbles slightly. Stevens catches her elbow to steady her, but she has already steadied herself, frees her arm from him, and walks on.' (TS p. 206.) Her expression of independence from Stevens suggests that she has now, finally, become a morally responsible adult, that she has exorcised the Temple Drake part, the destructive part, of her personality, and is now fully Mrs. Gowan Stevens.

In this way, the first version of Scene iii places Nancy Mannigoe and Gavin Stevens at the moral center of *Requiem*, since its 'moral' coincides in almost every particular with Nancy's catechism in Act III, and makes Stevens, as Mrs. Vickery has put it, 'the attendant priest' who forces Temple to take 'the long journey of redemption'.[38] In fact, paradoxically, most of what criticism has written about *Requiem,* that it is a morality play in which the vacuous Temple Drake of *Sanctuary* achieves salvation, is actually true *only* of its original, unpublished form.

The second version is considerably more complex. Here, as in the published book, Gowan replaces the Governor behind the desk; he listens to all the details of Temple's experiences in the Memphis brothel and of her attempt to leave him on the night their child was murdered. Temple is outraged when she discovers his presence and understands that she has been betrayed; and Stevens compounds the betrayal when he reveals, as he does not do in the first version, that he has known all along the Governor would refuse to save Nancy. In the second version, then, Temple is not humbled but humiliated, not saved so much as sacrificed to Stevens' warped vision of Truth; whatever purgatorial value her confession might have had is cancelled, since, her low opinion of people confirmed, she becomes much more cynical and much less likely to be able to reestablish and maintain a healthy relationship with Gowan. When Stevens quotes to her the words of the Governor's refusal, for example, her response is scornful and bitter:

Oh yes, he made it good too, didn't he? Round and ringing too. So it was not even in hopes of saving her life, that I came here at two oclock in the morning. It wasn't even to be told that he had already decided not to save her. The reason I came here was not just to confess to my husband, but to do it in the presence of two strangers, something I had spent eight years trying to expiate so that my husband wouldn't have to know about it. Dont you see that that's just suffering? Not for anything: just suffering? (TS #2, p. 2–3–50.)

She has, on the one hand, a sense of uncertainty about her future, that there is to be some considerable change in her life, perhaps even legal separation from Gowan; and when Stevens tells her that good not only can but must come out of evil, she responds, still bitter, though perhaps not a little relieved that her dilemma is at last finding resolution.

[38] Olga Vickery, *The Novels of William Faulkner: A Critical Interpretation,* rev. ed. (Baton Rouge, 1964), p. 123.

I'm sorry. Because it's all right. It doesn't matter. Your heart just has to break, and then it's all right. You can go on. You can forget it.

(to Gowan)

I would have told you. I —

(quickly; to neither of them directly)

But it's all right, it doesn't matter; all that will save until tomorrow or whenever it'll be when we are through with this and. . . .

(she stops a moment: then to Stevens)

You see. I started to say 'Get back to chewing the old hair shirt again.' Then I knew that was wrong, so I started to say 'The new hair shirt.' Then I knew that was wrong too, because it wont last that long now, since you and his honor finally thought about hiding him behind the door or under the desk or wherever it was; it will be quick now, just painful, like a piece of glass or a box of carpet tacks — (TS #2, p. 2–3–47.)

She has at the same time the bleak contradictory feeling that things probably will not change: her only words at the end of the scene occur when she looks at Gowan: 'Oh God. Again.' (TS #2, p. 2–3–48.) The bachelor Stevens, however, suggests that she should rather be grateful she still has her husband — grateful, indeed, that Nancy has 'saved' the marriage. During her exit she again stumbles; this time it is Gowan who aids her, and from whom she frees herself in order to walk out alone. Her gesture of independence here, in the context of the scene, is not a stoic resolution to face her future, but is rather a bitter, resentful resignation to the continuation of a way of life she had been led by Stevens to hope she could change.

The second version, then, is considerably darker than the first, but it is not nearly so dark as the published version, which achieves its darkness primarily on the strength of even further inversion in, a rethinking of, Gowan's character. At the end of Act I, scene ii, Gowan undergoes a kind of ritualistic baptism, which apparently symbolizes his emergence into moral adulthood: the question of what he is to do with his now seemingly undeluded view of the relationship between himself and his wife, however, is left unanswered until the final scene of Act II. The original version did not answer that question at all, or, perhaps, expected us to accept his 'conversion' as structurally parallel to Temple's. The question is answered in the published version, and the answer helps to make *Requiem* one of Faulkner's most tragic books.

Part of Temple's burden in the second version is that Gowan changes completely, becomes the opposite of his former self: he becomes the indignant husband, self-righteously seizing on the revelation of Temple's unsavory past as an opportunity to change their relationship from one in which he is the weaker member, to one in which he is the stronger. But in his new-found strength he becomes rude and domineering. Therefore it is *he* who passes on the Governor's judgment that Nancy 'cant' be saved. 'Cant?' Temple asks, 'The governor of a state, with all the legal power to pardon or at least reprieve, cant?' Her question is addressed to Stevens, but Gowan interrupts before the lawyer can answer: 'That's law', he says. 'If it was just law, Uncle Gavin could have plead insanity for her at any time, without bringing you here at two oclock in the morning——'. Temple immediately responds: 'And the other parent too; dont forget that. I dont know yet how he got you here, and besides, it doesn't matter. But just dont forget it.' (TS #2, p. 2–3–48.) Her bitterness and resentment is primarily a reaction to Gowan's harshness, and the tragedy of the second version is therefore a limited one in which Temple's suffering is not seen as a necessary condition of life, but is rather attributed to her and Gowan's specific human failure to forgive each other. The fact that forgiveness is a viable alternative — perhaps what Stevens had in mind when he brought Gowan to the Governor's office — makes absolutely unnecessary the suffering Temple faces in all her 'tomorrows'.

In the published version, however, the tragedy is complete. And what completely darkens it is the fact that nothing changes. Originally, everybody — Temple, Gavin, Gowan — changed for the better; in the first revision, they all changed for the worse. In the final version, they do not change at all — Stevens remains his harsh, implacable self; Temple, who has suffered much, is not purged and cannot cry, though she very much wants to (pp. 195, 198, 199).

Gowan too, and therefore Temple's actual and metaphorical burden, remains unchanged. Despite his 'conversion' at the end of Act I scene ii, and despite his knowledge of Temple's completely unselfish attempts to protect and even exonerate him during Act II, he is still, at the end, the irresponsible, selfish person he has always been, trying now to salvage what is left of his badly mangled vanity; apparently nothing — not even the suffering of his wife — can touch him, can make him face up to the world the way Temple must. As the three of them begin to leave the Governor's office, Gowan stops short of leaving by the front door: 'That's right,' he says, 'I'm probably still supposed to use the spy's entrance.' Then he 'turns back . . . toward the door at rear, sees Temple's gloves and bag on the desk,' takes them and gives them to her. 'Here', he tells her, 'This is what they call evidence; dont forget these.' As he leaves through the rear door, Temple asks, 'Did you have a hat and coat?' but he ignores her, and exits. His behavior is childishly spiteful, and it is also reflected in his designation of her bag and gloves as 'evidence'. She understands that he has not changed, and realizes therefore that her future is to be no different from her past: 'Oh God', she says, 'Again. . . . Tomorrow and tomorrow and tomorrow,' she starts, and when she falters Stevens finishes her thought for her: ' — he will wreck the car again against the wrong tree, in the wrong place, and you will have to forgive him again, for the next eight years until he can wreck the car again in the wrong place, against the wrong tree — ' (pp. 205–06).

Thus Stevens' simplistic dictum, borrowed from the Governor, that good 'not only can, it must' come out of evil (p. 208), is, at least in the context he makes it, absolutely wrong; nothing good has come from the suffering he has caused for Temple and Gowan — in the name of love — and certainly nothing good has come from Nancy's murder of that baby. Even the fulfillment of Nancy's stated intention to preserve that 'normal and natural' home (p. 208) for the benefit of the remaining child has not necessarily been accomplished, as Temple suggests:

Of course he wouldn't save her. If he did that, it would be over: Gowan could just throw me out, which he may do yet, or I could throw Gowan out, which I could have done until it got too late now, too late forever now, or the judge could have thrown us both out and given Bucky to an orphanage, and it would be all over. But now it can go on, tomorrow and tomorrow and tomorrow, forever and forever and forever — (Pages 209–10.)

And, given Gowan's state of mind after Act II, she may be right. No good whatsoever has come from the evil; but a great deal of evil has been created by the fanatical and misguided idealism of Gavin Stevens and Nancy Mannigoe.

Temple's humiliation at Stevens' hands is complete. Abject and defeated, she no longer has the strength to object to Stevens' insistence that she came to Jackson not just to suffer, but to 'affirm the very thing which Nancy is going to die tomorrow morning to postulate: that little children, as long as they are little children, shall be intact, unanguished, untorn, unterrified.' Temple responds to this 'quietly': 'All right. I have done that. Can we go home now?' (Page 211.) Her exit in this version is much like the one in the first, but her gesture of independence, though bleak, is a responsible one, since she leaves the Governor's office full in the knowledge that there is no relief from the burdens she bears, the same burdens she has borne for the years of her marriage; she knows too that there is no salvation from that burden, by suffering, by confession, or by any other means, save death.

This knowledge places Temple directly at the moral center of *Requiem for a Nun*. Not Stevens, whose sophistry and glib romanticism have turned a crazed 'nigger dope-fiend whore' and a murdress into a martyred saint. And certainly not Nancy, who commits the single most vicious crime in all of William Faulkner's work, and justifies it in the name of a rote and senseless theology whose central tenet is simply to 'believe'. 'Believe what?' Temple asks, in the final act. 'I dont know,' Nancy replies, 'But I believes.' (Page 281.) Only Temple, the terribly misused and bereaved mother, of all the characters, attempts in any way to come to grips with the 'vast and terrible burden' (p. 261) of reality; she alone is fully alive to the tragic and insoluble complexities of life.

The manuscripts, then, record both the deepening of Faulkner's vision and the degree to which he was committed, morally and artistically, to *Requiem;* and they demonstrate that he is here as fully in control of his materials as at any time during his career. Thus the evidence of the manuscripts indicates that Faulkner, far from being a glib and shoddy craftsman, far from being a theologically naive moralist, was a tough-minded artist who saw that he had written a simplistic novel with no real dramatic force, and then changed it, revised it directly toward a view of the human condition which is as complex and profound as anything he ever wrote.

Of course the published work does not need the testimony of the unpublished material to support its claims to complexity and artistic integrity, nor is it necessary to look beyond the published book for them. The manuscripts do prove with as much certitude as possible that Gavin Stevens is not, as critics have claimed, Faulkner's hero, and that Faulkner did not get lazy and simple-minded in his late career; but these truths should be self-evident to anybody who reads the published book with the care that any book of Faulkner's deserves.

Perhaps not all of the Faulkner manuscripts provide evidence as striking as that of the *Requiem for a Nun* materials, but all of the papers can have a decided effect on attitudes toward him and his work. The manuscripts, then, might be viewed not so much as a key to his artistic achievement as an index to the kind of man he was. The man who in 1933 described the writing of *The Sound and the Fury* as the 'travail of invention and drudgery of putting seventy-five or a hundred thousand words on paper'[39] was not being merely metaphorical seventeen years later when he spoke of the whole act of artistic creation in terms of 'agony and sweat'[40] — and the man who in 1957 proposed the title 'Man Working'[41] for an exhibition of his papers at the University of Virginia was yet again calling attention to an important aspect of his life and art. His papers do indeed provide crucial insights into his writings, particularly into those works which were editorially marred in one way or another. But equally important is that they record the cold-blooded effort, the sheer amount of work that went into the writing: William Faulkner was an artist capable of the profoundest reflections on the human condition, and he was committed to his art not just in terms of his overpowering vision of the world, but also in terms of his dedication to his craft, to the actual drudgery of putting the vision down on paper in a form which would adequately convey it. His manuscripts, which he took a great deal of trouble to preserve, prove this; and even if they do no more than this, properly studied they can keep us from making and perpetuating the glib generalizations about him that marred his reputation while he was alive, and which have kept us, even a decade after his death, from fully coming to grips with the depth and complexity of William Faulkner in all phases of his career.

[39] William Faulkner, 'An Introduction for *The Sound and the Fury*,' ed. James B. Meriwether, *Southern Review*, 8 (October 1972): p. 119.

[40] William Faulkner, 'Address Upon Receiving the Nobel Prize for Literature'; reprinted in *Essays Speeches & Public Letters*, p. 119.

[41] Linton R. Massey, comp., *"Man Working," 1919–1962* (Charlottesville: Bibliographical Society of the University of Virginia, 1968).

SOBER SECOND THOUGHTS: FITZGERALD'S 'FINAL VERSION' OF TENDER IS THE NIGHT

BRIAN HIGGINS and HERSHEL PARKER

Tender is the Night HAS BEEN THE TARNISHED HERO OF ONE OF THE MOST curious textual episodes in American literary history. After a composition which took Fitzgerald almost a decade, the serial form appeared in *Scribner's Magazine* during the first four issues of 1934 and the book version, somewhat revised, was published on 12 April of that year.[1]

[1] *Tender is the Night: A Romance* (New York: Charles Scribner's Sons, 1934). For bibliographical details, see Matthew J. Bruccoli, *F. Scott Fitzgerald: A Descriptive Bibliography* ([Pittsburgh]: University of Pittsburgh Press, 1972, pp. 78–81). A conscientious study of Fitzgerald's labors on this novel is Bruccoli, *The Composition of 'Tender is the Night'* ([Pittsburgh]: University of Pittsburgh Press, 1963). Since this article deals rather minutely with the differences between the first edition and the one prepared by Malcolm Cowley (New York: Charles Scribner's Sons, 1951), while many of our readers will most readily lay hand on the paperback Scribner Library text (New York: Charles Scribner's Sons, 1960), based on the 1934 first edition, we adopt the cumbersome but serviceable procedure of referring to all three of these editions except when certain quotations do not occur in all three. Page references not prefixed by a letter

Its comparative failure led Fitzgerald to make a number of now-familiar comments. In a letter to Maxwell Perkins (11 March 1935), he confessed to problems in his artistic control both during the overall construction and the final periods of revising: 'It has become increasingly plain to me that the very excellent organization of a long book or the finest perceptions and judgment in time of revision do not go well with liquor. . . . I would give anything if I hadn't had to write Part III of *Tender Is the Night* entirely on stimulant. If I had one more crack at it cold sober I believe it might have made a great difference. Even Ernest [Hemingway] commented on sections that were needlessly included and as an artist he is as near as I know for a final reference.'[2] On 13 August 1936, when there was talk of putting the book into the Modern Library, using the Scribner plates, Fitzgerald wrote Bennett Cerf of his desire to change the 'alignment of the scenes' without changing their order: what he intended was the insertion of 'sudden stops and part headings' with certain pages 'inserted bearing merely headings'. He had already thought about the problem seriously enough to have prepared a plan for the changes, which included some local resetting with 'equivalent line lengths' as well as alterations 'within a printed line'.[3] In his still more significant letter to Perkins on 24 December 1938, Fitzgerald wrote: 'Its great fault is that the *true* beginning — the young psychiatrist in Switzerland — is tucked away in the middle of the book. If pages 151–212 were taken from their present place and put at the start, the improvement in appeal would be enormous. In fact the mistake was noted and suggested by a dozen reviewers. To shape up the ends of that change would, of course, require changes in half a dozen other pages'.[4] About this time he made a notebook 'Analysis of *Tender*' in which he marked pp. 151–212 as the opening of the novel, added headings such as he had mentioned to Cerf, and marked minor deletions. He cut loose the

---

are to the 1934 edition; those preceded by 'C' are to the Cowley edition, and those preceded by 'SL' are to the Scribner Library edition. But the reader should take warning: as we explain later, the Scribner Library 'O' and 'Q' printings (so identified on the copyright page) are printed from the Cowley plates; strictly speaking, our abbreviation 'SL' refers to any Scribner Library printing other than 'O' and 'Q'.

[2] *The Letters of F. Scott Fitzgerald,* ed. Andrew Turnbull (New York: Charles Scribner's Sons, 1963), pp. 259–60.

[3] *Ibid.,* p. 540.

[4] *Ibid.,* p. 281.

pages from a copy of the book, rearranged them, made small changes and corrections, and wrote on the inside front cover: 'This is the *final version* of the book as I would like it.'[5] It was this version — or approximately this version — which Malcolm Cowley printed in 1951.[6] (Besides rejecting Fitzgerald's plan to delete the Divers' visit to Mary Minghetti, Cowley made numerous copy-editing changes, many of them obviously desirable). For the next two decades, his edition served at least as a conversation piece among Fitzgerald critics, though it did not meet with that unanimous approval Cowley had expected.

Cowley was probably right in his Introduction to hold that 'Fitzgerald could never have revised *Tender* into the perfect novel that existed as an ideal in his mind. . . . No matter how often he threw his material back into the melting pot, some of it would prove refractory to heat and would keep its former shape when poured into the new mould'.[7] Cowley maintained nevertheless that the version of the novel presented in his edition was a considerable improvement on the original. One 'fault' the new version remedied was the original's 'uncertainty of focus'. In the new version from 'beginning to end Dick is the center of the novel'; Fitzgerald 'sacrificed a brilliant beginning and all the element of mystery but . . . ended with a better constructed and more effective novel'. The 'principal virtue of Fitzgerald's new arrangement' is that 'the new beginning . . . prepares us for the end and helps us to appreciate the last section of the novel' more than the 1934 version. Cowley confidently asserted that there was 'no escaping the judgment' that the revised version was superior. Critics have been seconding or opposing him on these issues ever since, though it was not until the 1960s that the merits of the two versions were seriously debated again.

Wayne C. Booth in 1961 lent support to Cowley's notion that the revised edition put Dick more clearly at the center of the novel. Fitzgerald 'wanted to show the destruction of a man, not simply give a

[5] Cowley, Introduction, p. xii.

[6] During the 1950s the Cowley edition was available in England as a Penguin paperback and in various Scribner issues in the United States, where the only available editions based on the 1934 book version were the Viking Portable and the Bantam. The Scribner Library edition was steadily available beginning in 1960. See pp. 78–92 of Bruccoli's descriptive bibliography, which is the source of almost all our information about the various editions and issues of the novel.

[7] Cowley, p. xvi. Subsequent quotations in this paragraph are from p. xv, except those in the fifth sentence, which are from p. xvii.

convincing impression of this or that character or milieu'; consequently 'any technical stroke should be judged on its service in realizing Dick's tragedy'. The change to the straightforward chronological progression served this end:

> our intellectual picture of this man and of the two worlds he moves between is identical in the two versions. Whatever moral or social themes help to hold this work together are left unchanged from version to version. What is changed, radically, is the reader's emotional attachment to Dick. To begin the novel part-way down the slope, as it were, confined to the confused vision of a secondary character, is to sacrifice some of our attachment to Dick and consequently a good deal of the poignant dramatic irony as we watch him move to his doom.[8]

Two years later Matthew J. Bruccoli took the opposite view in his landmark study, *The Composition of 'Tender is the Night'*, maintaining that 'Cowley's feeling that the novel wants focus is puzzling because the 1934 version is clearly Dick's book.'[9] He also took issue with other aspects of Cowley's Introduction, claiming, for example, that the causes of Dick's deterioration 'are sufficiently probed', while Cowley had held that we were never certain of the reasons for his decline. Bruccoli argued that the original version was 'unified by Fitzgerald's view of his hero', and found support for his claims in his detailed study of the manuscripts. The preliminary sketch of Dick Diver which Fitzgerald prepared in 1932 showed 'that he knew the causes of Dick's decline', while the first holograph draft of the Dick Diver version of the novel contained 'no discarded sections which show contradictory views' of the hero. Bruccoli regularly 'extended' the scope of his study to comment on the way Fitzgerald's revisions pointed up 'his interpretation of his protagonist.' He also 'interrupted' his account of the composition 'to comment on — and to defend — Fitzgerald's original structure', allowing that the evidence was 'mainly negative' but pointing out that there was 'no other discarded structure' and 'no indication that Fitzgerald had any doubts about his narrative plan while he was writing the novel.' For the most part, Bruccoli contented himself with painstakingly laying out evidence which other critics could — but in

---

[8] Wayne C. Booth, *The Rhetoric of Fiction* (Chicago: University of Chicago Press, 1961); the previous two quotations in this paragraph are from p. 192, and the following quotation is from p. 194.

[9] *The Composition of 'Tender is the Night'*, p. 10; subsequent quotations in this paragraph are from p. 14.

fact did not — use to argue against the revised edition. Then in 1964 Bruccoli published a model textual article containing materials for a critical edition of *Tender is the Night,* a kit by which any scholar lucky enough to own one could improve his copy of the first edition without waiting for Scribner's to reset a corrected edition.[10] Here Bruccoli simply stated his conclusion as to which version was better, still without focusing his great amount of evidence on a specific point-by-point rebuttal to Cowley: 'Since my study of the composition of *Tender is the Night* has convinced me that the structure of "The Author's Final Version" does not represent Fitzgerald's best judgment, the first edition should be used as the copy-text for a projected critical edition.'

Critics pretty much ignored Bruccoli's book and his pioneer article (which is oddly missing even from *Fifteen Modern American Authors*[11]), but a few of them ventured their own impressionistic observations about faults of the revised version. James E. Miller thought neither version was obviously superior, but remarked that 'Putting events back in their chronological order sacrifices far more in dramatic effect and suspense than it gains in lucidity.' For Henry Dan Piper there were 'strong reasons (historical as well as aesthetic) favoring *Tender Is the Night* in its original 1934 form.' Robert Sklar formed a judgment similar to Miller's: 'when the revised version was posthumously prepared and published it lost the dramatic energy of the novel without gaining the formal clarity that only a textual revision could have attained'; and Milton Hindus thought that Fitzgerald's 'suggested change of the order of various chapters . . . not only fails to improve upon the 1934 version, but, on the contrary, weakens it still further. The earlier edition, by beginning in the middle of the story . . . had a dramatic tension and interest which the later version lacks.'[12]

The first full-scale defenses of the revised version — much more

[10] Matthew J. Bruccoli, 'Material for a Centenary Edition of *Tender is the Night'*, *Studies in Bibliography,* 17 (1964): pp. 177–93; the quotation in the next sentence is from p. 180.

[11] *Fifteen Modern American Authors: A Survey of Research and Criticism,* ed. Jackson R. Bryer (Durham: Duke University Press, 1969); the Fitzgerald chapter is by Bryer.

[12] See Miller, *F. Scott Fitzgerald: His Art and his Technique* (New York: New York University Press, 1964), p. 135; Piper, *F. Scott Fitzgerald: A Critical Portrait* (New York: Holt, Rinehart, and Winston, 1965), p. 226; Sklar, *F. Scott Fitzgerald: The Last Laocoön* (New York: Oxford University Press, 1967), p. 291; and Hindus, *F. Scott Fitzgerald: An Introduction and Interpretation* (New York: Holt, Rinehart, and Winston, 1968), pp. 52–53.

elaborate than Cowley's own or Booth's — were published by Milton R. Stern in 1970 and John F. Callahan in 1972.[13] Stern was convinced that 'Fitzgerald's own instincts about the relationship between the structure and what the book is all about remain most trustworthy, and he was right in wanting to tear the book apart and reassemble it.' Stern attacked the 'antirevisionists' first for their 'argument on the basis of evidence' (by which he meant the manuscript materials), insisting arbitrarily that Bruccoli's evidence was 'not negative evidence but simply no evidence at all. Of anything.' His second objection was to Arthur Mizener's early argument that the revised order would destroy the suspense of the original: 'Whatever is lost in "suspense" — and suspense for its own sake is quite beside the point in this novel — in abandoning the first edition is gained in. exactly what Fitzgerald wanted to achieve in the revision: the central, step-by-step disintegration of Dick, so that the whole sweep of his life is the documentation of excruciating personal, national, human loss.' John F. Callahan, in an analysis which ignored all evidence of Fitzgerald's immediate motivations for rearranging the novel, contended that the author 'changed structures because he perceived historical context rather than impressionist form as the novel's unifying mode.' Fitzgerald's 'revision strategy counterpoints the traditional focus on the individual from youth to maturity, with its implications of order, causality, and inevitability, against an aesthetic focus which fragments consciousness and annihilates individual and historical continuity.' The one clear tendency in all the commentary of the last two decades is that the critics who prefer the Cowley edition have often argued their points at some length while the antirevisionists with the exception of Bruccoli have been content to assert the greater 'dramatic energy' and 'suspense' of the original version and to deny the compensatory 'lucidity' of the Cowley order, without ever mustering much supporting evidence; and because of the rather stringent way he delimited the subject of his book and article, Bruccoli's opinions were usually tacit in the documentary evidence he presented — not, as it turned out, the surest way of engaging the consciousness of literary critics.

Meanwhile, in 1970, the Cowley edition received its apotheosis —

[13] See Stern, *The Golden Moment: The Novels of F. Scott Fitzgerald* (Urbana: University of Illinois Press, 1970) and Callahan, *The Illusions of a Nation: Myth and History in the Novels of F. Scott Fitzgerald* (Urbana: University of Illinois Press, 1972). In this paragraph quotations from Stern are from pp. 391, 389–90, and 393; those from Callahan are from pp. 68, 70.

not from defenses of ardent critics but from a blundering employee of the publisher. For the 'O' printing (May 1970) of the Scribner Library edition someone erroneously substituted the plates of the Cowley edition.[14] In the 'P' printing, Scribner's reverted to the 1934 order, but the Cowley plates were again used inadvertently for the 'Q' printing. 'R' and subsequent printings revert once again to the 1934 order. The Cowley plates have now been destroyed, and unless someone photo-offsets the edition for Scribner's to bedevil professors of American literature still again (or unless the English Penguin edition, based on the Cowley text, infiltrates this country in significant numbers), the 1934 order will prevail. As bad luck had it, it was just when the Cowley defenders were becoming most assured in their arguments that the Cowley plates were destroyed. These partisans who wrongly thought their cause was won will have to abandon their positions or else mark the pages of their Cowley texts to correspond with the pages in their students' copies (which have the 1934 order) and defend their favorite anew against each fresh crop of paperbacks. In some ways, not to speak too ironically, the whole question has become at last academic, having never engaged close attention of many critics during the years when it was more of a genuine issue. Most teachers perforce will use the 1934 order, and one may even hope that they will someday have a corrected, if not a definitive, edition based on the original text. Indeed, someone dedicated might take on the massive challenge of deciding once for all whether or not a definitive edition ought to use the *Scribner's* serial as copy-text (perhaps supplemented by some manuscript pages) rather than the 1934 book version, no matter how many revisions would have to be adopted from the book.

However, since scholars are still analyzing the effects in *Billy Budd, Sailor* of a 'Preface' which is not and never was a preface, one must expect that the Cowley text will haunt criticism for decades. Before we even attempt to lay the edition to rest as a historical curiosity, we need to look at some of its biographical, textual, and critical ramifications. With the best of intentions, Cowley had blundered his way into the textual history of *Tender is the Night*, inattentive not just to the

---

[14] Bruccoli's descriptive bibliography notes (p. 89) that 'The Scribner Library series normally used the original text, but in the "O" printing of 1970, the plates of the revised text were used inadvertently.' The subsequent comedy of errors, ending in the destruction of the Cowley plates, was kindly detailed by Philip C. Coleman, the manager of Scribner's College Marketing Division, in a letter to Parker on 26 January 1973.

biographical exigencies that made Fitzgerald plan the 'Author's Final Version' but also to the history of the composition of the book — insensitive to *Tender is the Night* as the product of years of Fitzgerald's life, a thing growing slowly, being reworked, but being finished at last in accordance with a long-held plan. Cowley altogether failed to distinguish between a writer's sense of his novel as a work of art and his attitude toward it as a marketable product. As far as aesthetics went, Cowley barely asked such superficial critical questions as the effect of moving a particular scene about, much less more profound questions about how any literary work is constructed and how any piece of literature affects its readers. In short, Cowley trampled on or blithely sidestepped a hoard of problems involving biography, textual and aesthetic theory, and criticism.

At the outset, Cowley failed to formulate two basic questions: 'Would the public in 1934 have responded much differently to the book if it had appeared in a form similar to the "Author's Final Version"?' and 'Would Fitzgerald have thought of rearranging the book if it had been as comparatively successful as *The Great Gatsby?*' Cowley's assumptions were somewhat contradictory: on the one hand, the book 'dealt with fashionable life in the 1920s at a time when most readers wanted to forget that they had ever been concerned with frivolities; the new fashion was for novels about destitution and revolt'; on the other hand, he implied that the book failed because the Rosemary section came first.[15] (The issues here need much attention: Bruccoli points out that even *The Great Gatsby* was not a big bestseller by the standards of the time, and also reminds us that the bestsellers of 1934 did not in fact deal very often with either destitution or revolt.)[16] At any rate, Cowley assumed that the public and the hostile portion of the critics were right: 'Fitzgerald didn't blame the public or the critics. It was one of the conditions of the game he played with life to accept the rules as they were written; if he lost point and set after playing his hardest, that was due to some mistake in strategy to be corrected in the future. He began looking in a puzzled fashion for the mistake in *Tender Is the Night.*' Cowley's admiration of the plucky author is touching enough, but in truth Fitzgerald probably should have blamed both his readers and his reviewers. In a more confident period he might have found strength within himself to justify what he knew was 'good,

[15] Cowley, p. x.
[16] *The Composition of 'Tender is the Night,'* pp. 3–4.

good, good',[17] just as he was never tempted to accept the sales figures of Edna Ferber's books as conclusive proof that she was on the right literary path and he was not. During the years following 1934, Fitzgerald was hardly in a position to be the strongest defender of his own achievement. Hemingway had found fault with the book and soon included the demeaning reference to Fitzgerald in the *Esquire* version of 'The Snows of Kilimanjaro'. Zelda Fitzgerald was in hospitals except for brief paroles; Fitzgerald himself, at times suicidal, was also hospitalized for long stretches, and unable even to judge the relative merits of his stories for inclusion in *Taps at Reveille*. The letter to Cerf in which he suggested adding headings was written at the Grove Park Inn at Asheville, North Carolina, where he was visiting his wife; he had climaxed a wasted year by injuring a shoulder so that he was nearly incapacitated for weeks. The letter to Perkins outlining the faults of the first edition was written toward the end of a period of disappointment and discontent at MGM where his best efforts had been cavalierly rewritten by people like Joseph Mankiewicz. At the time of writing, Fitzgerald was waiting with mixed feelings to learn whether MGM would renew his contract (within the next two days he learned they would not). But he was perhaps even more concerned with his literary standing, whatever of it was left to him, and determined to find ways of keeping his books in print. His particular concern with *Tender is the Night* must be seen in the context of his frustrating sense that such reputation as he still had was needlessly dwindling further and as part of a general effort to salvage what he could of both reputation and career as a serious writer.[18] There is no denying that he did some good thinking and writing during times of illness and drinking, but nothing in the circumstances of these years following the publication of *Tender is the Night* was apt to bolster his self-esteem against the critics (he retrospectively increased the number who disliked the flashback construction) or against the man he thought of as his artistic conscience. In short, Cowley neglected a great deal of evidence that the 'Author's Final Version' was the product of wan rationalization, the attempt of a physically and psychically battered man to recoup a few of his losses.

Even more serious was Cowley's neglect of the information about

[17] Cowley, p. x.
[18] See the surveys of these years in chapters 13–15 of Arthur Mizener, *The Far Side of Paradise* (Boston: Houghton Mifflin, 1951), pp. 238–86, and chapters 14–16 in Andrew Turnbull, *Scott Fitzgerald* (New York: Charles Scribner's Sons), pp. 241–97.

Fitzgerald's attitudes during the composition of *Tender is the Night*. Here Bruccoli's evidence is full and conclusive. All the time Fitzgerald was composing the Dick Diver versions of his story, he had in mind the 1934 order. In his first working notes for the seventh version of the manuscript (the first Dick Diver version), he specifically intended to have the 'hero treated 1st entirely from without and then entirely from within.'[19] Before actually writing the seventh draft, Fitzgerald elaborated his plan. Part I was to be 'From outside mostly'; Part II was 'Nicole from Dick' (that is, Nicole seen largely from Dick's point of view); and III was to be 'Dick' (presumably Dick from the narrator's point of view if not also from Nicole's).[20] Bruccoli summarized and interpreted Fitzgerald's notes in a way that clearly suggested their textual significance: they embodied 'the rationale behind the long introductory flashback which Fitzgerald later came to reject under critical fire, although the notes and the manuscripts clearly show that at no time during the composition of the novel did Fitzgerald alter the basic structure.'[21] Bruccoli could hardly have been more explicit: 'the flashback structure is the only scheme represented in the manuscripts.'[22]

It is clear, therefore, that from the start of the Dick Diver version Fitzgerald was working with a definite plan in mind, seeing the hero first from the outside. All through the writing of the Dick Diver drafts, he held to that plan. One cannot argue that every word of the book was written with that plan in mind, for pages here and there — especially in the early chapters — were salvaged from typescripts of pre-Diver stages (Fitzgerald later seemed to think he was reclaiming more than he had); yet even these pages from earlier drafts were altered to fit his purposes for the Diver story. Aside from small amounts of salvaging and even lesser amounts of late interpolating and shifting, *Tender is the Night* was written pretty much consecutively. By and large the early pages were written early, the middle pages written afterwards, and the late pages written last of all. Cowley neglected altogether the aesthetic implications of these simple facts. One cannot declare unconditionally that every word which Ftizgerald wrote from the seventh version onward affected every word that follows in the book as it was published in 1934: one must make exception of the

---

[19] *The Composition of 'Tender is the Night,'* p. 78.
[20] *Ibid.*, p. 84.
[21] *Ibid.*, p. 85.
[22] *Ibid.*, p. 103.

salvaging and tinkering. But, aside from such exceptions, after the opening of the book each sentence of any length, each paragraph, certainly each extended passage and chapter, is written the way it is because of what Fitzgerald had already written and because of what he knew the reader would already have read at a given point. When control over materials is as steady as Fitzgerald's was in the Diver drafts, when the writer knows both in general outline and in a good deal of specific detail where he is going, every passage he actually writes not only fulfills but in subtle ways alters the entire scheme. What Fitzgerald was writing at any stage was written precisely the way it was because he had in mind the general way and even particular ways it was affected by what he had already written and would affect what he was yet to write. When he started the later chapters of Book I, the earlier chapters were in his mind as something achieved (aside from any later insertions into these chapters after they were first completed); even when in a given chapter he used typescript pages from earlier drafts, he did so with a sense of how they fitted with what he had already written in the seventh draft or what he had already salvaged for insertion in earlier parts of that draft. By the time he got to Book II, almost every detail of what he chose to write was to some extent a consequence of what he had already written and was designed to cause certain effects in the mind of the reader who had already read certain scenes.

Book II provides a major example. Fitzgerald calculated just what degree of psychological shock he wanted the reader to experience as he passed from the largely romanticized view of Dick in his maturity to the section on Dick's wartime days, where the author played ironically with the similarity of his hero's alliterative name and exemplary school career to the names and careers of the heroes of boy's fiction. Having set up the situation, Fitzgerald provided a precise definition of the reading experience: 'it is confusing to come across a youthful photograph of some one known in a rounded maturity and gaze with a shock upon a fiery, wiry, eagle-eyed stranger'. His effect achieved, Fitzgerald set himself 'to be reassuring' to the bewildered reader.[23] (Fitzgerald necessarily omitted these comments from the 'Author's Final Version'.) Very obviously, the special characteristics of the prose of chapter 1 in Book II of the original edition would never have existed if that chapter had not been conceived of as following the Rosemary

---

[23] P. 155; SL, p. 118.

section. The boy's-book prose and the boy's-book name (the latter altogether more conspicuous and significant in the early Zurich scenes — and even more so in the reordering) suggest one source of Dick's ideals and 'illusions' which Fitzgerald stresses in his commentary. To give such indications of what amounts to Dick's immaturity before the Rosemary section rather than after it radically alters the nature of the reader's response to Dick throughout the novel. Furthermore, while the reader of the Cowley edition receives some sort of shock in coming (less abruptly) from the pages on the younger Dick to the Rosemary section, the shock is merely adventitious; the reader still undergoes a verifiable aesthetic experience, undoubtedly, but not the one Fitzgerald had thoughtfully conceived and arranged for and then had explicitly commented upon.[24]

As this example shows, arguing that the order of composition affected the substance and style of what was composed is anything but picky theorizing: it takes into account Fitzgerald as a working novelist and the work of art as a thing in-progress until it is finished. About the time this book was published, John Dewey was saying that 'the artist is controlled in the process of his work by his grasp of the connection between what he has already done and what he is to do next.'[25] The artist must 'at each point retain and sum up what has gone before as a whole and with reference to a whole to come.' Otherwise, 'there is no consistency and no security in his successive acts.'[26] For all the need of having a sense of direction, only the most mechanical sort of writing can be totally outlined in advance of actual composition; finer artists, Dewey argued, 'learn by their work, as they proceed, to see and feel what had not been part of their original plan and purpose.'[27] None of this is to deny that effective rejuggling can be done

[24] Even with the change in point of view it is unnecessary and clumsy in this arrangement of the novel for Dick's name to be produced at the end of Book II, chapter 3, with something of a flourish, after being withheld for more than a chapter, since we already know from the conclusion of Nicole's stream-of-consciousness section (Book II, chapter 1, in the Cowley edition) that the Divers have seen Rosemary on the beach and recognized her (p. 212; C, p. 57; SL, p. 162). Fitzgerald has indeed been playing with certain old-fashioned conventions of story-telling ('an isolated railroad stop, whence one morning in June 1925'), but the Cowley reordering falsely suggests that he is coyly involving the reader in a little guessing game according to the convention self-indulgently used in many nineteenth-century novels.

[25] *Art as Experience* (New York: Minton, Balch & Co., 1934), p. 45.

[26] *Ibid.*, p. 56.

[27] *Ibid.*, p. 139.

after a work is first completed, but it *is* to argue that in any large-scale rearranging almost any artist will leave telltale signs of the earlier order. Fitzgerald certainly did in his reordered version of *Tender is the Night*. Without unduly praising his craftsmanship, a critic can acknowledge that during his work on the Dick Diver drafts Fitzgerald set up an intricate series of verbal echoes which gradually swell into thematic reverberations; reordered, echo sometimes becomes original utterance,[28] and thematic reverberations, while undeniably continuing to sound, are not precisely authorial in the new combinations: they come from Fitzgerald's own words still, but not from his own careful patterning. It seems irrefutable that when Fitzgerald reordered his book he set discords ringing haphazardly, out of control. But rather than focus analysis on the way the new order distorted individual verbal echoes, concentrate for the most part on some of the larger consequences of Fitzgerald's — and later Cowley's — treating *Tender is the Night* as if it had been created simultaneously in the form of disparate blocks.

Most obviously, in the 1934 order the Rosemary section allows the reader to receive his first impression of Dick and his entourage largely (though by no means wholly) through Rosemary's glamorizing eyes, introduces them at that heightened period of time when the reader can nearly believe in their untarnished splendor, with Dick poised at what seems perfection, before it becomes apparent (as it does in this section even in the original order) how their health is illusory and their vitality is waning. By the end of Book I the reader can no longer cherish any belief in Dick's perfection, but to the end of chapter 15 Dick's extraordinary qualities of consideration, sensitivity, and restraint over-

---

[28] In the original order, Rosemary makes her judgment of Dick early: 'But Dick Diver — he was all complete there. Silently she admired him' (p. 24; C, p. 75; SL, p. 19). During the rest of the Rosemary section the attentive reader begins gathering evidence that Dick is indeed not complete; but in the original order it nevertheless comes as a rather rueful shock to be told (p. 153; C, p. 5; SL, p. 117) 'that the price of his intactness was incompleteness'. (The echoes do not stop here; for instance, the mentally ill are referred to as 'the incomplete' [p. 159; C, p. 9; SL, p. 120], while Dick later says that ' "The manner remains intact for some time after the morale cracks" ' [p. 368; C, p. 304; SL, p. 285].) In the Cowley order, Rosemary's admiration of Dick as 'all complete' becomes in the reader's mind something like an authorial jibe at Rosemary for vacuousness, if not an authorial jibe at Dick. The same words are retained in both versions, but while the reader ends up with the same quantity of words whether he reads in one order or the other, he ends up with a quite different quality of reading experience.

shadow all doubts about him. The worst we have learned about him is that he tends to excite himself too much about people. Furthermore, we read Book I with considerable suspense and come to Book II with a mixture of trepidation and nostalgia — emotions which cannot exist if we read the early Zurich scenes first. We read the early chapters of Book II with the pleasure of resolved suspense, then read the romance of Dick and Nicole with the pity and irony of knowing she will not remain cured — again responses a reader cannot have if he comes to the Zurich scenes first. More importantly, even while the original Book II is defining more clearly the flaws in Dick's character, it renews and intensifies the reader's sense of the good that is (or was) in him through its revelation of his personal and professional potential. Feeling this way, we come to the later chapters of Book II with a despairing sense of precipitous fall: Dick's failings come thick and fast. We go from his heroic period to his disastrous period with great poignance, our sense of tragedy inevitably heightened, moreover, by our almost having believed Rosemary's view of his perfections.

Just as inevitably, the 1951 order diminishes the poignance of this period of collapse, since in this edition we go from the heroic period to the Rosemary section (in which there are ominous signs of decay) then to the fall — a *steady,* fatalistic progression, with no hint that it could have been different, with no sense of a magic, poised moment when Dick could be idolized. Doubts about Dick are raised from the first chapter of the Cowley edition. ' "That's going to be your trouble — judgment about yourself," ' the young Rumanian intellectual tells Dick,[29] and thereafter we wait for signs of this questionable judgment. After the first such sign — Dick's involvement with Nicole against his better professional judgment — every hint of something wrong is intensified as we go on to read the earlier parts of the Rosemary section. We know that Nicole has had relapses and we suspect that Dick is sacrificing or has sacrificed his career. The reference to Dick's 'waste and extravagance' sounds more ominous than in the 1934 order.[30] Rosemary's sense of Dick's completeness and self-control, which sounds plausible enough in the original order, appears now to reflect her naïveté if not authorial irony at Dick's expense,[31] and our response to his consideration in his dealings with her is different. We have been

[29] P. 154; C, p. 5; SL, p. 117.
[30] P. 35; C, p. 84; SL, p. 27.
[31] P. 24; C, p. 75; SL, p. 19. See note 28, above.

prepared to view Dick more critically and to expect lapses; we wait for his lapse with Rosemary, especially since she is 'Daddy's Girl'.[32] Dick's invitation of Rosemary to Paris, his gradual involvement with her, his failure to guard against involvement on Rosemary's part (in spite of his knowledge of his own attractiveness and his awareness of her disposition to fall in love) are all clear indications of that same questionable judgment — signs of the second stage in a gradual deterioration we witness from the very beginning. All this is apparent before we come to the more explicit signs of his moral confusion and immaturity in the later parts of the Rosemary section. We move into these accounts of Dick's confusion over Rosemary not with an alarmed sense of his starting to lose control, as in the 1934 version, but with a grim sense of the predictability of this yet further deterioration.[33]

[32] P. 90; C, p. 130; SL, p. 68. The revised order makes the ironic title of Rosemary's movie offensively lurid, since already in the reader's mind is the memory of Devereux Warren's confession of incest with Nicole and the knowledge that her insanity is the consequence of that incest. It is worth pointing out that Fitzgerald does not play altogether fair with the reader here even in the original version, for he gives part but not the main part of what Dick would most naturally feel while watching *Daddy's Girl:* he should wince not only for all psychologists but also for Nicole. In the revised version, the reader, knowing of the incest, is sensitive (more so than Dick is shown to be) to the movie as very likely an embarrassment to Nicole and — even worse — the potential cause of another 'pousse' of her illness. After all, only a short time has passed since her relapse at Villa Diana (and any reader of the Cowley edition will have guessed what sort of scene Violet McKisco witnessed there). What was a minor flaw in the 1934 version, brought about by Fitzgerald's handling of point of view, becomes a serious flaw in Dick's characterization in the revised order, since it is unbelievable that he would not at this moment consider his wife's feelings and since there is now, without the mystery to sustain, no reason for Fitzgerald to withhold Dick's thoughts from the reader.

[33] One measure of our changed reaction to Dick is the battlefield episode, where we regard his sentimentalities and simplifications indulgently in the 1934 order (at least until we see him retrospectively from the latter parts of the novel) but very critically in the revised edition, since we come to the episode affected by Franz's comments on the superficiality of Dick's books on psychiatry. (Even a casual remark like Dick's later one to Rosemary about Abe, ' "Don't you know you can't do anything about people?" ' [p. 103; C, p. 140; SL, p. 78] is given added significance by the earlier suggestion in the Zurich scenes that his professionalism is not complete.) One major function of the battlefield episode in the original order, that of making Rosemary serve as partial surrogate for the reader so that he shares some of her uncritical love for Dick, cannot possibly be accomplished in the revised order, in which we are already much more skeptical of Rosemary's judgment. In the Cowley

A direct consequence of such changes is that Dick's attractive qualities, which affect us so forcefully in the original order, affect us less strongly in the Cowley edition or else are vitiated by their being put to the service of his questionable judgment. Ultimately, then, we cannot feel as tragic about Dick's final period of collapse as in the original edition because we have scarcely been allowed to think well of him, either in his personal or his professional judgments.

Further evidence of the revised edition's disruption of Fitzgerald's original intentions and effectiveness can be seen in the change in function of a character as important as Abe North. In the 1934 order, as Dick comes more and more to resemble Abe in his irresponsibility, drunkenness, unfulfilled promise, bitterness, and — finally — deathwish, there is an obvious contrast with the earlier Dick who 'drank' but 'not too much',[34] the 'only sober man with repose',[35] who next to Abe seemed all strength and self-control. In that order the gradual revelation that Dick is *like* Abe, not different from him, underscores the novel's progression: we see that what we thought was real strength is illusory. In the Cowley edition, Dick's resemblance to Abe, in spite of his relative sobriety, is suggested from the beginning of the Rosemary section. Rosemary, for example, learns that Abe is 'a musician who, after a brilliant and precocious start, had composed nothing for seven years',[36] and the several years' unproductiveness seems now to make pointed reference to Dick's parallel case, which it could not do in the 1934 edition. In the Cowley order, the revelations of Dick's further similarities to Abe emphasize the continual process of Dick's slow decline without the initial impression of real strength. In short, the 1934 order creates initial contrasts between Dick and Abe; only later — with much poignance — do we see that Dick has become nearly as bad as Abe. From the start the Cowley edition shows Dick and Abe as parallel characters, as much as contrasting ones, so that a good deal of Abe's original purpose in the novel is lost.

Still more, if less striking, evidence of the revised edition's weakened

---

order, the reader might well be anxious to know just where Nicole is during the scene, while in the 1934 order he either does not think of her at all or only later realizes that she is strangely silent, though she is always with the others.

[34] P. 80; C, p. 122; SL, p. 61.

[35] P. 67; C, p. 110; SL, p. 51.

[36] P. 43; C, p. 91; SL, p. 34. (Only the Cowley edition has commas after 'who' and 'start'.)

effectiveness is the way the reordering destroys the original purposes
for certain pairs of incidents or images, as by increasing the distance
between the early Zurich scenes and the period of Dick's disaster.[37]
In these pairings the second, contrasting, passage of the 1934 edition
makes all the more distressing our awareness of the imminent or actual
collapse of a man we have seen in his heroic period a comparatively
short time before. Thus after Dick's earlier scorn of 'shell-shocks who
merely heard an air raid from a distance', his 'half-ironic' self-diagno-
sis of 'Non-combatant's shell-shock' comes as a relatively quick and
poignant contrast;[38] so does the episode in which Dick is compromised
by having liquor on his breath after he has joked to Franz about
smelling of garlic.[39] Even the image of Dick the lone cyclist in Switzerland, uninvolved, ambitious, and energetic (though already behaving
as if his body were in top condition when it is not) is succeeded more
quickly in the original edition by the related image of a victorious lone
cyclist, 'toiling intent and confident', while Dick has become one of

[37] The pairing of images, incidents, and even whole scenes is, of course, one
of Fitzgerald's major structural and thematic devices in the novel; he cannot
have realized how seriously the reordering would affect these pairings. Destruction of the original purpose can result from the decrease of distance
between them as well as increase. In the case of the opening and closing beach
scenes, the decrease of distance naturally affects our response to the last one,
which no longer can give the sense of bringing the action full circle. The scene
thereby loses much of its elegiac flavor — though that loss also arises from our
inability to respond in a favorable way to Dick during the opening beach scenes
in the revised edition because his incompleteness has already been suggested.
We can hardly be deeply moved by Dick's being the deposed ruler of his beach
at the end when the malaise underlying his earlier rule was apparent from the
first scenes at the beach in their revised placement. Similarly, the closer jux-
taposition in the revised version of the Rosemary section and the later parts
of the original Book II (chapters 11–23) upsets the painful contrast between
Dick's zestful if reckless plottings at the Riviera (p. 35; C, p. 84; SL, p. 27)
and his sodden plottings with the two women in Naples (p. 269; C, p. 224;
SL, p. 206). In the reordered text, the earlier social efforts seem hardly zestful
at all, and the reader is later denied the sense that Dick's social schemings in
Naples are the actions of only the ghost of the man so long ago and so
hopefully encountered. By the time the reader gets well into Book III in the
1934 edition, the Riviera days seem very remote; in fact, the Rosemary section
deals with a more recent period of Dick's life than the first Zurich scenes, but
for the reader the chronology of Dick's life in this respect is irrelevant: what
counts is the order in which he reads the book.
[38] P. 157; C, p. 8; SL, p. 119; and p. 236; C, p. 196; SL, p. 180.
[39] P. 174; C, p. 21; SL, p. 131; and p. 327; C, p. 271; SL, p. 253.

the 'dupes of accident and defeat';[40] and likewise the comparison of Dick to Grant at Galena (on the verge of being 'called to an intricate destiny') is closer to Nicole's mistaken self-reassurance that Dick's career in upstate New York again bides its time like Grant's.[41] The total effect from the greater separation the revised edition puts between related passages such as these is to contribute to the new slower, more relentless process of deterioration in this version, which replaces the sense of precipitous fall conveyed in the original text.[42] From every standpoint, our experience of Dick's collapse is more vivid, more painful, and more overwhelming in the 1934 edition.

Pervasively, then, in ways large and small, the reordering of the sections of *Tender is the Night* alters or altogether destroys the effects Fitzgerald elaborately calculated, and absolutely no evidence shows

[40] P. 194; C, p. 39; SL, p. 147; then p. 400; C, p. 328; SL, p. 309; and p. 400; C, p. 329; SL, p. 310 (though the word 'dupes' becomes 'victims' in Cowley).

[41] P. 155; C, p. 6; SL, p. 118; and p. 408; C, p. 334; SL, p. 315.

[42] The 1934 version moves in a much shorter span than the Cowley version from the introduction of the idea of the Warrens' buying Nicole a doctor to Dick's sense that Baby thinks they have bought *him* and his impotent rebellion against her (p. 201; C, p. 45; SL, p. 152; and pp. 232–33; C, p. 193; SL, p. 177). The effect of rapid collapse is again created in the original text and destroyed in the revised. Similarly, a number of ideas are associated in the flashback with Dick's ambition as a psychiatrist: that 'it's a confession of weakness for a scientist not to write' (p. 211; C, p. 56; SL, p. 161); that time is important ('a man knows things and when he stops knowing things he's like anybody else, and the thing is to get power before he stops knowing things' [p. 212; C, pp. 56–57; SL, p. 162]); and that potential can quickly evaporate, particularly through drinking (' "I don't want to let my current ideas slide away with a few dozen glasses of beer" ', Dick says [p. 182; C, p. 29; SL, p. 138]). Then in the first chapters after the flashback in the original version, we learn of the stagnation of Dick's work and his fretful sense that 'patient Germans were sitting close to the libraries of Berlin and Vienna callously anticipating him' (p. 216; C, p. 178; SL, p. 165); we witness the start of his heavy drinking (p. 218; C, p. 179; SL, p. 167), and then in the next chapter we see him 'listening to the buzz of the electric clock, listening to time' (p. 223; C, p. 183; SL, p. 171) — time when he is obviously accomplishing nothing. This effect of his marriage to Nicole is clearly another instance where the original version gives the impression of more rapid deterioration than the revised version, where Dick's work is not mentioned between the end of Book II, chapter 1, and Book III, chapter 14, except when he says to Abe that he may abandon his ' "scientific treatise" ' — then qualifies that remark by adding more lightly that he may ' " — abandon it for another one" ' (pp. 81–82; C, p. 123; SL, p. 62).

that he desired or even foresaw the full consequences of his reordering. But there is still a need to examine some basic ways in which the experience of reading the 'Author's Final Version' is not merely different and largely adventitious but is actually illogical or even nonsensical. For example, the point of the first beach scenes in the 1934 order is to throw Dick and his group into pleasant relief by contrast with the distasteful McKisco set — to make the reader respond to the Divers with Rosemary's sense of how fine they are by contrast. In the Cowley edition, the reader will suspect from the start that Dick and his own group, while superficially showing more elegance and distinction, have weaknesses of their own. Here as elsewhere Fitzgerald's strategy of encouraging a certain kind of judgment — a strategy built into each part of the first, second, and fourth chapters — is baffled by what we already know, so that the scenes cannot fulfill their function in their new place. The same words are in each scene but they cannot have the same effect.

This loss of coherence in a particular scene is bad enough, but a lack of logical development pervades the reordered version up to Book III, chapter 14 (Book II, chapter 11 in the original edition). The initial emphasis in the revised order is on Dick's moral potential and his ambition as a psychiatrist, despite his 'American' incompleteness. His first personal and professional test is the allurement of marriage to Nicole (and the Warren money). So at the end of the first book of the revised version, where Nicole's problem 'was one they had together for good now',[43] what the reader is interested in discovering is the kind of relationship that Dick and Nicole achieve, the kind of difficulties involved in it (and whether or not they are overcome), the effect of each one on the other, and the effect, if any, of Nicole and her money on Dick's work. Yet in the Cowley edition during the considerable interval between Book II, chapter 2, where Rosemary's point of view is assumed, and Book III, chapter 14, we learn, in fact, very little about Dick and Nicole's relationship. We are told early that Rosemary was unaware that the Divers' 'simplicity of behavior', their 'nursery-like peace and good will' and 'emphasis on the simpler virtues' was 'part of a desperate bargain with the gods and had been attained through struggles she could not have guessed at.'[44] All this appears to hold promise of further elaboration — but none is forthcoming. We con-

[43] P. 206; C, p. 50; SL, p. 157.
[44] P. 27; C, p. 77; SL, p. 21.

tinue to learn about Dick and Nicole, certainly; we learn about Dick's great social virtuosity, his developing love for Rosemary, and the complex emotions that it inspires; we learn about Nicole's appearance, her lavish spending, her tendency to be rather silent, and her being tired of Abe. But beyond their qualities as host and hostess, their continuing passion, and Dick's insistence to Rosemary that he and Nicole 'have got to go on together' (though he has become 'intensely critical' of Nicole), we do not learn about their relationship.[45] (Rosemary, we are told, thought that 'it was a rather cooled relation',[46] but she is an unreliable source, especially so here because a short time previously she had overheard the passionate exchange between the Divers in the restaurant cloakroom.) We know that Nicole has had relapses, but we do not know how Dick has met the obvious demands and strains of his situation; we do not know precisely why he is becoming so critical of Nicole. Certainly we suspect that Dick is failing to fulfill his early potential; we have the ominous revelation in Nicole's stream-of-consciousness section (Book II, chapter 1, in the revised order) that he is not finding time for his writing, and we have Dick's own later casual mention of possibly abandoning his ' "scientific treatise" '.[47] But we are left merely to guess at the nature and extent of Dick's work (which receives only the most fleeting of references), to infer his neglect of it, and to infer the relation of this neglect to his marriage to Nicole, the nature of which remains itself largely a matter of speculation. In other words, our central concerns from Book I have become the subject of mere conjecture — in spite of the fact that Fitzgerald continually breaks into Rosemary's point of view to make authorial comment, including long passages devoted to Dick and shorter passages to Nicole. We have continual shifts in point of view but are not furnished with the kind of information the opening chapters (in the revised edition) have led us to expect. The Divers remain at or near the center of our consciousness, yet are undeveloped in the areas of their lives which most interest us. To use Dewey's words again, the Rosemary section notably fails, in the 'Author's Final Version', to 'retain and sum up what has gone before'; the result is that 'there is no consistency'.

This lack of logical development in spite of the author's unconcealed omniscience makes more conspicuous what Cowley refers to as the

[45] P. 98; C, p. 136; SL, p. 75; and p. 129; C, p. 161; SL, p. 100.
[46] P. 99; C, p. 137; SL, p. 75.
[47] P. 211; C, p. 56; SL, p. 161; and p. 81; C, p. 123; SL, p. 62.

'mystery-story element' of the Rosemary section — an element which he regarded as easily dispensable.[48] But the 'mystery-story element' is not in fact so simply and entirely sacrificed in the 1951 edition as Cowley suggested. The original mystery of the section has disappeared for the reader in the revised version because he already knows the background of Nicole's illness, but the mystery element remains written into the section. For despite the flexible use of point of view, what Violet McKisco saw in the Divers' bathroom at the Riviera is not revealed until the conclusion of the Peterson episode, even though a duel is fought as one of the indirect consequences of this first bathroom scene; the duel, of course, and certain remarks by Abe and Tommy (for example, ' "It's inadvisable to comment on what goes on in this house." ') raise curiosity even higher.[49] Furthermore, the conclusion to the mystery retains its sense of climax: 'Rosemary, back in the salon, heard the bathroom door bang, and stood trembling: now she knew what Violet McKisco had seen in the bathroom at Villa Diana.'[50] The reordered text, in withholding information the reader desires, seems to be luring him into the expectation of significant revelation beyond what he already knows of Nicole. Naturally, the false climax falls flat and the mystery and its solution seem absurd. For the reader has previously learned of Nicole's insanity and of her relapse after Topsy's birth and this second bathroom episode merely lets him know what he has naturally assumed since the occurrence of the first — that Nicole is still liable to fits of madness, though more violent in the symptoms than he had realized. The element of mystery seems all along to be working against the reader's natural assumption, which is then finally and perversely confirmed. Clearly, to make any mystery of Nicole's continuing illness is inappropriate, given the knowledge the reader has from Book I. Again the failure to retain and sum up what has gone before results in a lack of coherence.

Subsequent parts of the novel in the 'Author's Final Version' maladroitly emphasize the presence of the absurd mystery and false climax in the Rosemary section, for they now supply the reader with the information about Dick and Nicole that had noticeably been held back since the second chapter of the new Book II. Cowley objected that in the original version the 'psychoanalytical case study is finished by p.

[48] Cowley, p. xiv.
[49] P. 47; C, p. 93; SL, p. 36.
[50] P. 148; C, p. 174; SL, p. 112.

212, when the reader has all the pertinent information about the past life of the Divers.'[51] But far from finishing the study of Dick and Nicole, the section presenting the young Dick arouses those interests and expectations already mentioned: the kind of relationship that Dick and Nicole achieve, the effect of Nicole's problems and money on their lives. These questions are answered just after Nicole's breakdown in the bathroom in Paris, in the part of the book beginning 'Doctor Richard Diver and Mrs. Elsie Speers sat in the Café des Alliées in August, under cool and dusty trees' (Book III, chapter 14, in the Cowley edition).[52] Here the focus is on the relationship of Dick and Nicole and its effect on Dick. We learn of Dick's dissatisfaction with his work, an uneasiness apparently connected with the luxury in which the Divers live. We also learn of the unprofessional agonies Dick suffered during Nicole's long relapse after Topsy's birth, the cleavage he had to make between Nicole sick and Nicole well, his difficulty in distinguishing between 'his self-protective professional detachment and some new coldness in his heart'.[53] Then chapter 15 elaborates on Dick's problems, his struggles for financial independence in the marriage, Nicole's wanting to own him and encouraging slackness toward his work, which has become confused with Nicole's own mental problems. The next chapter keeps the focus on strains in the relationship, the 'dangerous subject' of young girls, Dick's resentment of Baby Warren's 'cold rich insolence', the 'unavoidable series of strains' from living on the Divers' scale.[54] After this follows the account of Dick's deterioration. In the Cowley edition all these scenes are separated from the chapters on the young Dick Diver by the entire Rosemary section — so late does the 'Author's Final Version' hold back information the reader desires. The original version of the novel develops this information in a logical and satisfying manner, presenting it when it is expected (directly after Dick's decision to marry Nicole against all considerations to the contrary), while the revised edition delays it for no legitimate reason at all.

None of these arguments is meant to defend the 1934 version of *Tender is the Night* as a perfect work of art. As Cowley and others have pointed out, the Rosemary section in the original version is to some

---

[51] Cowley, p. xiv.
[52] P. 213; C, p. 175; SL, p. 162.
[53] P. 220; C, p. 180; SL, p. 168.
[54] P. 226; C, p. 188; SL, p. 172; then p. 232; C, p. 193; SL, p. 177; and p. 235; C, p. 195; SL, p. 179.

extent misleading, since it causes many readers to think that Rosemary has rather greater importance than she actually has.[55] An uncertainty of focus may well detract from the total impact of the book. Perhaps the fault of the original edition is more one of balance than ordering: Rosemary's point of view may be emphasized too much for too long, so as to become out of proportion to the stress given to Nicole's critical view of Dick at the end of the novel — a view with which it seems meant to contrast. Fitzgerald made something very close to this point in a letter to H. L. Mencken on 23 April 1934, just as the reviews were accumulating:[56]

[55] The fact is that the revised order is at least as confusing, since after the Zurich section the reader has every reason to feel sure that he is being told a story devoted almost exclusively to Dick Diver. He can only be bewildered by the sudden, belated shift to Rosemary.

[56] *Letters,* p. 510. Throughout his discussion of the two versions of the novel in *The Golden Moment,* Stern confuses the evidence dating before the end of 1938 which deals with Fitzgerald's desire to strengthen his presentation of Dick with the evidence dating from 24 December 1938 or afterwards which deals with Fitzgerald's decision to reorder the book. More than most of Stern's evidence, this letter seems to support his position that Fitzgerald thought at a very early time in the history of the book's publication that his opening was wrong, for Fitzgerald did say that there was a 'deliberate intention' in every part of the book except the first. Stern comments: 'In the month he published the book, he was already unhappy about the first part of the novel, already aware that introducing Diver's story through Rosemary's point of view was a false beginning' (p. 376). But this letter is not an altogether satisfactory account of Fitzgerald's composition of Book I or his estimation of it. In the first place, although he made concessions about the early part of the novel, he was most concerned in this letter to defend the ' "dying fall" ' of the conclusion. In the second place, when he said that ' was a deliberate intention in every part 'except the first', that was of course not literally true, for despite his heavy reliance on previous drafts (which he integrated very well into his new version), he did hold rather closely to the original plan for the Dick Diver version, which was to present Dick first from the 'outside mostly'. It is quite likely then that Fitzgerald's phrasing was at fault, and that he meant to concede no more than he does in his next sentence — that the Rosemary section became 'too long and too elaborated'. Thirdly, when he said that 'everything else in the book conformed to a *definite intention'* and that if he 'had to start to write it again tomorrow' he would 'adopt the same plan', his use of 'it' was ambiguous. He meant he would adopt the 'same plan' for writing either the entire book again or for writing 'everything else' besides the first part again. If he was thinking of the entire novel, the 'same plan' would mean the original conception of seeing Dick in three different ways in the three books. This amounts not to an awareness that the romantic introduction was a 'false beginning' or 'misplaced' (as Stern would have it) but to a defense of it — both its point of view

I would like to say in regard to my book that there was a deliberate intention in every part of it except the first. The first part, the romantic introduction, was too long and too elaborated largely because of the fact that it had been written over a series of years with varying plans, but everything else in the book conformed to a *definite intention* and if I had to start to write it again tomorrow I would adopt the same plan, irrespective of the fact of whether I had in this case brought it off or not brought it off. That is what most of the critics fail to understand (outside of the fact that they fail to recognize and identify anything in the book): that the motif of the "dying fall" was absolutely deliberate and did not come from any diminution of vitality but from a definite plan.

Fitzgerald's later decision to switch the beginning and part of the middle of the book around, while it gave a more powerful focus to the opening, caused great damage, in the long run, to all parts of the novel. Rewriting, reshaping parts of *Tender is the Night* might indeed have produced a better novel; reordering it caused far more problems than it solved. But one of the curiosities of scholarship is that Cowley was not quickly challenged by biographers, textual scholars, and critics. Art may not be magical or mystical but, as someone should have reminded Cowley, good art is subtle and coherent, is the way it is for good reasons, even if the artist himself under later compulsions loses part of his faith in — or recollection of — his original design and the validity of his first 'final' intentions.

---

and its location — even while conceding that it was faulty in execution, 'too long and too elaborated'. Alternatively, Fitzgerald may have been using 'it' to refer to 'everything else' (and his concern with the ' "dying fall" ' in the next sentence suggests this possibility); in this case, he is defending Books II and III but again still not rejecting the strategy or position of Book I.

In short, the letter to Mencken offers scant evidence that at this early date Fitzgerald was already troubled by the ordering of the novel. He did not repudiate the chronology or the basic strategy of opening with a romantic introduction. He may have felt when the book was published — though what follows in the letter casts this in doubt — that he had not followed a plan in the first part. In that case, he was wrong — just as he was wrong later in wanting to reorder Book I and a part of Book II.

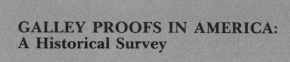

GALLEY PROOFS IN AMERICA:
A Historical Survey

JOHN BUSH JONES

ALTHOUGH IT REMAINS SOMETHING OF A MYSTERY PRECISELY WHEN,
where, and by whom galley proofs were introduced into printing practice in Britain, let alone in America, the printers' manuals and trade
journals of both countries provide a fairly full and, hopefully, accurate
index to their spread during the nineteenth century and the first
decades of the twentieth.[1] The growth pattern of 'proofs in slips', as
they were then generally called, was similar in England and the United

[1] A preliminary history of galley proofs in Britain is provided by Geoffrey
D. Hargreaves, ' "Correcting in the Slip": The Development of Galley Proofs',
The Library, 5th ser., 26 (1971): 295–311. The author admits that 'far more
examples are clearly needed' (p. 310): his survey draws information from only
a few of the major English printers' manuals of the nineteenth century. Hargreaves is unable to pinpoint with accuracy for Britain, as I am unable for
America, the precise date of the introduction of galley proofs.

The present study was made possible, in part, by a Newberry Library grant-
in-aid in the summer of 1971. In the summer of 1972 I consulted additional
sources in the Printing Library of St. Bride's Institute, London.

States, receiving their first widespread acceptance for newswork, and only considerably later — and, seemingly, somewhat grudgingly — for book work.[2] A survey of American manuals and trade papers reveals not only trends in the adoption of galley proofs, but also something of the uses to which they were put, whether they were strictly for the benefit of proofreaders in the printing houses themselves or for sending out as author's proofs, the latter function having particular bearing on questions regarding the transmission of texts.

In the earliest American printers' manuals, those of the first four decades of the nineteenth century, galley proofs or their equivalents are conspicuous by their absence. The reason for this absence is simple. Of the three manuals from this period available to me — Van Winkle, Adams, and Saunders — the first two are thinly disguised, though at least openly acknowledged, adaptations of early British manuals which pre-date the rise if not the inception of galley proofs;[3] the third is simply the New York imprint of a current English manual of a slightly conservative stamp.[4] In 1816 Van Winkle, naming Stower's *Printer's Grammar* of 1808 as his source just as Stower had acknowledged Smith's 1755 *Printer's Grammar* as *his*, makes it clear throughout his manual that what he means by 'proof-sheet' is precisely that — a proof of the sheet with the pages properly imposed in the form.[5] Similarly, Thomas F. Adams, citing Smith directly as the origin of his own 1837 text, paraphrases him with only such revisions necessary to

[2] The question of galley proofs in jobbing, though touched on by some of the manuals, is not considered in detail in the present survey.

[3] Such acknowledgment of sources is rare. In large part, the history of nineteenth-century British *and* American printers' manuals is a history of plagiarism — unacknowledged borrowings from Moxon, Smith, Stower, and Johnson. Accordingly, unless advances in techniques and methods were even slower and more conservative than is sometimes supposed, the usefulness of many of the manuals even at their date of publication must be questioned. They are, furthermore, a trap for students of printing history who may not be aware of the borrowings. Generally speaking, those manuals which are more wholly original must be taken to reflect most accurately the actual practice of their day.

[4] The earliest English manuals with explicit references to galley proofs are G. Cowie, *Cowie's Printer's Pocket-Book and Manual* (London: W. Strange, n. d. [ca. 1830, according to the catalog of the St. Bride's Printing Library]), and [C. Knight], *The Guide to the Trade: The Printer* (London: Charles Knight & Co., 1838).

[5] Cornelius S. Van Winkle, *The Printers' Guide; or an Introduction to the Art of Printing* (New York: C. S. Van Winkle, 1816), *passim.*

154

accomodate the idea of a proof-press: 'Our form, or forms, being now locked up, and become portable, we remove them to the proof-press and pull a proof of them. . . . a proof sheet ought to be pulled as clean and as neat as any sheet in a heap that is worked off.'[6] That the notion of proofs only in sheets is not simply an accident of borrowing is clear from a statement presumably written by Adams himself that 'when a proof is pulled, the compositor who imposed the sheet ought to collect and arrange the copy.'[7] Concerned exclusively with book work, Adams seems oblivious to proofs in any form other than sheets. If galleys were indeed gaining ground in news or periodical work by 1837, we could not discover it from Adams's manual.

Like Adams's, Saunders's volume two years later concentrates entirely on book work.[8] Strictly speaking, it is not a printers' manual at all, but a somewhat watered-down guide to printing and publishing designed for authors. As an American imprint of an English title, what it describes, naturally, is current practice in British book houses, and it may not, therefore, be a good index to American procedures at all. Nevertheless, what Americans in 1839 could learn from Saunders about proofs is that 'When a sufficient number of pages have been set to form a Sheet, they are what is called *Imposed*, and the *Form* is removed to the Press-room, where the first impression, technically called the first Proof, is taken off.'[9] As late as 1855 a book intended for an even more general readership shows that one major American book house was working entirely with proofs in sheets or, at least, in unimposed pages. In *The Harper Establishment; or, How the Story Books Are Made*, Jacob Abbott describes the process:

When the galleys are full, the *matter*, as the mass of type set up is called, is formed into pages in a frame called a *chase* to be proved.

* * *

[6] Thomas F. Adams, *Typographia: A Brief Sketch of the Origin, Rise, and Progress of the Typographic Arts; with Practical Directions for Conducting Every Department in an Office* (Philadelphia: Thomas F. Adams, 1837), p. 216. Despite Adams's claim that his primary source was Smith, the text shows clearly that most of his borrowings are from Johnson's *Typographia*.

[7] Ibid., p. 236.

[8] Frederic Saunders, *The Author's Printing and Publishing Assistant: Including Interesting Details Respecting the Mechanism of Books* (New York: Frederic Saunders, 1839). This is the American imprint of the same book published in London by Saunders and Otley.

[9] Ibid., pp. 2–3.

In the Harper Establishment almost everything at present is electrotyped. The pages of type are therefore only locked up in small chases containing one to four pages each, for the electrotyping process. . . . In order to correct the errors, the form containing the page to be produced is placed upon a small hand press, and an impression taken.[10]

It seems quite possible that the nature of the electrotyping and stereotyping processes may have been partly responsible for the virtual absence of galley proofs from book houses at the same time that they were approaching universality in newswork. Two issues of *The Printer* in 1858 and 1859 attest to this discrepancy. An article quoting 'an English work' (unnamed) concludes by observing that 'the compositor whose matter is last in the sheet then locks it up, and carries the forms [sic] to the proof press. (The general practice of stereotyping in American book offices will here suggest a slight modification.)'[11] Clearly, this 'slight modification' could have been nothing as radically different from proofs in sheets as galley proofs would be. Rather, it was probably something similar to the proofing of matter made up into pages — often in pairs, but not fully imposed in the sheet — for stereotyping, or for electrotyping as described by Abbott. I would suggest that the electrotyping or stereotyping of small groups of pages allowed for proofing much sooner than the older procedure of having to compose enough pages to make up a full sheet. This new measure of convenience may have retarded the adoption in book houses of the even more convenient galley proof.

Less than a year later, in April 1859, the first explicit reference to galley proofs in an American manual or journal appears in the same trade paper; the context is clearly that of news work. A piece on 'New Improvements by Hoe & Co.' calls a new proof-press 'a decided improvement upon the kind usually met with in newspaper offices merely intended for galley slips.'[12] If proof-presses in newspaper offices were 'usually' producing galley slips by 1859, they assuredly had to go through the initial and intermediate phases of 'never', 'seldom', and 'frequently' in the preceding decades. By the outbreak of the Civil

[10] Jacob Abbott, *The Harper Establishment; or, How the Story Books Are Made* (New York: Harper & Brothers, 1855), pp. 65, 67.

[11] ' "Companionships" in a Book Office,' *The Printer*, 1 (May 1858): 9. The English source has not been located, though the article is by no means of recent date; it will be found almost verbatim — excepting, of course, the final parenthetical editorial comment — in Adams, p. 270.

[12] *The Printer*, 1 (April 1859): 286.

War, then, galley proofs in American news work must have been an established fact.

This assertion gains support from Thomas Lynch's *Printer's Manual* of 1859, in his discussion of galleys:

The galleys are of two kinds: wood, and brass. The former has ledges on two sides, and is generally used in book- and job-offices, for holding the types until the "make-up" is passed to it, or containing parts of a job until it is all composed. The brass galley, having ledges on three sides, can be used in proving the types in slips, besides being used for the same purpose as those made of wood.[13]

and in his discussion of proofing American newspapers:

In daily papers published in this country the compositors have nothing to do with the taking of the proofs, it being the business of the foreman or his assistant to fill out short galleys, and, after having pulled an impression, to put them where they will be readily found when wanted.[14]

The first excerpt unequivocally places wooden galleys in book houses and assigns to them the sole use of holding type before make-up. Lynch fails to state here in what kind of printing the brass galley was used, but the second excerpt appears to isolate galley proofs as a phenomenon peculiar to news work. That such proofs *could* occasionally be used elsewhere is barely implied in Lynch's description of proofreading book work: 'The form [i.e., imposed pages] being ready, the next thing to be done is to pull a proof. . . . If the types be on a galley, they should be carried to the case and corrected there.'[15] By mentioning correcting in the galley in the context of a passage clearly on book work, Lynch suggests at least a limited use of galley proofs in book houses.

Nothing substantial, however, about galley proofs in book work appears until three years later, and once again it is the trade journal *The Printer* leading the way in making known their use and, this time, even urging the expansion of their function. The August 1862 installment of a regular feature column called 'The Youthful Printer: A

---

[13] Thomas Lynch, *The Printer's Manual: A Practical Guide for Compositors and Pressmen* (Cincinnati: Cincinnati Type-Foundry, 1859), p. 67.

[14] Ibid., p. 148.

[15] Ibid., p. 136.

Department for the Apprentice' contains this detailed account of proofing book work:

When the galley is filled, it is "quoined up" for proving. That is, a "side-stick," or strip of beveled wood, is placed alongside the matter composed, and wedged with "quoins," or small pieces of wood, beveled to the same angle as the side-stick. A proof is then taken on a "proof-press," hereafter to be described — on a slip of damp paper, and handed, with the copy, to the "proof-reader," . . . The first proof having been corrected, another is pulled for the examination of the author. This proof being read and corrected, a "revise" is taken for a final critical examination, which is denominated the "press-proof." The few remaining errors or inaccuracies are now corrected, and the matter is ready for "making-up" into pages. Most printers make up after the first proof is corrected; but *we prefer having the author's proof corrected before dividing the matter into pages* [my italics] — for the obvious reason that important alterations, involving the over-running of whole sheets, may be made by him.[16]

This passage not only implies that the use of galley slips for first proofs was general in book houses by 1862, but also the hortatory tone of its remarks on author's proofs has the air of a radical — though certainly practical — departure from the more limited common practice of the day. By the next month's issue, however, that same column is speaking of author's proofs in galley form as if they were a normal occurrence: 'When the author's or editor's proof is corrected, if book-work, the running title and folio is set up. . . . The page is then made its proper length.'[17] And the article extends the similar application of galley proofs to periodical work by reference to the production of *The Printer* itself: 'We generally have two proofs before making up, and one after, which we call the "press proof." '[18]

If these articles alone could be accepted as sufficient evidence, it would seem that galley proofs had become the norm in book work for both first and author's proofs by the second year of the Civil War. Yet the second edition of Thomas Mackeller's influential manual, published four years later, indicates that 'The Youthful Printer' may have been too sanguine in painting his happy picture of the rapid rise of galley proofs. As far as Mackeller is concerned, 'proof' and 'proof-sheet' always refer to impressions of imposed pages, as when he in-

[16] *The Printer,* 4 (August 1862): 68.
[17] *The Printer,* 4 (September 1862): 84.
[18] Ibid.

structs, 'When a first proof is pulled, the compositor who imposed the sheet ought to collect and arrange the copy.'[19]

The several entries touching on proofs in Ringwalt's *American Encyclopædia of Printing* (1871) are at times ambiguous and occasionally contradictory (or seemingly so), yet the overall thrust is that the galley proof had by that date become a well-established, if not universally accepted, part of all branches of American printing. The entry for 'proof' defines it as

A single impression of type-matter, taken for the purpose of examination and correction by the proof-reader or author. The first impression taken for this purpose is called the first proof; the second which is compared with the first to see that all the errors marked in it are corrected, is called the revise. In careful work other proofs are frequently taken, such as an author's proof, a re-revise, and a press-proof, obtained from the form after it is made up and placed upon the press on which it is to be printed.[20]

The careful description of the nature of the press-proof (made-up pages imposed in the form) and the omission of such a description for all earlier proofs tempt one to assume that these could all take the form of galley slips, though there is, of course, no way to be certain. They could just as well be proofs of individual pages, or of series of pages.

Again, under 'Proof Press' appears the equally vague reference to 'the ordinary galley press in general use,'[21] with no indication whether this 'use' is in news work, book work, or both. And the 'Ready Proof Press' is defined as 'A press especially designed for taking proofs of small jobs, or of matter on galleys for newspapers,'[22] perhaps leading one to believe that galley proofs were used exclusively in news work. The explanation for such discrepancies may lie in the encyclopedic nature of Ringwalt's book, the editor possibly careless in establishing uniformity in what may be supposed to be the work of several contributors.

In comparison with the entries already cited, the lucidity and precision of that under 'Galley' suggest it may be most valuable for accurately viewing the scope of American galley proofs by 1871. The

[19] Thomas Mackeller, *The American Printer: A Manual of Typography*, 2nd ed. (Philadelphia: L. Johnson & Co., 1866), p. 181. Cf. Adams, p. 236, quoted above.

[20] J. Luther Ringwalt, ed., *American Encyclopaedia of Printing* (Philadelphia: Menamin and Ringwalt, 1871), p. 373.

[21] Ibid., p. 373.

[22] Ibid., p. 376.

wooden galley, useless for taking proofs, was becoming obsolete, though 'still used to some extent in book and job offices.' 'Brass galleys,' however, 'which are now used universally in newspaper offices and extensively in book and job offices, provide facilities for proving matter before it is made up or tied up, thus lessening the difficulty of making corrections, and avoiding troublesome overrunning of pages.'[23] Like 'The Youthful Printer' nine years earlier, Ringwalt finds galley proofs widespread, though by no means universal, in book work, but absolutely *de rigueur* for newspapers. Can the observations in his impressively handsome *Encyclopaedia* be trusted?

Possibly not. Tracing the development of American galley proofs through the printers' manuals is something like the game of 'May I?' — taking a giant step back for every one or two forward. Slightly more than a decade after Ringwalt's publication, the master American printer of the century's closing years, Theodore Low DeVinne was still writing of the proofing of book work in sheets, only conceding the galley proof to periodical printing: 'Proofs of serial matter on galleys must be numbered consecutively by the prover. . . . the proof of a book form must be folded accurately by the print. . . . Before making-ready, the pressman must get . . . a readable proof of the form to be printed, on its own paper, and with right margins.'[24]

Two works from the nineties argue strongly that Ringwalt's view of post-Civil War galley proofs may indeed have been more accurate than that of the then conservative DeVinne. 1894 saw the publication of the anonymous *American Dictionary of Printing and Bookmaking* whose entry for 'Proofs in Slips' (interestingly, there is no listing for 'Galley Proofs' even at that late date) begins with a paraphrase of C. T. Jacobi: 'Where corrections and alterations are likely to be heavy proofs are asked for in slip form — not made up into pages,'[25] and continues with the words of its own anonymous author: 'Nearly all proofs in America are taken in slips, it being regarded as an injustice to the compositor to force him to correct his matter in the form.'[26] Another passage provides

[23] Ibid., p. 179.

[24] Theodore Low DeVinne, *Manual of Printing Office Practice, reprinted from the original edition of 1883, with an introductory note by Douglas C. McMurtrie* (New York: Press of Ars Typographica, 1926), pp. 31, 39.

[25] The paraphrase is acknowledged; it is from Jacobi's *The Printers' Vocabulary: A Collection of Some 2500 Technical Terms, Phrases, Abbreviations and Other Expressions Mostly Relating to Letterpress Printing, Many of Which Have Been in Use Since the Time of Caxton* (London: Chiswick Press, 1888), p. 105.

[26] *American Dictionary of Printing and Bookmaking* (New York: Howard Lockwood & Co., 1894), p. 474.

insight into the historical development of what by then appears to have become virtually universal practice: 'Almost all work done in the United States is proved upon the galley, the practice which existed before the [Civil] war of imposing and then proving having died out.'[27] And still another entry illustrates the comparative states of current American and British practice: 'Correcting in the form . . . was formerly much practiced in America, and is still the common method of British book offices.'[28]

As an Englishman writing in 1899, the great printing historian John Southward could view the development of American galley proofs from a distance and with a clear perspective. His findings corroborate (seemingly paraphrasing in part) those of the *American Dictionary:* 'In the United States, where expedition is regarded of so much importance, almost all work is proved upon the galley, the practice which existed up to about twenty years ago of imposing and then proving the matter in the chase having died out.'[29] The tenor of Southward's remarks on contemporaneous British practice indicates that while he personally favors galley proofs for all book work, they have not as yet gained universal acceptance.[30]

Only with the turn of the twentieth century do American printers' manuals show unanimity on the prevalence of galley proofs in book work, at least as far as first proofs are concerned. Some discrepancies remain on the varieties of author's proofs, but this seems only natural since it is to be expected that those presses with which the several writers were familiar had different methods of conducting business.

In 1904 DeVinne virtually reverses the position he held twenty years earlier on the role of galley proofs in book work. *Modern Methods of Book Composition* describes the preparation of the first proof in 'American book-houses': 'Compositors deliver their copy and the matter as it is set to the maker-up, who has their galleys proved, and then passes the copy and proof to the proof-reader. Illustrations furnished with copy that cannot be proved on the galley are put by him in the proper place as attachments to the proof.'[31] (An interesting footnote to this passage

[27] Ibid., p. 466.
[28] Ibid., p. 469.
[29] John Southward, *Modern Printing: A Handbook of the Principles and Practice of Typography and the Auxiliary Arts* (London: Raithby, Lawrence, & Co., 1898–1900), 2 (1899): 181–82.
[30] Ibid., 1 (1898): 202; and 2 (1899): 178.
[31] Theodore Low DeVinne, *Modern Methods of Book Composition* (1904; rpt., New York: Oswald Publishing Co., 1921), p. 80.

contains what is quite possibly the first published account of the modern form of page proofs: 'In some book-houses proofs are not taken upon the galley. Matter is made up in pages as fast as it is set, and the pages are proved in strings on a press or with a proof-planer or stone. This method saves the employer the cost and care of many galleys, but it does not quicken or improve composition, for the correction of outs or doublets will compel the overrunning of many pages.'[32]) After acknowledging first proofs in galleys as accepted practice, DeVinne, with only slight reservations regarding the nature of the copy, gives the nod to their utility as author's proofs as well. His remarks on this matter, though lengthy, bear fairly full quotation to illustrate the meticulousness and sense of his argument:

For manuscript copy that may receive changes in the text, another proof should be taken in the galley, and this proof should be sent with the first proof corrected to the proof-reader, who adds his queries, stamps it with the proper date, and forwards it to the author with the copy. The author returns it with his alterations, but it may require another proof containing the correction of these alterations. It is always a great risk to make up before the author has finished corrections, or before the cuts or diagrams are ready. Overrunning of type in made-up pages is slow and expensive.

When the author has nothing more to add, . . . the matter may be made up in pages. . . . In a few houses the second reading of the printing house is done by the foundry-reader upon the page proof sent to the author. This can be done with safety when it is surely known that nothing more will be added to the proof by the author. A reading of the page proof by the office reader before it will be seen by the author gives the latter more time to consider queries and to approve or disapprove proposed suggestions. In other houses the final reading or the reading for foundry is given only when the author returns the proof as entirely corrected. This is a better method, but it takes more time and may compel the resubmission to the author of another proof.[33]

If I read DeVinne correctly, he is proposing that the author receive at least one set of galley proofs and, subsequent to their correction and alteration, at least one of page proofs, the system currently employed by most contemporary American book publishers of my acquaintance.

[32] Ibid., p. 80, n. 1.
[33] Ibid., p. 84.

Three years after DeVinne's work appeared, the first of two specialist manuals devoted entirely to the subject of proofs was published. This work by Alexander A. Stewart agrees in the main with DeVinne on the use of galley proofs for first proofs, while differing somewhat on the extent to which they were employed as author's proofs. The normal order of proofs taken for use *in* the printing house is outlined by Stewart:

When the compositor finishes his work of setting the lines and they are locked in the galley by means of a side-stick and quoins, the *first proof* is usually taken on a roller press. . . . After the galley-matter is corrected and made up into pages, with headings, page numbers, notes, etc., the pages are again proved on a hand-press. . . . [then] if they are to be electrotyped . . . they are locked up in a foundry chase (in pairs, if they are pages of ordinary size) and *foundry proofs* are pulled. The final proofs are taken when the pages are imposed and locked in the chase ready for the press.[34]

He later adds the refinement that 'in bookwork two or three revisions may be made of galley proofs, then as many more when pages are made up.'[35] When author's proofs are required, they 'are commonly sent in page form, unless there are likely to be many corrections, in which case galley-proofs are sent.'[36] The language of DeVinne and Stewart on this point may be little more than a subtle shift of emphasis, yet one gets the distinct impression that the former writer finds — and advocates — a more widespread use of author's proofs in galleys than does the latter.

About twenty years after Stewart, Hugo Jahn's *Printer's Proofs* — the last manual to fall within the scope of this survey — describes what has remained in American book houses the normal practice down to the present. Jahn's definition of galley proofs encompasses 'first proofs, revises, author's proofs and page-proofs used for making dummies,'[37] the last named item suggesting that for him the term galley proof refers generally to proofs of any matter taken on long strips of paper

[34] Alexander A. Stewart, *Printers' Proofs: A Brief Description of the Methods by Which They Are Taken, Marked, and Corrected* (Boston: School of Printing of the North End Union, 1907), pp. 4, 5.

[35] Ibid., p. 26.

[36] Ibid., p. 30.

[37] Hugo Jahn, *Printers' Proofs* (Chicago: United Typothetae of America, 1925), p. 6.

on a galley press, regardless whether the matter has been made up into pages or not. Yet in his account of author's proofs, he makes the modern distinction between galley and page proofs, though both are taken on a galley-press:

In book-printing houses, two sets of galley proofs are sent to the author, and these are returned by him with his corrections or changes, . . . After the author's proofs have been O. K.'d, the type is made up into pages of the required length, and the headings, page numbers, footnotes, etc., are added. The type which is still on galleys, is again taken to the proof-press and three or four sets of proofs are taken. Two or three sets are sent to the author, and one set is kept in the print-shop. These are called page-proofs.[38]

The conclusions to be drawn from this survey, while not startling, may at least prove interesting to the student of printing history and useful to the editor dealing with transmission of texts. An overview of nineteenth-century printers' manuals and journals reveals that while galley proofs may have been mentioned for the first time later in America than in England, their adoption for book work was quicker, earlier, and more general here than in Britain,[39] their widespread use coinciding roughly with the end of the Civil War. The prevalence of author's proofs in galley form seems to be a somewhat later phenomenon, gaining a foothold in the 1870s, but perhaps not becoming firmly established practice till the turn of the century. Even such tentative observations as these may be helpful in knowing what sorts of documents to look for or to hypothesize at particular points in time when dealing with the transmission of nineteenth- and early twentieth-century texts. The manuals and trade papers provide a convenient starting point for the study of American galley proofs, but their opinions, observations, and instructions can ultimately be tested and, hopefully, corroborated only by the discovery and analysis of proofs themselves. The investigation of such primary evidence would be a vital and welcome complement to this historical survey.

[38] Jahn, p. 29.
[39] Hargreaves observes that as late as 1926, a year later than Jahn's manual, galley proofs in Britain were still used extensively only for books requiring considerable alteration (pp. 310–11).

PRACTICAL EDITIONS III:
A *Proof* Seminar

THE EDITOR

Proof SEMINARS ARE CONFERENCES AT WHICH PEOPLE CONSIDER NEW OR expanding directions in bibliographical and textual studies. The current series on practical editions began in 1971. 'Practical editions' are defined generally as those editions which are directed at students, teachers, and the general reading public — not editions for scholars or collectors. The intent of this series is to evaluate practical editions of important works or important writers. After discussion and revision, the evaluations presented at the *Proof* Seminars are published in the following volume of *Proof*.[1]

The third *Proof* Seminar was held on Friday, 28 December 1973, at the annual meeting of the Modern Language Association of America in Chicago. Joseph Katz substituted for Robert T. King, scheduled to preside. The following two papers were presented at the Seminar.

[1] 'Practical Editions', *Proof*, 2 (1972): 285–318; 'Practical Editions — II', *Proof*, 3 (1973): 369–94.

PRACTICAL EDITIONS:
Washington Irving's
The Sketch Book

HASKELL SPRINGER

WASHINGTON IRVING'S *The Sketch Book* HAS ONE OF THE MOST COMPLEX publishing histories in nineteenth-century American literature. As a result of the various non-authorial influences on the text of *The Sketch Book* (as well as of some authorial tinkering and oversight), Irving's best book has come down to us in very corrupt form. Though most of the corruptions are not what many readers — even scholarly readers — would think of as significantly affecting the meaning of the book, they do have some serious cumulative results which are worth considering not only for their significance to the textual critic, but particularly as they affect the teaching of *The Sketch Book* in the college classroom.

The Sketch Book was first published in seven parts, in the United States in 1819–1820, and before American publication was complete, it appeared in two volumes in England (1820). This first British edition was the most heavily revised and, for the history of the text, the most important of the many editions of *The Sketch Book*. Also, long before the last number of the first American edition was published, a second edition in seven parts began appearing in the United States. Since the British edition and the second American edition texts had been separately revised by Irving, who had also added material to the British edition alone, *The Sketch Book* was, within a year of its first appearance, available in three distinct texts. Then the third and fourth American editions of 1822–1823 and 1824 respectively were published. They did not follow the texts of their American predecessors, but were based on that first British edition — and so were all future printings, on both sides of the Atlantic.

To further complicate matters, by the time of the fourth American edition, the popular *Sketch Book* had come out in at least six editions in England, and had been once again worked over by the author, who in 1821–1822 made perhaps one hundred substantive changes. But Irving was not the sort of person who, even at this point, could leave a good thing alone. When he was approached in 1823 for permission to print another edition, utlimately published in Dresden (1823), he once again read proof and made further changes. But he used one of the 1821 British editions as printer's copy and thus bypassed his own revisions of the British text made in 1821–1822, while introducing new readings that dead-ended in the Dresden publication.

In that same year (1823) a Paris edition in English appeared, but this time Irving had had nothing to do with it. It was based on an 1823 British edition and thus incorporated the author's 1821–1822 changes. To see the significance of this Paris edition one has to look forward twenty-five years to 1848 when Irving was going over his books to prepare the Author's Revised Edition, to be published by G. P. Putnam in New York. He made many major and minor changes in *The Sketch Book* in 1848, and from some surviving, authorially annotated leaves of the printer's copy for that edition one can see that Irving worked with a page-for-page reprinting of the Paris edition of 1823. From this 1848 Author's Revised Edition, derived from the Paris edition, itself derived from an early British edition, come the scores and scores of nineteenth-century reprintings of *The Sketch Book* in America, and, ultimately, the editions, both British and American, in print today. Though no authoritative changes were introduced into the book after 1848, some of its errors were corrected, and, of course, a large number of new ones created. Such, in very brief and simplified summary, was the printing history of *The Sketch Book*.

Now, after all these years, Irving's book is available to the teacher and student in several forms. Aside from expensive, fancy editions (which, by the way, are as textually corrupt as any other), unsuitable for ordinary use, there are two complete texts of *The Sketch Book* currently in print: one by Dent (Everyman's Library), and the other by Signet. Measuring them by the tests for reliability and honesty advocated by Joseph Katz in *Proof* 2, one would have to say that the unreliability of the texts makes the question of honesty moot.[1] They do not reprint authoritative sources and they do not state the sources they reprint. The question of the accuracy of their reproduction is therefore not worth asking; and of course any emendations made in these editions are silent ones. There is also a separate edition of 'Rip Van Winkle' and 'The Legend of Sleepy Hollow' (David McKay Company) which is similarly anonymous, unauthoritative, and corrupt. In addition, of course, many anthologies reprint portions of *The Sketch Book*. It is through these anthologies that most students, graduate and undergraduate, have their brief acquaintance with Irving.

I examined the following six major anthologies which include portions of *The Sketch Book:* Bradley, Beatty, and Long (Norton); Meserole, Sutton, and Weber (Heath); Irving Howe (McGraw-Hill); Milton Stern and Seymour Gross (Viking); Poirier and Vance (Little, Brown); and Brooks, Lewis, and Warren (St. Martin's). All of them reprint both 'Rip Van Winkle' and 'The Legend of Sleepy Hollow', except for the Meserole, Sutton, and Weber volume, which substitutes 'The Author's Account of Himself' for 'Rip Van Winkle'. The Norton anthology contains the fullest sampling: it adds 'The Author's Account of Himself' and 'English Writers on America' to 'Rip Van Winkle' and 'Sleepy Hollow'. All of these anthology texts are based on one or another unauthoritative reprinting of the Author's Revised Edition of 1848, or selections therefrom; all contain careless substantive errors and corrupt readings. In addition, and more importantly, most illustrate in a particularly glaring way the effects of bad printer's copy. At least that is how I account for the fact that of the five anthologies which contain 'Rip Van Winkle' only two print the complete text of this deservedly famous tale, crucial both to the study of American literary history and to the understanding of Irving as an artist. Irving's concluding 'Note'

[1] 'Practical Editions: Stephen Crane's *The Red Badge of Courage*', *Proof* 2, (1972): 301–18:
    (1) Does it reprint an authoritative source?
    (2) Does it state clearly the source it reprints?
    (3) Does it reproduce that source accurately?
    (4) When it emends that source, does it record every change?

and his 'Postscript' to 'Rip Van Winkle' (constituting more than a full page of text) are printed only in the Little, Brown and St. Martin's anthologies. Norton, McGraw-Hill, and Viking omit them without a word of explanation. There are, of course, a few other anthologies, and some of them contain full, if otherwise corrupt texts of 'Rip Van Winkle'. But the incomplete versions, in collections edited by well-known scholars, stand as warnings to the teacher and student.

The specific and pervasive effects of a long and varied printing history on those editions of *The Sketch Book* (or parts of it) now in print can be summarized as follows:

1. Words and phrases which cannot be traced to the author himself.
2. Heavy punctuation, which is truly excessive when measured by Irving's own practice.
3. Dominant use of American spellings, whereas Irving's preference was for British usage.
4. Completely modernized spelling, in contrast to Irving's fondness for a number of forms which were antique or obsolescent even in 1820.

Taking these effects one by one, I'll begin by saying that, from the point of view I am taking toward *The Sketch Book* here, the various unauthoritative words and phrases of my first point do not constitute the book's most significant corruptions. Someone quite familiar with the book would be able to indicate to his students the most important of these substantive errors and their effects on meaning, such as the text's reference to 'a dreadful story' where Irving actually wrote 'a dreadful but true story'. One could also compare the implications of Geoffrey Crayon's comment on his own 'gratitude and goodness' in both complete *Sketch Books* now in print with his gratitude and good will' as Irving intended. Or students could be warned that they could search forever, in vain, for a book by Harvey Pierce entitled *Supererogation,* because Irving actually referred to Gabriel Harvey's pamphlet, *Pierce's Supererogation,* before a printer's error confused the matter. But the teacher who is not an expert on *The Sketch Book* need not despair, because the instances of significant substantive error, such as these, are scattered through the book's 350–400 pages; and though they loudly call for correction, they do not significantly affect the reader's response to the work as a whole or even in part as do my other three points. Punctuation, for one, which seems such a minor, even inconsequential matter to most readers, is actually, for *The Sketch Book* in the classroom, more significant than incorrect words.

Irving is usually taught as (among other things) a prose stylist; and until very recently his *Sketch Book* was still a model for English composition in a number of foreign countries. But the rhythms, at least, of Irving's *Sketch Book* prose are very often not his at all. It is impossible to illustrate this point by brief quotation, but when one compares several pages of Irving's manuscript with the corresponding passages in the editions in print, the differences are readily apparent. The manuscript is rather lightly, even erratically, punctuated; and its rhythms might be called 'loose' — verbal rather than written — 'informal', even 'personal' or 'idiosyncratic'. That is, on the whole the punctuation gives the prose a personality. To some careful readers Irving's pointing suggests a certain romantic cast of mind very much in keeping with the attitudes expressed in *The Sketch Book* essays. But the personality thus evoked, because the idiosyncratic punctuation catches the attention of the reader, is missing from the editions in print, where the heavy punctuation is above all correct. In its standardized blandness it is ignored by the reader, and therefore suggests little or nothing about the writer.

We should be concerned about this heavy pointing, because Irving himself was. The process of overpunctuation began with the printing of the first number of the first edition of *The Sketch Book;* and when Irving (who had not read proof because he had been in England) saw his first installment in print, he mildly complained in a letter to New York, saying: 'the work appears to be a little too *highly* pointed. . . . High pointing is apt to injure the fluency of the style if the reader attends to all the stops.' Irving had earlier warned, in a note accompanying his manuscript, that there might be errors in the punctuation, but the print shop did much more than correct errors: in about 250 short pages of text Irving's American printer added nearly 1,000 commas and semi-colons. And later editions further 'corrected' the pointing by increasing it. The problem Irving had complained about, therefore, got worse as time went on, and the fluency of the prose, as he suggested, is definitely affected. However, in later years Irving, at that time a busy and successful author, did nothing to change the situation.

The particular textual problem of punctuation, then, gives the teacher of *The Sketch Book* the opportunity to discuss in class some ideas of formality and informality in prose, to expand on the concept of 'Romantic', and to begin to present the notion of the ideal book which exists in the author's head versus the printed document we read. This subject opens up the question, quite interesting to most students, of the author as both an artist deeply concerned that his book be what he ideally intends it to be, and, conversely, a businessman who must negotiate contracts, think about copyright and advertising, read proof, and live on royalties. This general topic, of course, once introduced by way of *The Sketch Book,* can be used again and again to advantage in almost any course in American literature (Poe, Melville, and Mark Twain are obvious examples who come immediately to mind).

Spelling is another matter considered completely trivial by many of my colleagues and nearly all of my students. But in fact the spelling of *The Sketch Book* is more than a pedantic concern of textual scholars, for it has particular relevance to the understanding of Irving's mind and of the emerging literary self-consciousness in America in the early nineteenth century. Irving's *Sketch Book* manuscripts are spelled in the British fashion. That is, they usually use an *-re* rather than *-er* ending, *-our* vs. *-or, -xion* vs. *-ction.* In fact, all the editions of *The Sketch Book,* British and American, until 1848, used Irving's own predominantly British spellings. But under the influence of Noah Webster's dictionary the Author's Revised Edition changed the orthography to the American manner, and ever since, American editions (and some British ones as well) have used the American spellings. Only one modern edition of those mentioned above uses the British spellings, and that is the Everyman edition.

In 1806, in the first edition of his *Compendious Dictionary,* Webster's entries read 'honor', 'theater', 'connection', etc.; and his famous spelling books had even earlier advocated such new forms. These newer spellings were apparently quite current in 1819–1820, for most of the earliest American reviews of *The Sketch Book* used Webster's orthography. There was an element of pride and national consciousness involved in these American spellings: they were largely derived from the same sources and sorts of thinking that produced what we have come to call the American Literary Revolution. That protracted revolution was in full swing when *The Sketch Book* first appeared, and it is somewhat ironic that the first internationally acclaimed and financially successful book by an American author is a book written in England, by an anglophile, primarily about England and English scenes, full of quotations from British authors, and originally written with British orthography. For such reasons, some of Irving's American reviewers saw him as too genteel and conservative, lacking in true American vigor (not vigour) and independence. For the same reasons some of his English reviewers regarded him as the best British writer America had yet produced. Thus, to present *The Sketch Book* in American dress, as most students now have it, is not only to ignore the author's own prefer-ences, but also to misrepresent the personal views out of which the book grew, and the literary climate into which it was published.

Another orthographic practice of Irving's also has broad implica-tions. He regularly and repeatedly used various obsolescent and pic-turesque word forms such as *shew, traffick, chaunt, gulph, holyday,* and so forth, which are the orthographic concomitants of his often-expressed preference for 'the shadowy grandeurs of the past' over the 'common-place realities of the present.' Another concomitant of this attitude is his insistence that his printer retain precisely the quaint orthography of his many quotations from English literature of the fourteenth to eighteenth centuries. These preferences of Irving's also show him running counter to some of the dominant American literary trends of his day. He was patriotic enough toward his young, growing, demo-cratic country, but, as one of his early American reviewers noted when commenting on 'Rip Van Winkle', he preferred the old days to the new. The subjects, the scenes, the dominant tone of *The Sketch Book* are strongly antiquarian and conservative (in the sense of preserving the valuable past). Essay after essay looks back, in one way or another, to better, or more interesting, or more genteel times; and several of them are included in the book primarily for their antiquarian interest. Irving's whole cast of mind, then, differed from that of most American writers of his day, who practically saw newness as all. Therefore, the preservation of Irving's antique word forms is important to the full understanding of his mind, art, and historical context; but you will not find these authorial spellings in any form of the text now available to the teacher and student.

For the teacher of *The Sketch Book,* then, or of the anthologized segments thereof, there is not very much choice. The Everyman edi-tion is preferable to the Signet because of its British spellings and its avoidance of several errors committed by the Signet (such as reversing the proper order of the headnote and epigraph to 'Rip Van Winkle' — an error shared by the anthologies — and printing the 'Notes' to 'Westminster Abbey' at the end of the book rather than with the sketch itself). But still the spelling is modernized, the punctuation is grossly excessive, and many substantive errors are present. Among the an-thologies, only those which include the complete text of 'Rip Van Winkle' can be considered minimally acceptable as far as the study of Irving is concerned. But again, in every case even a complete text is a corrupt one, since each has modernized and Americanized spellings, is excessively punctuated, and substantively unauthoritative. Unfortunately, then, only when in God's good time the University of Wisconsin Press resumes publication of Irving's complete writings, including a fully edited and authoritative text of *The Sketch Book* which becomes the source for teaching texts, will the teacher and student be able to deal with Irving and his *Sketch Book* in the way they both deserve.

PRACTICAL EDITIONS:
Henry D. Thoreau's *Walden*

JOSEPH R. McELRATH, JR.

THE SONG THAT I HAVE TO SING WILL BE A FAMILIAR ONE TO THOSE WHO regularly attend the annual *Proof* Seminars. That is, practical editions of Thoreau's *Walden* — the texts that we and our students usually use — are not exceptions to the rule of general corruption among this breed. For, in examining ten practical editions of *Walden,* I found still more evidence that Thoreau was simply wrong when, in the 'Reading' chapter, he presumed to make some rash declarations about the uncorruptibility of the classics, such as: 'A written word is the choicest of relics . . . [which carry] their own serene and celestial atmosphere into all lands to protect them against the corrosion of time.' And in the same chapter, 'For what are the classics but the noblest recorded thoughts of man? They are the only oracles which are not decayed'. Despite the quasi-religious veneration that Thoreau and *Walden* have had for approximately a half century, and despite the voluble adulation rendered by the Thoreau cult, Thoreau's masterpiece is a shoddilymaintained 'relic'. Its text — American classic though the work is — has not been well protected against the 'corrosion of time.' Like other American works given 'oracle' status, it has been *made* to decay in practical editions, through the agencies of poor setting-copy choices by editors, publishers' house-styling, compositors' errors, and uninformed or half-informed editorial meddling. In seven out of the ten texts I have examined *Walden* is in bad shape.

To begin on a positive note, though, I would like to point out and, to some degree, celebrate, three of the more reliable practical editions. The first is the *Walden* published by the Charles E. Merrill Publishing Company in 1969 as part of its 'Standard Edition' series. It is a photo-offset printing of the first edition, introduced by Willard Thorp. I mention it first because for the modest sum of ninety-five cents any professor, student, or general reader can, in effect, own an uncorrupted copy of the first edition. Moreover, this text of *Walden* meets all of the very reasonable standards for judging the quality of a practical edition which Joseph Katz set forth during the first *Proof* Seminar of 1971. These criteria are:

First, *Does it reprint an authoritative source?* For the Merrill edition the answer is, 'yes'. It is the first edition, first impression text.

Second, *Does it state clearly the source it reprints?* The Merrill edition is a model of clarity in this regard: on the verso of the title page Thorp declares, 'This text of *Walden* is a facsimile of the first impression published by Ticknor and Fields, 1854.' Thorp even identifies the copy used: that of The Ohio State University Libraries, PS 3048/A1.

Third, *Does it reproduce that source accurately?* Yes, the Merrill text is a clear copy, free from any significant distortions that might result from photo-offsetting.

Fourth, *When it emends that source, does it record every change?* Thorp makes no emendations.

Thus the Charles E. Merrill edition delivers all that it promises. So too does *The Annotated Walden* published in 1970 by Clarkson N. Potter and introduced and annotated by Philip Van Doren Stern. Like the Charles E. Merrill edition, it is a photo-offset printing. Like the Charles E. Merrill edition, its source is the first impression, clearly identified as such. And like the Charles E. Merrill edition, it reproduces the first impression accurately, with no emendations. Unfortunately it is not yet in paperback; but because it is a 'must' for college and university libraries, due at least to the wealth of data provided in its notes, I include it for consideration here. All serious students of *Walden* should, and I think will, use it from time to time. Hopefully, it will someday be issued in paperback, as *The Annotated Alice in Wonderland* of the same series was.

The Charles E. Merrill *Walden* and *The Annotated Walden* are the only two offset printings of the first impression available — and therefore the only two texts which do not introduce deliberate emendations, and corruptions. The remaining eight texts are genuine new editions — that is, newly-reset texts. And the best of them is the one published in 1966 by the W. W. Norton Company, *Walden and Civil Disobedience*, edited by Owen Thomas. It has faults, but compared to other emended *Walden* texts, it represents virtual perfection: it contains only thirty-two unacknowledged accidental variants and only eight substantive variants. That may give you an intimation of how bad the other practical editions are.

What is most remarkable about Thomas's Norton edition, though, is that as an editor Thomas seems to be pretty much aware of what he is doing — despite the forty variants he should have caught in a final collation. He has chosen an authoritative text of *Walden,* the first edition, as his source; he identifies the copy owned by the Oberlin College Library as the setting-copy which he used, and in 'A Textual Note on *Walden*' he lists all of the emendations he has deliberately made. These emendations are all derived from Thoreau's personally marked copy of the first edition, now in the possession of the Library of Middlebury College. Thoreau made sixteen changes in the text and added five comments that might be considered notes, which Thomas includes in his text. When arrangements were being made for an 1862 second printing of *Walden,* Thoreau did not ask that these twenty-one alterations be made; all that he requested of Ticknor and Fields was that the subtitle be dropped. But since just about everyone (myself included) accepts the markings as expressions of Thoreau's final intent, Thomas is to be not chided but congratulated for including them — especially since he is the only editor who has fully incorporated these apparent corrections and additions in his text. (I am, of course, excepting J. Lyndon Shanley's scholarly edition, the Princeton-CEAA *Walden* of 1971, from discussion here since it has not yet been made into a practical edition.) Thomas has done his work well. Now if he can only get Norton to make the necessary plate corrections for the unintentional variants, he will have produced a splendid practical edition of *Walden.*

My reason for praising the somewhat faulty Norton edition to the degree I have may become clearer when I turn to the edition that one would expect to receive potent accolades: *The Variorum Walden,* edited by Walter Harding. It was first published by Twayne Publishers in 1962. And then, in 1963, another edition of it was published by Washington Square Press. The apparent reasons for the almost immediate paperback publication would seem to have been the weight of Walter Harding's reputation and the fulsome claims for the fineness of the text made by Twayne Publishers. It *must* have been for those reasons since apparently no one thought to check closely the quality of the text; for its textual achievement does not match that of its advertisements. A Twayne copy-writer blurbs on the dust jacket that, 'it is the first *Walden* with its text printed exactly as Thoreau wished it to be.' We are also told that this 'is the first time that . . . Thoreau's own corrections and additions to the first edition have been completely followed.' And to make sure that the point is clear, the dust jacket again tells us, 'The only edition of WALDEN which is based directly on the first edition and includes Thoreau's own corrections of the text'. In 'A Note on the Text' Harding himself declares, 'The text of this edition is based on the first edition published by Ticknor & Fields in Boston in 1854. It is the first edition of *Walden* to incorporate all the corrections Thoreau made in his personal copy.' Now this is where things get tricky, for the unsuspectng reader may not immediately realize that the 'text of this edition' and the 'edition' itself are two different matters altogether. Thoreau's corrections and additions *are* in the edition — but *in the notes, not in the text of the edition.* One has to keep ones guard up when reading such notes on the text. Else one might come to the conclusion which the blurb writer did: that this *Walden* is 'printed exactly as Thoreau wished it to be.' It is not.

So we do not have Thoreau's final intentions in the texts of the Twayne and Washington Square publications. Rather, what we do have is a text derived from the authoritative first edition, into which Harding and his publishers have silently worked their corrections and errors. In the Twayne edition of *The Variorum Walden* the text contains thirty-eight accidental variants from the first edition, and twenty-six substantive variants. These substantive variants are not trifles, either. For example,

THE FIRST EDITION	THE VARIORUM WALDEN
the words of the catechism	the catechism
this oracular sentence	this sentence
such great impropriety	such impropriety
fellow-men	fellow-man
a snow storm	a storm
tinkled	tingled

And an unauthorized change of 'from' to 'for' creates a situation in which, instead of looking from his window to the pond, Thoreau looks out to see his window floating by. *The Variorum Walden* by Twayne is a book which promises much and delivers little, textually. It is a great disappointment. But worse yet is the Washington Square Press publication: thirty-nine substantive variants and one hundred accidental variants, an increase which resulted because no one seems to have exercised control over Washington Square's galley and page proof. As in the Norton edition, no one seems to have done that final collation against the setting-copy which *must* be performed before a book goes to press. High quality is virtually impossible otherwise.

Five practical editions of *Walden* remain to be discussed. They can be dispatched quickly, for the majority of *Walden* texts now in use fail to meet the first standard for judging the quality of a practical edition: the sources of the five practical editions are all non-authoritative. The two sources used are the 1906 'Walden Edition' of *Walden* published by Houghton Mifflin, and the *Walden* volume of the 'Riverside Edition' of 1889. Two practical editions I have examined which were set in type from the 1889 Riverside Edition are Sherman Paul's 1960 Houghton Mifflin Riverside *Walden and Civil Disobedience* and Larzer Ziff's *Walden: A Writer's Edition,* published by Holt, Rinehart and Winston in 1961. Neither editor apologized for using this non-authoritative source. In fact, both seemed proud of it. In *'A Note On The Text'* Ziff writes, 'The text of *Walden* which follows is that of the 1889 Riverside edition, which is the result of Thoreau's own revision of the first edition, published in 1854.' In his 'Bibliographical Note', Sherman Paul writes, 'The text produced here . . . is that of the 1889 Riverside edition which first incorporated many of Thoreau's own corrections and revisions of the first edition.' Wrong. Both wrong. Of Thoreau's alterations, only one appears: 'brisk' became 'frisk' in 1889. That's it. But the 1889 Riverside did 'add' a good deal more to the text: house-styling of the first edition's compound words, punctuation, and spell-

179

ing; and arbitrary and unjustifiable editorial tampering of the nine-teenth-century variety.

I began this report by indicating that I would have a familiar song to sing: and this is the most familiar part — what happens in so-called 'standard' editions. The 'relic' is updated and 'improved' — that is, corrupted. The upshot is that Sherman Paul's Riverside edition gives three hundred and ninety-three accidental, and twenty-two substantive, variants from the first edition — only one of which represents Thoreau's correction. I made my collation of Paul's text against the first edition, and thus I have no answer for Katz's third criterion: *Does it reproduce that source accurately?* I only made spot-checks in the source — enough so that I can say, 'I'm afraid so.' As to Katz's fourth criterion, *When it emends that source, does it record every change?*, there is *no* practical edition of *Walden* that lists all of its variants. The point is, though, that these two criteria are minimally-relevant when a truly corrupt source is employed. What is relevant here is that Paul's Riverside edition is significantly distant from the *Walden* that Thoreau wrote and intended. And spot-checks in Ziff's edition reveal the same basic situation. If you are interested in an *authoritative* practical edition, avoid these two.

This brings us to the three texts based upon what is frequently referred to as *the* standard edition: the 1906 'Walden Edition'. The three practical editions derived from this text which I have examined are those of the Modern Library edited by Brooks Atkinson (1950), the Signet (1960), and the Viking *Portable Thoreau* (revised edition, 1964) edited by Carl Bode. All three editions are as poor as they are mainly because somewhere along the line the editors did not learn that 'standard edition' is in most cases synonymous with 'corrupt editions'. The 1906 Houghton Mifflin *Walden* is a non-authoritative source which is even more house-styled, and error-ridden, than the 1889 Riverside text. And it is almost as though the editors knew this, for none announces what the source of his text is.

As in the case of practical editions derived from the Riverside edition, I again did not apply Katz's third and fourth criteria. A complete collation of the Modern Library text against the first edition text rendered the staggering total of ninety-five substantive variants, and eight hundred and sixty-six accidentals — though I hesitate to call the eight hundred and sixty-six 'accidentals'. When one reaches that magnitude of corruption, one surely is discussing some kind of substantive effect. Think of it: eight hundred and sixty-six instances in which the spellings and punctuation of the first edition were silently disposed of. At this point we might recall Thoreau's query in 'The Ponds' chapter: 'Walden, is it you?' As for the Signet edition, I only spot-checked it to find that it was derived from the 1906 text.

The Viking *Portable Thoreau* text, however, received a full collation against the first edition. But, how I wished that I had only spot-checked it. It was an experience beyond compare. This collation was not to be measured in terms of hours or days spent — but in weeks, and in varying degrees of outrage and amazement. All of this is appropriate preface to announcing that the Bode's *Portable* edition of *Walden* contains one thousand three hundred and six accidental variants from the first edition, and forty-one substantive variants! The job I faced in recording so much error is painful to recall; consider the energy that Bode had to expend in *making* a text so bad. One wonders what his 'unrevised' edition was like.

Such is the situation of practical editions of *Walden* today. To sum it up, there are two offset printings, the Charles E. Merrill *Walden* and Clarkson N. Potter's *The Annotated Walden,* which present perfectly reliable reproductions of the first edition. There is a good edition published by Norton which incorporates Thoreau's final alterations for the text and identifies all of those alterations in a table. When its faults, forty of them, are corrected it will be a very good edition. The two editions of Walter Harding's *The Variorum Walden* are not especially good. Paul's Riverside; Ziff's Holt, Rinehart and Winston; Atkinson's Modern Library; the Signet; and Bode's Viking text do not merit any respect at all. As far as practical editions of *Walden* are concerned, the commendable revolution for which we hope has still a long way to go.

But the first step has perhaps been taken. On 28 December 1973 I spoke with representatives of the publishers of seven of the practical editions of *Walden.* I expected some hostility when delivering the bad news to them, but I instead met with interest, concern, and a desire for more data about what, exactly, was wrong. To be particular, these were the responses:

Twayne Publishers — Mr. Jack Steinberg and Dr. Walter Harding wished to see a table of errors I had found in *The Variorum Walden.* They say that in the next offset printing by Twayne corrections will be made. (I was also assured by Dr. Harding that the errors in the Washington Square Press edition will be corrected.)

Norton — Mr. John Francis said that Norton would be very interested in eliminating blemishes at the next printing. I was invited to send Norton and Dr. Owen Thomas my suggestions.

Holt, Rinehart and Winston — Miss Harriet Nolte of the College Department was surprised that *Walden: A Writer's Edition* was derived from a non-authoritative source. I was invited to submit suggestions for a better edition. She also invited me to report on the 'Rinehart Edition' text, edited by Norman Holmes Pearson — which has not been discussed here.

Signet (New American Library) — The 'Signet Classics' series is not very 'active' now, they said, but I was asked to contact the appropriate editor about the possibility of a new edition.

Modern Library — I wrote to Vice President Jason Epstein on 4 December 1973 to see what he would do about his *Walden*. On 12 December his assistant informed me that he was not interested in publishing a new edition at this time. The representative of Random House at the MLA Convention, however, directed me to an editor who might be concerned.

Houghton Mifflin and The Viking Press: Both wished to receive full reports. They will.

The short of it is that if *Proof* continues to inform publishers that there is a new demand for accurate and authoritative practical editions, and if users of practical editions follow *Proof*'s cue by informing publishers of their desire for reliable texts, we may someday be able to work with texts of classics like *Walden* that are truly free from the 'corrosion of time.' Publishers might be willing to produce them if they knew that there was a clear call for them in the market place. And the publishers I have reported on here might be even more anxious to produce either revised or new editions of *Walden* if this single call were joined by others.

THE CASE WESTERN RESERVE EDITION OF SHERWOOD ANDERSON:
A Review Article

G. THOMAS TANSELLE

THREE VOLUMES HAVE NOW APPEARED IN THE EDITION OF 'The Major Fiction of Sherwood Anderson', edited by Ray Lewis White and published by The Press of Case Western Reserve University: *A Story Teller's Story* came out in 1968, *Tar: A Midwest Childhood* the following year, and *Marching Men* three years after that.[1] Each volume is labeled, on its title page, 'A Critical Text'; each is based on manuscripts in the Anderson Papers at The Newberry Library and contains an appendix recording variant readings. Mr. White, who has been an energetic Anderson scholar (having brought together a number of other collections of material by and about Anderson), has thus added to his formidable program the task of producing a 'definitive critical edition' (as one dust

[1] The first volume does not contain the series title, but it is listed as the first volume of 'The Major Fiction' in the later two volumes. Just why the edition is entitled 'The Major Fiction' is not clear; although Anderson's autobiographical writings can be regarded as fiction, Mr. White in his introductions refers to the first two of these books as autobiographies.

183

jacket says) of Anderson's major work. With such an aim, the edition occupies a special position: for while students of American literature have now become accustomed to scholarly critical editions of nineteenth-century authors (particularly those prepared under the auspices of the MLA's Center for Editions of American Authors), this Anderson edition is at present the only instance of an attempt to provide for a twentieth-century novelist the same kind of comprehensive scholarly treatment.[2] The undertaking is a worthy one; and because the edition, by virtue of its special place, could have an influence on future textual work in twentieth-century American literature, it deserves to be examined carefully. Such an examination, I am sorry to have to report, reveals that the edition is thoroughly unsatisfactory. A number of previous reviewers, noting the use of manuscript material and the presence of variant readings, have hailed the series as 'meticulously and expertly edited' and 'undoubtedly definitive'; but Walter B. Rideout's unfavorable review of the first volume, citing many instances of inaccuracy, suggests the unpleasant truth.[3] It is doubly disturbing to have to render such a harsh verdict: in the first place, one wishes to encourage the textual study of twentieth-century authors and would like to take the Anderson edition as a hopeful sign for the future; in addition, the publication of these volumes may serve as a deterrent to the re-editing of the same works in the near future, and pronouncing the present job a failure amounts to saying that it has actually performed a disservice to Anderson scholarship. The fact is, however, that these three volumes are both inadequate and unreliable: their editiorial plan leaves much to be desired, and the execution of that plan is both inconsistent and inaccurate.

I

To begin with, it is necessary to understand what the textual situation is for each of the three books and what approach Mr. White has taken. In the first volume, *A Story Teller's Story* (originally published in 1924), he explains that, while the holograph manuscript and the proofs for this work do not survive, the Newberry collection does contain the typescript which served as printer's copy (or *'the printer's actual text'*, as

[2] Copyright problems often make it impossible for textual work on twentieth-century figures to result in actual critical editions; for that reason, the CEAA has established a procedure for approving the apparatus for such editions and encourages the separate publication of apparatus.

[3] *English Language Notes*, VII (September 1969): 70–73.

he calls it). This typescript contains numerous revisions in ink in Anderson's hand, a few small changes in ink in Paul Rosenfeld's hand, and a great many penciled alterations by E. T. Booth, who edited the book for the publisher, B. W. Huebsch. Because the published text naturally incorporates Booth's alterations, Mr. White decides, quite rightly, that the typescript should be the copy-text for a critical edition, since the goal is, as he says, 'to print *A Story Teller's Story* as Sherwood Anderson wrote the book' (which, despite the ambiguous wording, does not mean to exclude Anderson's own later revisions). Thus Mr. White rejects Rosenfeld's and Booth's revisions; so far his rationale is defensible, although various underlying issues are not discussed.[4] But there is a further — and expected — complication in the textual history: the text of the first printing does not conform to the revised typescript, as a result of changes which apparently were made on the now lost proofs. Deciding who made each of these changes clearly involves critical judgment and is the heart of the process of producing a critical edition of this book. Mr. White, however, chooses not to make any decisions. Here is his entire discussion of the matter:

> But that aim [printing the text Anderson intended] is complicated by the loss of proofs corrected by Anderson, who did make new sectional divisions in the galleys. In addition, Anderson cut several passages and many phrases from the galleys. The present edition restores these cuts, some of which *may* have been made by editorial and printing proofreaders, by bracketing such material, along with authorial cuts in the typescript. Anderson occasionally added material in galleys; such material is bracketed and marked with asterisks. (Pages xvii–xviii.)

The logic of this passage is impenetrable. In the first place, what is the evidence that Anderson was the person who 'cut several passages and many phrases from the galleys'? Then, if that statement can be made, how can one go on and say that some of 'these cuts' (those made

----

[4] One question which Mr. White ought to have raised is this: To what extent did Anderson approve of the editing done at the publishing house? Even if Anderson not merely acquiesced to but actively encouraged the regularizing of his eccentric spelling, punctuation, and grammar, an editor could still argue that Anderson was reacting to external pressure and that a great part of the flavor of his work was lost by such alteration. In any case, Mr White should have faced the issue. Furthermore, it would be unwise to reject Booth's revisions out of hand, for Booth on occasion might have noticed an obvious slip on Anderson's part which a later editor might not happen to notice otherwise.

185

by Anderson) may have been made by someone else? In any case, if the likelihood is strong (as the editor's statement suggests) that Anderson himself made most, if not quite all, of the deletions, what is the justification for restoring them? Finally, as for the added material, why is the flat statement that Anderson was responsible not similarly qualified by the suggestion that someone else might have made insertions as well as deletions? By printing these alterations in brackets in the text, Mr. White is simply avoiding any responsibility for making decisions; he is not offering a critical text but the material for a critical text. His immersion in the textual study of Anderson surely places him in a better position than other readers for deciding which of these changes are Anderson's; and if he claims to be producing a 'critical edition', one has a right to expect the benefit of his critical insight on these matters.

Discussion of editorial principles here cannot be separated from a consideration of the editorial apparatus, for the arrangement of the apparatus is a reflection of editorial decisions about what kinds of information are relevant and worth recording. First of all, the presence of bracketed material in the text means that Mr. White is not aiming for what is usually called a 'clear text' — a text free of all editorial intrusions. Texts which incorporate brackets and other symbols obviously have their place, especially in editions of letters or journals (or of complicated manuscripts in which it is important to show the growth and development of the text). But one may question the wisdom of utilizing anything other than clear text for a finished literary work, particularly when the textual problems are relatively simple, as they are here. The brackets and asterisks must surely be a distraction to the general reader, and they pose a problem for the scholar in making quotations. If one is quoting a passage that contains brackets, one must either explain what the brackets signify (no easy task in this case) or else omit the brackets (if one decides that Anderson wanted to include the words involved) or the whole bracketed phrase (if one decides that Anderson did not finally intend to include those words) — again with an explanation. The situation is awkward, whatever one does, and the responsibility for establishing the text of the passage has been shifted from the editor to the quoter.

Now one might argue, in Mr. White's defense, that the aim of his edition (despite its label 'critical edition') is not to present an easily-readable finished text but to show the stages in the growth of the text. The fact that he includes in brackets words known to have been deleted by Anderson in the typescript and the fact that material added later is distinguished by an asterisk might seem to support this view. If such is the case, however, he has hit upon a most inefficient system for accomplishing his purpose, for brackets without asterisks are used to mean two different things, as the passage quoted above indicates. Words enclosed in brackets may be either (1) words canceled by Anderson in the surviving typescript or (2) words omitted from the first printing and presumably canceled in proof by Anderson or by someone else. Not to distinguish these two categories makes the system worthless as a means for tracing the development of the text. Aside from that, the first category is a definite one, consisting of words which Anderson unquestionably deleted, while the second is a tentative one, consisting of words which Anderson may have deleted but which, in some instances at least, he may have wished to retain. If Mr. White is going to leave it up to the reader to determine the extent of Anderson's responsibility in the second category, he should at least indicate which items fall in that category, so that the reader will not waste energy pondering those which are in fact not debatable.

It happens in *A Story Teller's Story* that there are places where an example of the first kind of omission falls within an example of the second kind, and Mr. White's system is incapable of reflecting the true situation in such instances. For example, one of the major deletions from the typescript made in the first printing is a long passage at the end of Book IV, Note VI (277.33–286.2 of Mr. White's edition),[5] and Mr. White encloses this passage in brackets; but an examination of the typescript shows that parts of this passage (283.18–20, 285.5–20) had already been deleted in ink by Anderson on the typescript, though the editor's system gives no indication that some of the passage was deleted earlier than the rest. Then there is a further confusion: in the deletion at 285.5–20, the fifth line of the passage ends in the middle of a sentence, with the sixth beginning a new paragraph, and Mr. White provides a footnote explaining that 'Pages 392–93 are missing from the typescript.' What he does not say is that Anderson deleted a passage running from the bottom lines of p. 391 of the typescript through the top lines of p. 394; he therefore marked out the proper parts of pages 391 and 394 and simply discarded the two intervening pages, making a note on p. 394 explaining that fact. A reader might infer from

[5] All page and line designations throughout refer to Mr. White's volumes; in counting lines I omit chapter or section headings, so as to conform with the system used by Mr. White. *Cf.* n. 8, below.

Mr. White's footnote that two pages have been lost from the typescript, whereas the truth is that Anderson himself eliminated these two pages in the process of making a deletion — a deletion from the typescript which eventually turned out to be only a part of a still longer deletion from the proofs.[6] Precisely the same situation exists (twice) a few pages later in the other principal passage deleted from the typescript in the first printing (290.12–302.23). Within this large passage, Anderson marked out two passages in ink on the typescript (294.31–295.22, 299.7–300.3), and in each case he discarded pages of the typescript as part of the deletion (four of them in the first instance, one in the second); at each point Mr. White gives a footnote pointing out that a page or pages are 'missing' from the typescript. It is good, of course, to have these passages — amounting to over twenty pages of reflection on the relation of the American writer to his country — but whether or not they should be printed as part of the body of the text is a complicated issue which Mr. White fails to discuss (he does not even note, as Rideout's review points out, a 1924 letter in which Anderson talks about his reasons for deleting some of this material).

Besides the brackets and asterisks in the text itself, there is more — equally confusing — apparatus following the text. The principal list which appears there is described in the introduction as containing 'substantive original readings from the typescript, unusable in this text because of Anderson's revisions' (p. xviii). No explanation is provided to help one follow the logic of including some deleted passages in brackets in the text, when they will fit, and placing others, which will not easily fit because of the nature of the revision, in a list at the end. If the text is to be a genetic transcription, showing the growth of the manuscript, all deletions would seem to belong in brackets in the text, whether they fit grammatically or provide alternative wording; on the other hand, if the edition is intended to establish a reading text of Anderson's final intention, deletions certainly or most probably made by Anderson would not seem to belong in the text at all, even in brackets. When the reader turns to this list (of seventy-one entries) at the end (pp. 348–50), he finds it entitled, without a single further word of explanation, 'Deletions from the Typescript and Unincorporated Typescript Readings'. It is difficult to imagine a more confus-

[6] Mr. White does say in the introduction that 'a few pages of the complete typescript are lost, having been deleted by the author'; but the presence of this comment on p. xvii does not prevent the footnote on p. 285 from being an inadequate statement of the situation.

ing and misleading title. In the first place, only one category is speci-
fied for this list in the introduction (typescript readings made 'unusable' by revisions), whereas two are named in the title of the list. Which
of the two corresponds to the previously announced category is not
easy to say, since both seem more inclusive: (1) First, one might regard
the 'unusable' original readings as 'deletions from the typescript' —
which they obviously are, if they are superseded by revisions entered
on the typescript. But then one would recognize that 'deletions from
the typescript' would also include words deleted but not replaced
(some of which are restored to the text in brackets and, despite the
title, not found in this list at all). (2) Alternatively, one might regard
the 'unusable' original readings as 'unincorporated typescript readings' — meaning that they are not incorporated into the present text
and therefore appear in this list. But then one would note that some
entries in the list occur at points where an asterisk is present in the
text, signifying an 'addition' made in the galleys rather than in the
typescript; since some of these revisions in the galleys could have been
made by someone other than Anderson, this category, too, is larger
than one described as readings 'unusable in this text because of Anderson's revisions'. This much would be seen by any reader who makes
a determined effort to understand Mr. White's system; but anyone who
looks at the typescript itself will see still another problem. Even a
cursory examination of the typescript shows that a great many small
alterations made by Anderson are not reported in this list at all. Perhaps Mr. White, in claiming that his list includes 'substantive original
readings', is using 'substantive' to mean 'substantial', despite the fact
that in discussions of textual matters 'substantive' is now generally
used to refer to variants of words themselves as opposed to variants
in punctuation or spelling. If Mr. White does indeed intend to record
only the 'substantial' variants created by revision of the typescript and
of the proofs, what is missing is any indication of how he defines
'substantial'. Some of the listed variants consist of changes of single
words; and whether all of them are more significant than such unlisted
changes as Anderson's revision in typescript of 'that' to 'it' at 19.33
or someone's apparent revision in proof of 'older' to 'oldest' at 10.28
is a matter of individual opinion. One is at the mercy of Mr. White's
subjective decisions about what is important, and anyone interested
in making a close analysis of Anderson's stylistic revision at this stage
of his career would find that a great deal of the relevant evidence is
not reported. What this list contains, therefore, can be stated in this

way: (1) a partial printing of words deleted by Anderson in the type-script (and not already incorporated, within brackets, in the present text) and words superseded by Anderson's revisions in the typescript; (2) a partial printing of words replaced by revised wording in the published book (and thus altered, presumably on the proofs, by Anderson or by someone else) — but not including straightforward deletions or additions in the published book, for they are incorporated in the text, marked with brackets (deletions) or brackets and asterisks together (additions).[7]

Another question, aside from the puzzling one of trying to determine what rationale could have resulted in such a list, concerns the usability of the list. It is inconvenient to use not only because of the difficulty of working out and keeping in mind the complicated kind of explanation presented above but also because of the inefficient form of the individual entries. Each entry consists merely of a page-line reference followed by a word or words; there is no indication of just which word or words in the body of the text are at issue. Of course, at those points where brackets and an asterisk appear in the text, the brackets indicate what words are involved; but at other points the reader has only the context and Mr. White's usual inclusion of one additional unchanged word for help in locating the words under consideration. One can readily imagine the problems which this system might produce, and they do in fact occur. Here is the way the opening of the list looks:

5.10	not flashy . . . a "sign-painter"
8.3	waiters, harnessmen
9.2– 3	Some say she
14.2	soft bark
14.9	soft yielding bark
19.4	some role

The third item illustrates the way these entries typically work: in the text the end of 9.2 and the beginning of 9.3 read, 'It | was said she had shuffled'; the repetition of 'she' in the list entry is meant to indicate

---

[7] One must keep in mind that asterisks mark the revisions at this stage as well as the additions, so that entries do sometimes appear in the list at the point of an asterisked reading in the text.

the position of the revision, and the entry is thus saying that this sentence originally began, 'Some say she had shuffled'. Or at 14.9 the text reads 'deep into the yielding bark'; thus the list entry means that the word 'soft', just before 'yielding', was deleted by Anderson in the typescript (though why it is necessary to repeat two words — 'bark' as well as 'yielding' — in the entry is not clear). But some entries are not so straightforward. At 8.3 the text reads, 'eyes of others, of waiters, horsemen, thieves, gamblers, women'. Does the list entry mean that (like the entry for 9.2–3) the word 'harnessmen' was replaced by 'horsemen', or does it mean that (like the entry for 14.9) the word 'harnessmen' was simply deleted and that 'horsemen' was originally the third item in the series? The meanings of the two words, along with the absence of a comma after 'harnessmen' in the entry, might suggest that the former is probably the correct explanation, but an editorial apparatus which requires readers to draw inferences about its meaning cannot be regarded as a very desirable one. How simple and unambiguous this entry would have been if Mr. White had chosen to follow the standard procedure of first listing the reading of the text before providing the variant:

8.3   horsemen] harnessmen

At 14.2 the complete line reads as follows: 'bark of the tree. And it must enter the bark of the tree at just'. Since the word 'bark' appears twice in this line, one does not at first know to which occurrence the list entry for 14.2 refers; then one notices that the preceding line ends with the word 'soft', so the first occurrence of 'bark' still has the adjective modifying it, and the entry is recording the deletion of 'soft' before the second occurrence. Such entries, though awkward, can at least be figured out by a painstaking reader, but others cannot be understood at all without recourse to the typescript itself. For instance, the end of 19.3 and the beginning of 19.4 read in the text, 'in some | part not his own. Was there a role of his own'. I would presume that any reader, looking at the list entry for 19.4, 'some role', would conclude that 'a role' in the text had previously read 'some role' — but he would be wrong. The typescript shows that the revision involves the word 'part' at the beginning of the line and that the original reads 'some role' rather than 'some part'; 'some' is the word Mr. White intends as the locating word here, not 'role', yet it appears on the preceding line, and no one could possibly know this without going to The Newberry Library and consulting the typescript.[8]

This list is followed by one other short list (of eleven entries), entitled 'Variant Readings from Printings One and Two' (p. 351). The editor explains in his introduction (without specifying the date of the letter or making any other precise reference to his documentation) that Anderson, 'having seen copies of the first printing of his book, noticed several errors in the text and asked that Huebsch correct such mistakes in time for the third printing' (p. xviii). The third-printing readings are therefore incorporated in the text, and this list records what the first two printings had in each instance. (The title of the list might be clearer if 'from' were changed to 'in'.) Since this list is presented in the same form as the previous one, it involves the same kinds of problems. But there is the further problem of the relation of these readings in the first two printings to the corresponding readings in the typescript. The entry here for 218.6 reads 'hurriedly — thrown-together', and the text reads 'hurriedly thrown together'. One would naturally conclude that the revision made in the third printing was the deletion of the dash and the hyphen. Actually, however, only the dash was deleted in the third printing; the hyphen is not printed in the present text for a totally different reason — because it was added to the typescript in pencil and is therefore one of E. T. Booth's altera-

---

[8] Another example of this kind calls attention to two further difficulties. There is an entry labeled '59.12' which presents two complete sentences deleted by Anderson in the typescript (but does not give any additional locating words outside these two sentences). Page 59 in the text begins with the heading 'NOTE VI'; if one counts that as the first line and goes on down eleven more lines, one will find a line which contains the end of a sentence and may assume that these two deleted sentences originally stood at that point. But then one might notice that the next line also contains a sentence break — in fact, two of them — and that if one excluded 'NOTE VI' in the counting, *this* would be the twelfth line. A check of the typescript shows that the latter explanation is the correct one and that the two sentences originally occurred after the first of the periods in that line. But Mr. White does not explain his system of counting lines, nor does he say where in the twelfth line (by his count) the deleted reading goes. The second difficulty here is that the text of these two deleted sentences is presented in its earlier form; before deleting those sentences, Anderson revised the second sentence opening from 'They' to 'It might well be they'; but only 'They' appears here. Not only is a stage of revision not reported, but it is an intermediate stage: thus the text of these sentences, as printed here, does not represent Anderson's final wording of them before his decision to delete them altogether.

tions. The true situation can only be discovered by referring to the typescript; yet Mr. White's entry would not have been misleading if he had simply left out 'thrown-together'.

What becomes abundantly evident as one examines this volume is that no clear conception of the aims of the edition lies behind it. The volume does not offer a reading text representing Anderson's final intention, because the text restores passages known to have been deleted by Anderson and because it incorporates revisions made in the now lost proofs without attempting to decide which of them may have been made by someone other than Anderson. Neither does the volume present a genetic text, for the record of revisions does not report all the extant evidence. It would seem, however, judging from the attention given to typescript deletions and revisions and from the way in which deletions and additions in proof are distinguished, that Mr. White's primary concern is in showing the development of the text. But, if so, why are Anderson's *additions* in typescript not identified? Why are we informed about some of his deletions and revisions in typescript without being told which words in the present text were added at that same stage? (For example, the words 'now that you are an author' at 7.36 and 'toward solid respectability' at 8.8 were added by Anderson to the typescript.) Further, if Mr. White is truly interested in the history of the text, he could extract much more information from the typescript than he gives in his brief description in the introduction. It is true, as he says, that 'the pages are renumbered by Anderson to total four hundred forty-eight, although some pages are inserted extras. . . . Several pages are pasted insertions'. But what he does not say is that there is further evidence in the typescript which might prove useful in reconstructing the earlier development of the book: some pages have typed numbers replaced by Anderson's renumbering, and other pages have typed numbers which conform to the final sequence of numbering; a close study of the earlier numbers and the interpolation of newly typed pages would surely have enabled the editor to present a more detailed history of the typescript than he has offered. As for the publication history of the work, Mr. White reports that the 1958 Grove Press printing reproduces the first (rather than the corrected third) Huebsch printing, but he makes no mention whatever of the 1925 English issue by Jonathan Cape. Any reader aware of the Cape issue would legitimately wonder what relation its text bears to the Huebsch text and whether it might possibly contain authorial revisions; why Mr. White does not report that the Cape publication consists of sheets of the third Huebsch printing with a cancel title page is inconceivable. Finally, one misses any precise accounting of the differences between Mr. White's text and the published text which has been read and studied for the last fifty years. It hardly seems sufficient to offer, as he does in the introduction (pp. xvi–xvii), a list of thirty-five examples (without any page-line references) of the 'over twenty-five hundred undesirable changes' made by Huebsch's editor in the typescript;[9] a more thorough categorization of these alterations would be helpful, and, if the edition is adequately to present the textual history of the work, a listing, at least of the substantive changes, would be essential. (After all, Booth may have hit on certain necessary alterations — necessary because they correct slips which cannot have been Anderson's intention, not because Booth's revisions carry any authority — and the reader should be provided with the means for examining Mr. White's decisions as to what constitutes 'undesirable' changes.) Unfortunately, then, Mr. White's attempt to outline and demonstrate 'the process of establishing a sound text . . . for the guidance of future editors of Anderson material' (p. xvii) has turned out to be a failure. This edition of *A Story Teller's Story* provides a disastrous start for a multi-volume edition.

II

Essentially the same editorial procedures are followed in the other two volumes, and essentially the same criticisms can be made of them. But there are a few differences in each case. For *Tar: A Midwest Childhood* (originally published in 1926), the second work to be edited, the surviving materials are somewhat more complicated, for the Newberry collection contains two heavily revised typescripts of most of the chapters. The order of the two can be easily established, since Anderson's holograph corrections and additions in one are incorporated in the typing of the other; Anderson then entered further alterations on the second typescript, and presumably a newly-typed copy of that revised typescript was prepared to serve as printer's copy. A collation of the latest surviving typescript against the published text reveals, according to Mr. White, 'the existence of several hundred undesirable, but not

---

[9] This list is said to 'illustrate errors uncorrected in the published text' — certainly an odd way of describing revisions purposely incorporated in the published text by the publisher's editor (even though it is true that those revisions may be regarded as errors by a present-day editor).

reprehensible, changes in the author's words and punctuation' (p. xvi), and he provides a sample listing (without page-line references) of forty-nine of them. He then adds that Anderson's 'loose punctuation meant to reproduce for the reader a flowing, simple style, was stand-ardized and "stiffened" by the Boni and Liveright editors, who also ignored the author's clearly marked episode spacings and paragraph-ing' (p. xvii) — forcing one to take his earlier remark that 'the printed text shows fairly careful handling by the original publisher' (p. xv) to refer to care in routine copy-editing rather than fidelity to Anderson's intention. (It is true that 'fairly careful handling', in the earlier context, might be interpreted to mean that the publishers performed carefully the standardizing which Anderson is said to have encouraged them to undertake; but in this sentence the standardizing is taken to be a departure from Anderson's intention, not a fulfillment of it.) In any case, though these changes are not 'reprehensible', apparently they are 'undesirable' enough to reject, for Mr. White says that the later of the two typescripts offers 'the closest extant guides to Sherwood Anderson's final textual intentions' (p. xvi) — and therefore it presum-ably becomes the copy-text for his edition, though he does not specifi-cally say so.

That choice is the correct one, but what he does after that is as hard to follow as it was in *A Story Teller's Story;* indeed, his entire statement of his textual procedure is equally brief and equally opaque:

The present critical text, therefore, makes over fifteen hundred corrections, restoring Anderson's words, personal spellings, punctuation, and spacing. Words and passages that occur undeleted in the late typescripts but not in the 1926 book are restored within brackets. Words and passages added by the author in the printer's copy or in the galleys are indicated herein with brackets and asterisks. Whenever revision prohibits inclusion of original substantive material, such passages are included in the third appendix [*i.e.,* the list of 'Deletions from the Typescript and Unincorporated Typescript Readings']. (Pages xvii–xviii.)

If the copy-text is indeed the later of the surviving typescripts, the first sentence of this paragraph is awkwardly worded, for it implies that the editor is working with the printed text, making 'corrections' in it and 'restoring' Anderson's intended words and forms; apparently what Mr. White means to say is that his newly edited text, based on the later typescript, *in effect* makes these corrections and restorations. The sec-

ond sentence reflects an improvement in technique over the previous
volume, for brackets without asterisks are now used for only one purpose and not two — they identify words omitted at some stage later
than the latest extant typescript but not also passages deleted by Anderson in the typescript. The third sentence, like the corresponding
sentence in the earlier volume, begs an important question, for it
casually refers to 'Words and passages added by the author in the
printer's copy or in the galleys' without explaining how an editor
determines, with only the evidence of the published text before him,
which alterations were made by the author. And the fourth sentence,
which mentions one category of material recorded in the list at the end
(the 'third appendix'), should be read in conjunction with a remarkable
sentence two pages earlier, which names the other category found in
that list:

> In order to arrive at the most useful critical text of *Tar,* it is necessary to
> consult the earlier typescripts only for evidence of substantive deletions of
> biographical importance (such deleted passages are printed in the third appen-
> dix of this volume) and for occasional copyist errors, made in re-typing the
> first revised fair copy. (Page xvi.)

Aside from an awkward shift in terminology (from a plural term, 'earlier typescripts', referring to the physical document, to a singular term,
'first revised fair copy', presumably referring to the text embodied in
that document), the principal question raised by the statement is this:
Why is 'biographical importance' a criterion in determining which
'substantive' deletions by Anderson in the earlier typescript are worth
examining and recording? The student of Anderson's life will of
course be grateful for the printing of such material, but an editor's
focus must be on the text itself and not merely on its biographical
aspects.

In any event, the difficulty which this procedure creates in utilizing
the list is obvious. The title of the list refers only to 'the typescript',
and one might assume that the reference is to the later typescript —
that is, to the copy-text. But if deletions of 'biographical importance'
made in the earlier typescript are also recorded there, then how is one
to know in any given instance which typescript is the source of the
reported reading? Once again, Mr. White's seeming interest in providing the data for a study of the growth of the text goes only so far and
no farther. What is the point of providing as much information about

deletions and additions as is given, if the stage at which some of the deletions were made is not indicated? The list does include a number of long passages marked out by Anderson in the earlier typescript (examples are the entries for 35.3, 66.19, and 70.15), but the reader who wishes to follow Anderson's process of revision has no way of knowing whether to assign these deletions to the earlier or the later of the surviving typescripts. Furthermore, some of these long deleted passages had been revised by Anderson before their deletion, but no reference to such revisions is made. In the entry for 70.15, for instance, the text presented is the unrevised text of the earlier typescript; but Anderson had made a number of revisions in the passage (such as changing 'Dick' to 'he' in the third line) before canceling all of it. The fact that Anderson discarded a whole page in the middle of this passage is handled somewhat differently from the way this kind of situation was handled in *A Story Teller's Story*. Mr. White merely inserts in brackets in the seventh line the notation 'One page missing', without pointing out that he has not reported the beginning of a sentence at the bottom of the page preceding the break and the end of a sentence at the top of the page following the break (such words were included in his text at corresponding points in the earlier volume) and that the first full sentence on that page does not begin a new paragraph, though it does in his transcription. To say anything more about this list would be to repeat what has already been said about the list in *A Story Teller's Story*, for this list of eighty-eight entries follows the same plan and again omits many smaller deletions — and in fact does not even include all the 'deletions of biographical importance' from the earlier typescript (e.g., a paragraph of thirty-five words following 36.25). Similarly, this volume does not attempt to analyze the physical evidence offered by the typescripts (nothing is said about the differences between the earlier typescript of chapter 2 and the earlier typescript of most chapters, or about the larger question of whether the earlier of the surviving typescripts of individual chapters all represent the same stage and whether the later ones all represent the same later stage, or about the group of manuscript fragments of this book available in the Newberry collection) and does not give a full account of the publication history (he 'surmises . . . that the work did not sell well enough to please either Anderson or Boni and Liveright, for the only [American] reissue . . . came from Boni and Liveright in 1931', but he does not mention the second impression of December 1926). In particular, one must complain about the fact that no comment is made regarding the status of the text in the six installments of *Tar* published in *Woman's Home Companion,* some of which appeared before the book was published (and even before Horace Liveright had read a typescript of the work); presumably these texts antedate the later of the extant typescripts, but their relationship to the surviving typescripts ought to be explained in detail.

By the time Mr. White got to his third volume, *Marching Men* (originally published in 1917), he must have decided — perhaps because of the increasing attention being paid to the CEAA editions — that he should make a longer statement about his copy-text and his textual principles and should point out differences between his procedures and those of the CEAA editions. For *Marching Men* the document which survives is a revised manuscript-typescript, containing many pages in Anderson's hand as well as two stages of typescript copy heavily revised in his hand. To suggest the complexity of this document (which may be called, for convenience, a 'manuscript') Mr. White provides on pp. xvii–xxiii of his introduction (1) a physical description of those parts of the manuscript comprising the first chapter of each of the seven 'Books' into which the work is divided; (2) a list of twenty-one items (without page-line references) illustrative of the 'several dozen' penciled alterations made in the manuscript by an unidentified person; (3) what he calls a 'stylized "genetic" text' of the first and last pages of the manuscript; and (4) a list of thirty-seven items (without page-line references) illustrative of the 'fairly large group of changes' in 'grammar, punctuation, diction, and general style' made by Anderson or a publisher's editor (or both) at some point between the date represented by the extant manuscript and the date of the final reading of page proofs. Although the usefulness of this material, in the form in which it is presented, is rather limited (the symbols employed in the genetic transcription are particularly awkward), at least the documentary form of this copy-text is more extensively described than are the corresponding documents in the two earlier volumes.

Following this seven-page account of the manuscript come three and a half pages on the textual principles to be followed (pp. xxiv–xxvii). Mr. White begins, 'The rationale for preparing critical texts of Sherwood Anderson's works is not simple.' Indeed, it would appear to be incomprehensible, judging from the ensuing discussion. First of all, he summarizes 'the recent but already "classical" theory of bibliographical editing closely identified with the work of Fredson Bowers', citing the first volume of Bowers's Stephen Crane edition. His statement is a fair summary: it makes the distinction between substantives and accidentals, defines copy-text as 'the printed form of the work (normally the first printing) demonstrably closest to the author's final manuscript or typescript, assuming that the actual manuscript or typescript is not extant', points out that later revisions 'definitely by the author' are accepted into the text, and recognizes that all emendations in the copy-text are to be recorded. But if Mr. White understands this rationale well enough to make such a summary, how is it possible for him to misunderstand it as drastically as he does in the paragraphs which follow? He asserts that this procedure 'is not the most desirable approach to Sherwood Anderson's work, and the reason springs from Anderson's own attitude toward his writing'. Anderson, he says, 'learned to apologize for his untutored prose' and thus 'continued all his life entrusting to his publishers final preparation of his writing'. The results of this professional standardizing, he says, are 'sad', and he concludes:

One would not exaggerate in speculating that almost no essay or book by Anderson was published as the author intended in his manuscripts. For this reason, the printed versions of Anderson's novels are not the most sound bases for critical editions. Instead, in distinction to Professor Bowers' theory of copy-text, one must return for authoritative readings of both accidentals and substantives to Anderson's manuscripts. (Page xxv.)

It is hard to know where to begin commenting on this passage. The implication that the theory of copy-text followed by Bowers (and the other CEAA editors) favors printed over manuscript texts is simply not true. Many of the CEAA volumes employ manuscripts as copy-text, and Mr. White's own earlier summary seems to suggest that he understands this point, for he says that a printed text is used 'assuming that the actual manuscript or typescript is not extant'. I do not know how to account for such a gross inconsistency within a brief passage of three paragraphs. Furthermore, the statement that Anderson's published texts do not reflect his intentions seems to contradict the earlier assertion about Anderson's 'entrusting' to his publishers the 'final preparation of his writing'. The argument as it stands appears to run like this: Anderson expected his publishers to put his prose into publishable shape, according to conventional standards of correctness; the result appears 'sad' to a present-day editor; therefore the editor should return to the intention embodied in the manuscript. Although Mr.

White's conclusion — that the manuscript should be the copy-text — would be affirmed, I believe, by most Anderson scholars and could be effectively supported, he has managed to arrive at it through the shakiest of arguments and to present it in the most unconvincing light.

After this general exposition of his rationale, 'best understood in its contrast with . . . the work of Fredson Bowers', he offers first a discussion of accidentals and then one of substantives. As for accidentals, he argues on the one hand that Anderson knew how 'to present his material effectively' and should be allowed such idiosyncrasies as his 'pet spellings'; on the other hand, he says, an editor must 'understand the need to supply a missing comma for a dependent clause or a phrase lacking one comma of a pair' and must 'decide that frequently occurring forms should coincide'. Apparently he is saying that standardizing and regularizing are necessary, but that one should not go as far with those activities as the original publisher of *Marching Men* did. No proof is offered for the seemingly inconsistent statement that the manuscript 'reveals Anderson's serious attempt to standardize his accidental forms', unless the fact that Anderson's secretary in Ohio 'clearly' made changes as she typed constitutes this 'serious attempt'. In the midst of this discussion is a sentence which I must quote here, for I have not been able to comprehend it sufficiently to paraphrase it. After pointing out that the typed passages inevitably incorporate corrections made by Anderson's secretary-typist, he declares:

The discarded original holograph passages of *Marching Men* being lost, one must accept the secretary's presumed corrections of Anderson's accidentals, incorporating into a critical text the author's paragraphing, punctuation, diction, word order, sentence divisions, and pet spellings. (Page xxv.)

Obviously at those points where holograph is missing, an editor must accept the typescript as the closest surviving document to Anderson's holograph manuscript; but the phrase beginning with 'incorporating' seems to contradict the first part of the sentence and to suggest that somehow Anderson's own usages can be inserted into the same passage. (Does it also mean to classify 'diction' and 'word order' as accidentals?) When Mr. White goes on to say that the 'extant holograph passages are incorporated without question', he seems to be contradicting the view that a 'literal transcription . . . would evade serious editorial responsibilities' and that an editor must do a certain amount of standardizing.[10] However unclear this discussion is, a complete listing of all the editor's alterations in the copy-text would at least have enabled the reader to see what has been done to the text. Mr. White mentions, in his summary of 'Bowers' theory', that lists of emendations in the copy-text are a feature of editions following that theory; presumably one of the ways in which his own procedure differs is that no such list is required.

The paragraphs on substantives (which offer 'a more difficult task') are equally unsatisfactory. Mr. White's unwillingness to take the central editorial responsibility of ruling on which revisions are Anderson's emerges in particularly striking form (despite the incoherence of the first of the following sentences, which says the opposite of what is meant):

Thus it would not be acceptable to reject substantive manuscript readings in favor of the printed forms, which *could* be the author's revisions. Nor can one fairly incorporate the printed forms and totally neglect the manuscript readings, which *might* be what Anderson intended. (Page xxvi.)

His solution, which he calls a 'compromise procedure', employs the same system of brackets and asterisks as the previous volumes. But his somewhat longer explanation of the system produces another misleading statement, not present in the other volumes. He says that, when the list at the end contains an entry for which no signal appears in the text, the reading in the list is one that 'presumably was rejected by Anderson during revision of the typescript'. This 'typescript', however, must be the copy-text document elsewhere called a 'manuscript', and since Anderson's deletions on it can be examined, the word 'presumably' is puzzling in this sentence. The entry for 166.1 is an example: the word 'ten', recorded in the list, is marked out on the manuscript, with 'six', the word now in the text, written above it in Anderson's hand. There is no reason to call this a 'presumable' change

---

[10] Another peculiar statement here is that 'one must remove from the 1917 printed text the British house-forms of the Lane company' — as if the text of the original edition were being used as copy-text. But since the manuscript is copy-text, the point is not to remove house styling but rather not to insert it.

by Anderson; it is certainly by him.[11] (Incidentally, if that revision is to be recorded, why is there no record of the fact that five lines later the phrase 'quiet, strong in her own kind of faith' is a revision replacing 'patient, kindly' or that 'reputation', a few words beyond, is a substitution for 'womanhood'?) The list at the end follows the same plan as that employed in the other two volumes, but now the word 'Substantive' has been added at the beginning of the title; but its 309 entries do not begin to account for all the small deletions and revisions made by Anderson on the manuscript, so the word 'substantive' cannot be intended here in the same sense in which it is used in the introduction (where it refers to 'words themselves'). Without arguing the merits of the principles and procedures employed in the CEAA editions, one can say that Mr. White would have been much better advised to follow them; it seems clear that he could hardly have done worse than to follow the system he has devised.

III

Even though nothing can be said in defense of the editorial policy of these volumes or of the inconsistent application of that policy, there yet remains, theoretically, one hope for salvaging something from them; for if their standard of accuracy were high, they could at least be relied upon for what material they include and could have a limited usefulness. It is my unpleasant duty, however, to report that none of them is reliable, either in its text or in its appended list. I shall present here a few examples of inaccuracies from each of the volumes. This listing is in no sense a systematic record, but I have tried to make it a representative sampling of the errors I discovered in a not particularly extensive collation of passages chosen at random.

[11] This section also points out specifically that the fair copy, made from the extant manuscript, does not survive. It is puzzling, therefore, to find the statement made seven pages earlier that the penciled changes by a 'foreign hand' on the extant manuscript 'were seldom rejected by the author, who accepted most of them into the new fair copy of his novel' (p. xix). Presumably, those which appear in the 1917 edition were accepted; but when a passage containing one of these revisions does not appear there, how can one say what was true of a document no longer in existence? (For example, compare the entry for 9.1–5 in the list with the text itself and with the first entry in the list at the bottom of p. xix.) The statement that Anderson accepted 'most of them' allows for the possibility that he rejected some of them in passages later canceled; but of course it is possible that he accepted all of them. The point is that this is an unacceptable generalization about a nonexistent document.

A Story Teller's Story[12]

11.2   The reading reported here in the list of 'Variant Readings from Printings One and Two' should end with an
exclamation point rather than a period.

19.3   The peculiar expression 'everlasting-strutting', in Mr.
White's text at this point, results from his misreading of
the typescript. He is correct in rejecting the revision to
'everlastingly strutting', made in the typescript but not
in Anderson's hand. But the original reading of the typescript has a spaced hyphen between the two words; since
spaced hyphens throughout the typescript are used for
dashes, the correct reading here is 'everlasting — strutting'.

28.1   Mr. White retains the comma in this line after 'is', although he reports exactly the same reading in his list of
the variants present in the first two printings. Since this
comma is deleted from the third printing and since Mr.
White is accepting the alterations of the third printing,
obviously the presence of the comma here is an oversight
on his part.

215.12   The entry in the list of 'Variant Readings from Printings
One and Two' labeled '215.2' should actually be keyed
to '215.12'. (In addition, the entry is misleading: it reads
'So-and-so' and the text reads 'so and so'. One would
conclude that the third printing made the 's' lower case
and eliminated the hyphens. What in fact appears in the
third printing is 'so-and-so', and Mr. White has deleted
the hyphens for a different reason — because they were
originally inserted in the typescript by Booth.)

249.3–23   The second sentence of the paragraph, reported as beginning 'Was it somewhat' (249.3), originally began, in
the typescript, 'That might be only'. In revising the typescript, Anderson deleted all the paragraph except the
opening sentence (and deleted the first four words of the
next paragraph as well) and wrote, above the opening

---

[12] I have purposely avoided repeating any of the errors noted in Rideout's
review, pp. 71–72; one should turn to that review, therefore, for a discussion
of six additional errors (including one in the subtitle of the book).

of the second sentence, 'Was it somewhat'. He meant these three words to connect with 'more sophisticated' (249.23) in the next paragraph. Mr. White, however, takes the words as a revision of the opening of the second sentence and thus prints a sentence Anderson never intended — to say nothing of mixing two stages of revision by not indicating that this passage was deleted before the larger deletion of 249.1–250.22.

283.19   'Americans' here is an error for 'Moderns', changing the meaning of the sentence. Errors such as this, occurring within one of the long important passages not elsewhere available in print, are particularly unfortunate, since a reader has to go to the typescript itself to check on them and cannot make a preliminary check against a more convenient printed source.

291.9   What Mr. White prints as 'it's' reads 'is' in the typescript.

292.40   Following this line in the typescript there is a row of dots, indicating a sectional division. Since Mr. White elsewhere reproduces these divisions simply with white space, and since this one falls at the bottom of one of his pages, there is no way for the reader to know that a division occurs here.

296.12   The typescript ends this sentence appropriately with a question mark, not a period as appears here.

300.8–12   The text here prints both Anderson's original wording and his replacement for it, as if the replacement were actually an addition. In the original version, the sentence continues from 'us' at 300.12 to 'of' later in the same line ('talk to us of himself'); then Anderson marked out the passage from 'Once' (300.8) through 'us' (300.12) and replaced it with 'I hungered to have him talk to me'. Mr. White has supplied the period after 'us' in order to use both the original and the revised versions simultaneously, producing a reading that Anderson never intended at any stage.

Tar: A Midwest Childhood

17.35   The text reads '[*it was to be]'; since the word 'it' is present in the typescript, it is not a later addition and should be outside the brackets.

24.4   The sentence 'Better let music alone.', not present in the typescript, should be enclosed in brackets and marked with an asterisk.

27.7–8   The words marked with brackets and an asterisk are present in the typescript; thus no symbols should appear here at all.

42.24   The text reads '[how many] many times'; but it ought to read either '[*how] [many] many times' or '[*how] many times', depending on whether one regards the added 'how' and the deleted 'many' as separate items or whether one takes the 'how' as a replacement for the first 'many'. As it stands, the reading signifies that the published version omits 'how many'; but the reading of the published version is 'how many times', and the 'how' is not present in the typescript.

62.32–36 There is a cluster of errors here too complicated to report in brief space. Perhaps the most important point to note is this: in the earlier version of the passage, printed in the list on p. 238, Mr. White has taken it on himself to capitalize the 'And' and create a new sentence, so that he will not have to include the earlier part of the sentence, which was less drastically revised. The original sentence reads, 'He made some remark about how much women and children cost and the farmers laughed.' Because the revised version (printed in the text) includes a sentence similar to the first clause of this sentence, Mr. White does not report the original clause and claims that the original reads, 'And the farmers laughed.'

196.14   The text reads 'the only negro in town'; it should perhaps read 'the only negro living in town', for 'living' is not canceled in the earlier of the manuscript-typescripts and its omission from the later was apparently the typist's error. While one could argue that Anderson's failure to restore the word at any later stage implies his approval of the deletion, one could also argue that he never happened to notice the omission and that no documentary evidence supports the reading without 'living' as his intended wording. In any event, the fact that 'living' is not reported here at all raises the question of how carefully Mr. White has checked for possible errors of

205

transcription in the preparation of the later of the surviving typescripts.

200.22 Although the text reads 'sold them [fast] stuff, fast enough', the bracketed 'fast' does not appear in the typescript and should be deleted. (Neither is the comma in the typescript, but it is present in the published book. Apparently this is one of the alterations of the typescript which Mr. White does not regard as 'undesirable'.)

202.19 Mr. White's text reads, 'getting all the dresses out of a big truck'; but since this scene takes place in a bedroom, the word 'truck' should obviously be 'trunk', as it is in the typescript and the first edition.

214.6 The text here omits the word 'in' (present in typescript and published book) preceding 'a car' and produces the absurd reading 'he would like to be a car like that'.

Marching Men

xxi.11 The word *'Standing'* in the genetic text should be in roman type, not italic, for it is Anderson's form, not a revision by the 'foreign hand'. In the same line, the dash after 'be' should be a hyphen.

38.33–34 Because the syntax was altered in the 1917 edition, it would seem that the text here should have '[*shook]' rather than 'shaking' and '[*and]' following 'hand'. There is nothing in the introduction which would explain why this kind of difference between the manuscript and the printed book should be entirely ignored.

135.12 In the deleted passage printed in the list of variants at this point, the words 'the blatant talk of taking' occur. Actually, 'taking' is Anderson's revision, written above the four preceding words, which he had marked out. (Furthermore, the passage ends in mid-sentence, and the editor does not explain that, judging from the manuscript page numbers, Anderson discarded three pages here as part of the deletion which included this passage.

161.9 The word 'his' is omitted, just before 'mind', in the transcription of the deleted passage here.

180.10 The main text reads 'grin [*appeared]'; but the entry in the list of variants gives the same reading, 'grin appeared'. That entry should read 'grin spread', however,

201.4   The deleted passage given in the list begins with the words 'court room', which are meant to provide the connection with 'court room' in the main text. But the words preceding 'court room' in the main text are 'From the', which do not fit as the opening words of the first sentence in the deleted passage. The original sentence begins 'In the' (later revised to 'From the'), and 'In the' is a necessary part of the deleted passage. This entry, therefore, should begin 'In the court room' — or, to provide a locating word, 'him. In the court room'.

207.10   There is perhaps no point in noting an unreported deletion in the manuscript, since there are so many of them and since I am primarily calling attention at this stage to errors of commission rather than omission. But this example suggests the importance of some of the unreported deletions. Following the word 'faces' a clause is deleted: 'as they turned them [*i.e.,* eyes] up to that other silent mover of men'. I cannot think what definition of 'substantive' would result in the absence of this clause from a list entitled 'Substantive Deletions from the Typescript. . . .'

Without multiplying examples, one can begin to see how thoroughly these volumes have failed to provide 'a scrupulously accurate text' — one of the goals announced in *A Story Teller's Story* (p. xviii). If it is true, as Mr. White says in the first volume, that 'few modern books have been published in such unreliable texts as *A Story Teller's Story*' (p. xv), he has done nothing to alter the tradition and has in fact extended it to two other books. In a recent publication he claims, 'Reading, transcribing, and editing manuscript material by Sherwood Anderson is by now no problem to me';[13] nevertheless, it was obviously a problem at the time when the work on these three volumes was carried out. I see no alternative to concluding that the volumes fail to make any contribution whatever to the study of Anderson's texts or to textual

[13] *Sherwood Anderson / Gertrude Stein: Correspondence and Personal Essays* (Chapel Hill: University of North Carolina Press, 1972), p. 118.

theory in general. Finding fault often requires more space than be-
stowing praise, and I regret that I have had to fill so many pages with
negative comments. But I regret even more having to announce that
what could have been a major scholarly contribution has turned out
an utter failure,[14] and in fairness such a harsh judgment should be
accompanied by a considerable amount of evidence. There is little I
can say at this point that would be constructive. It is a sad fact that
these three books of Anderson's stand in greater need of editing now
than they did before Mr. White embarked on his task. The first editions, after all, are historical documents of interest in their own right;
but these new editions are secondary sources which are as likely to
convey misinformation as clarification at any given point. What can be
done now is hard to say, for presumably copyright restrictions will
complicate the production of further editions for a time. The idea of
publishing editorial apparatus (keyed to a suitable printed text, such
as a first edition) separately from the text is growing in favor — under

[14] My concern has been solely with the text, not with the biographical and
historical annotation. The brief introduction to each volume does contain
some biographical background, and allusions in the main text to Anderson's
own life or to historical persons are identified in footnotes. I have made no
effort to check this kind of annotation; but Rideout's review lists a number
of errors in the footnotes in *A Story Teller's Story*. I should also point out that
each volume includes an appendix containing biographical material: *A Story
Teller's Story* offers a three-page piece labeled 'Sherwood Anderson's Earliest
Autobiography' and identified only as a '1918 publicity essay' (pp. 345–47);
Tar prints an analysis of 'The Diaries of Sherwood Anderson's Parents' by
William A. Sutton (pp. 219–30) and the text of 'The Death in the Forest',
edited by William V. Miller from the Newberry manuscript (pp. 231–36); and
Marching Men reprints a selection of Anderson's pre-1914 essays from *Agricul-
tural Advertising* and *The Reader* (pp. 229–61), along with 'his first professionally
published short story', 'The Rabbit-pen' from *Harper's Monthly Magazine* of July
1914 (pp. 262–69). (Mr. White says that he has selected 'twelve' of the 'over
thirty' early articles, but actually there are fifteen separately titled items taken
from eleven issues of magazines; and though he says they have been selected
'to show his [Anderson's] developing literary acumen' during this period, all
date from the years 1902–4. In his introductory comments to these essays,
something has obviously gone wrong with the first two sentences, which now
seem to say that Anderson joined the Crowell firm in two consecutive years.)
Finally, each volume contains a 'Selected Bibliography', listing all Anderson's
books (with the American but not the English publishers) and books (but not
articles) about Anderson, along with translations and reviews of the particular
book involved (the first two volumes also cite some other secondary sources,
and *Tar* includes a list of 'Comparable American Autobiographies').

the encouragement of the CEAA — and perhaps someone can undertake to re-edit these books in that fashion. Meanwhile, Anderson scholars face an awkward situation and will have to decide whether the better course at present may not be to make their quotations from the original editions.

THE PAPERS OF JOHN C. CALHOUN:
A Review Article

LAWRENCE S. THOMPSON

THE PRACTICE OF EDITING SIGNIFICANT WORKS OF FAMOUS MEN FOR convenient use in sets goes back to antiquity.[1] The Alexandrians did a generally commendable job with Homer, but the editorial policies of Plato and Xenophon were so loose that we can't be sure about what Socrates really said. The dependability of the collected letters of Saint Paul has often been questioned; he deserved better editors in the first and second centuries. In the nineteenth century German scholars, fascinated by what could be extracted from a chipped clay tablet or

[1] *The Papers of John C. Calhoun,* ed. W. Edwin Hemphill (Columbia: University of South Carolina Press):
    Volume III, 1818–1819 (1967)
    Volume IV, 1819–1820 (1969)
    Volume V, 1820–1821 (1971)
    Volume VI, 1821–1822 (1972)
For prices and formats see 'The Register of Current Publications', *Proof,* 1 (1971), 2 (1972), and 3 (1973).

a crumbling piece of papyrus or paper, carried the mania for editing everything about famous men to the ultimate extreme: the graffiti in the privy of Strindberg's Berlin flat were meticulously photographed, edited by competent scholars, and offered for publication — unfortunately, without verification by a graphologist.

The speeches, letters, and other writings of major American public figures of the latter eighteenth and nineteenth centuries were published selectively, and usually uncritically, soon after they died in many cases. Within less than a decade after John C. Calhoun's death, Richard K. Crallé offered a selection of some 150 speeches, reports, and public letters. Just before the turn of the century J. Franklin Jameson did a superb job of editing the correspondence which was available to him and which, in his mature judgment as a highly competent historian, were significant.

But scholarly editing had not yet been established as a major discipline within American historical studies. It was students of literature, using textual methods developed by the classicists, above all in nineteenth-century Germany, who first applied scholarly editorial methods to modern authors. The Shakespeare Variorum and the Weimar editions of Luther and Goethe are abiding and egregious examples of superior editorial work, although technology and some of the newer techniques will necessitate revised editions even here. There have been many refinements, both in hardware (*e.g.*, photographic equipment, mechanical collators, indexing by computer) and in methods, especially those developed for editing literary texts by Greg, Bowers, and their scholarly progeny of all persuasions. But the genius of the editor, his insight into the writer's mind and the physical evidence of it, are the basic elements for establishing dependable texts. Thus students in courses in the lyric of the Republic will use the 1959 text of Tibullus by Lenz, but the teacher will feel much more secure if he has a copy of Heyne's 1755 edition at hand for reference.

The editing of writings by prominent men in American public life had been given some attention by competent scholars, notably in the case of Washington and Lincoln, before the middle of this century, but it came to official maturity in 1950 with the appearance of the first volume of the Jefferson papers under the editorship of Julian P. Boyd at Princeton. It is not without significance that this prototype for other similar projects, including the Calhoun, was first sponsored by a great private university with private funding and published by that institution's press. The larger proportion of seminal movements, projects, trends, and ideas in American scholarship up to the present time can be traced to the Philadelphia–New York–Boston circuit. With the appearance of Boyd's Jefferson, the federal government, tax-supported institutions, and private foundations saw the urgent need for dependable and accurate collected editions of the work of leading Americans of the past. With the example of the Jefferson to show how the job could be done to satisfy the most exacting standards of American historical scholarship, the work of leading American statesmen of the last century (Calhoun and Clay being among the first) were singled out for editing, generally by scholars in the jurisdictions of which the statesmen were native.

The late Robert L. Meriwether, who planned the Calhoun edition and had edited the first volume before his death in 1958, applied Boyd's methods judiciously but did not imitate them in every detail, for he realized that every editorial job, just as every human mind, requires individual analysis. This is not the place for a eulogy of Mr. Meriwether, of which there were an abundance; but it cannot be too strongly emphasized that his great work in building the comprehensive Calhoun Collection of the South Carolina Library in Columbia made his work and that of his successor, W. Edwin Hemphill, much easier. This exemplary collection attempts to pull together in a single corpus the originals or some accurate copy of everything written by Calhoun. If there had been similar dedicated collectors at the universities of Kentucky and Tennessee, the editors of Clay and Johnson could have moved with much more dispatch.

It is not the purpose of this commentary to review the reviewers of earlier volumes. One significant point, however, has been brought out by two reviewers of the second volume. Both Holman Hamilton and J. A. Munroe felt that too many trivia were included and the selection of papers to be published might have been more judicious, although Munroe was satisfied for the policies set up for the third volume. The matter of inclusion and exclusion is one of the greatest problems of the editor and the enumerative bibliographer. To be sure, it will only be necessary for the editor of Patrick Henry to make a one-sentence reference to the tens of thousands of land grants signed by him that dot Kentucky mantelpieces as thickly as canvas over tobacco patches in April. But of the letters, speeches, official files, marginalia in books, nay, even graffiti of doubtful provenance — what is significant and what is not? We must depend on the editor, presumably the closest living intimate of the individual he edits. One can only dismiss Mr. Hamilton's criticism by asking who would make so bold as to question his own selections of those papers of Zachary Taylor which ought to appear in print.

There is not much more to say other than to express gratitude to Mr. Hemphill and to the University of South Carolina Press for a job well done. The national significance of the project is self-evident. The portrait of the ambitious, brilliant, sometimes dogmatic statesman is easily limned from his papers; and his role in the development of the Republic and of the South develops sharply against the backdrop of his associations with other leaders of equal or less stature. The bulk of the papers go beyond local history, but they are still a treasure trove for the student of South Carolina traditions and a special delight (particularly the first volume) for those of us privileged to trace our ancestry to the old Ninety Six District. Yet who save the antiquarian and the professional student of nineteenth-century American history will go through each volume, letter by letter, speech by speech, or even refer regularly to the carefully compiled index? What is needed for the literate South Carolinian and the general student of American history is a Calhoun reader. It is hoped that the University of South Carolina Press will be able to fulfill this pious chore.

Set in Linotype Caledonia with long descenders and designed with a simplicity consistent with Calhoun's own personal tastes, the set is a handsome one, a worthy decoration even for the shelves of non-readers.

THE FIRST TWO VOLUMES OF THE WRITINGS OF HENRY D. THOREAU:
A Review Article

JOSEPH R. McELRATH, JR.

THE GENERAL EDITORSHIP OF THE EDITION OF THOREAU'S WRITINGS being published by Princeton University Press has just recently changed hands, from Walter Harding's to William L. Howarth's, and it is thus especially appropriate to now consider how well the editors have so far fared. What has been accomplished? What can be accomplished under the guidance of a new general editor? By the time this review appears three volumes will have been published: *Walden* (1971), edited by J. Lyndon Shanley; *The Maine Woods* (1972), by Joseph J. Moldenhauer; and *Reform Papers* (1973), by Wendell Glick. The first two are available at the time of this writing; Glick's volume will have to be treated at a later time. Hopefully it will be a very strong piece of editorial work, one that will significantly increase the quality of The Writings of Henry D. Thoreau. For if one had to assign a grade to what presently exists, it would be a B-plus over an F. Despite one flaw in copy-text choice, *The Maine Woods* is, overall, a respectable volume, and in the main a truly admirable achievement. *Walden,* however, is the sad irony of the entire project. It is the book that made the Thoreau edition a historical necessity, the gem around which all of Thoreau's other literary efforts naturally arrange themselves. Like *The Maine Woods,* it has been granted the seal of the Center For Editions of American Authors; but, unlike Moldenhauer's work, Shanley's has instead earned censure. In claiming that his *Walden* is a 'definitive' critical edition, as the CEAA seal which it displays makes explicit, Shanley has, in effect, reduced Thoreau's brave chanticleer to a jackdaw, strutting in peacock's feathers. And because Shanley's *Walden* violates so many of the general principles of current editorial theory, especially those emphasized by the CEAA, one would imagine that its possession of the seal is only a temporary thing. It simply is inadequate to present expectations of a CEAA volume, or, indeed, to any truly 'critical' edition. One might term its publication something of a tragedy, for students of Thoreau — and for CEAA.

Would that the Thoreau edition had held off on publishing *Walden* first and resisted the temptation to make the big, dramatic splash at the beginning. If blunders had to be made in getting an edition of Thoreau's writings off the ground, why could not they have been made in a less 'essential' text, and not *the* Thoreau book that everyone reads? Indeed, why not wait until last, when all of the information on Thoreau's compositional idiosyncrasies and the characteristic editorial and compositorial interference with the transmission of Thoreau's texts was available? But, most important, why not wait until the Thoreau team — virtually an army — had passed beyond the pale of amateurishness to easy familiarity with modern editorial theory and practice? Shanley and Harding might at least have paused until Moldenhauer provided a healthy example of how a textual-bibliographic scholar functions. For the second irony of the Thoreau edition is that the textual apparatus of *The Maine Woods* almost point-by-point provides the kind and quality of essential information that *Walden* lacks at the most crucial nexi. The *sine qua non* of modern editing is the ability to ask the right questions of the textual situation at hand. Moldenhauer knew how to ask them and to clearly present the answers in the great majority of instances; Shanley did not.

A third irony is that the editing of the three essays and the appendix that constitute *The Maine Woods* seems a considerably more difficult task than the editing of *Walden.* Though the *Walden* situation is far more complex than the piece-of-cake to which Shanley has reduced it by his copy-text choice, Thoreau at least saw the book through the press and expressed a good many final intentions in surviving page proofs. *The Maine Woods,* however, like most of Thoreau's enormous literary remains, was posthumously-published from printer's copy finally readied by other hands than Thoreau's. The first two sections, 'Ktaadn' and 'Chesuncook', saw magazine publication during Thoreau's lifetime: the former as 'Ktaadn, and the Maine Woods' in *Union Magazine of Literature and Art* (1848), and the latter with the same title in *Atlantic Monthly* (1858). But the third section, 'The Allegash and East Branch', and the 'Appendix' remained in manuscript form until the 1864 first edition. Each of the four pieces was being prepared for book publication by Thoreau at the time of his death in 1862; but none, so far as we can now tell, was in its absolute final state, as intended by its author, when printer's copy was delivered to Ticknor and Fields by Henry's sister, Sophia. It was Sophia — and, to some as-yet-undetermined degree, Ellery Channing — who put the finishing touches on Henry's texts before submission. And then, of course, Ticknor and Fields (and its printers) made its editorial (and compositorial) contributions to what became the first-edition text.

The main task of the editor of *The Maine Woods,* as Moldenhauer clearly perceives, is to separate wheat from chaff, to identify and evaluate the particular instance in which the people at Ticknor and Fields and Sophia interfered with Thoreau's probable intentions. (Channing quickly drops out of the picture: 'Of Channing's role nothing specific has been recorded; he seems to have taken the publication lightly' [p. 355].) And it proves a pleasure to watch Moldenhauer expertly burrow through the layers of interference that were superimposed upon Thoreau's texts, especially since each of the four sections presents a unique set of demands upon the burrower as he works his way back to and attempts to reconstruct the forms of the texts that Thoreau left us.

The 'Appendix' to *The Maine Woods* proves the simplest section to handle. Printer's copy is not extant, nor is any working draft, and thus we do not know exactly what Thoreau wrote. Moldenhauer, however, has scrupulously researched the entries to determine what possible interferences occurred, digging into relevant journal and notebook entries and working copy of the three essays, as well as into Thoreau's printed sources of information. He was surprised to find that, 'despite its technical character, the 1864 "Appendix" is a fairly accurate publication'. The majority of mistakes have to do with misspellings of Indian terms which, 'even in Thoreau's most careful longhand, could easily have been misread by a compositor' (p. 366). The fact that

Thoreau's characteristic abbreviation of 'Mountain', an 'underscored "Mt." ' which Sophia regularly expanded to the full spelling, was allowed to stand gives Moldenhauer further cause to suppose that a scribal transmission did not intervene between Thoreau's final draft and typesetting. 'If', Moldenhauer reasons, 'Thoreau's last "Appendix" manuscript were reasonably clean and legible, there would have been no need to transcribe it for the printer; if the manuscript was rough, an intervening stage of transmission would have introduced a multitude of blunders' (p. 366). The first edition's 'Appendix' must serve as copy-text and Moldenhauer, because of its apparently close proximity to setting copy, conservatively limits the majority of his emendations of the copy-text to corrections of the most obvious errors of spelling and punctuation. In his 'Textual Introduction' and 'Textual Notes' he clearly identifies the sources of his spellings — Thoreau's reference works, his manuscripts containing material directly related to *The Maine Woods,* and general reference works of the period. In substantive matters, Moldenhauer is not reluctant to turn to pre-copy-text passages in Thoreau's journal to untangle probable editorial and compositorial confusions. For instance, in the *'Ranunculus acris* (buttercups)' entry at 309.21–22, the first edition reads, 'abundant at Smith's dam, Chesuncook, 1853.' Moldenhauer deletes 'dam' and then offers the following explanation in his 'Textual Notes':

The copy-text adds "dam" after "Smith's" but there was no dam at this settlement. The journal draft, MJ, October 8, 1857, reads simply "Smith's." In the journal for September 18, 1853, Thoreau notes buttercups along the Chesuncook shore near Smith's. He may have intended the word "farm" for this "Appendix" entry.

The manner in which Moldenhauer here explains his decision to emend is significant in several ways of his work throughout *The Maine Woods:* first, he is intimately familiar with the history and geography of the actual settings of the essays; second, he obviously has a strong command of all pre-copy-text material which may have a bearing on determining the nature of Thoreau's final versions of the texts; third, he is willing to run the considered risk of emending to a pre-copy-text reading when the copy-text's seems awry; and fourth, this willingness is tempered by a respectfully conservative attitude toward the copy-text. Yes, Thoreau may have penciled in 'farm', or something orthographically similar, in his characteristically execrable hand at some

218

stage of revision. That would explain the unlikely 'dam'. But Moldenhauer refrains from emending to 'farm'.

It is not in the 'Appendix', though, that Moldenhauer exhibits the
most fruitful results of his scholarship and textual savvy. It is in 'The
Allegash and East Branch' section that he encounters his most complicated problems, and his sophisticated response — as we shall see —
might have taught Shanley a good deal about the procedure of choosing and handling a copy-text. Moldenhauer here opts for a copy-text
in a way that may strike many as unconventional, and even radical.
Printer's copy and proofs do not survive, and thus the first-edition text
would seem to many the obvious first choice; such is the tendency
nowadays when the choice of 'foul' copy or a first edition text presents
itself, and it is unlikely that many would have raised serious objections
if the 1864 'Allegash' were chosen. But Moldenhauer instead turns to
extant last drafts of sections of 'Allegash' and, because of their apparently 'final' character as holographs, decides that they are more proxi-
mate to Thoreau's intended fair copy readings than the text which
passed through Sophia's and Ticknor and Fields's various hands:

From surviving "Allegash" drafts in the Henry E. Huntington Library and the
Houghton Library . . . it is apparent that when Thoreau died he left something very much like a finished (though not fair) copy. . . . Cancelled passages
on these sheets do not appear in the 1864 publication, the order of paragraphs
is final, and the wording duplicates that of the first edition in all but a few
particulars. . . . they are ink drafts with pencil cancellations and insertions in
Thoreau's autograph. Another hand — Sophia Thoreau's — has rewritten
many pencil notations in ink. Sophia also expanded abbreviations and numerals, and occasionally changed the wording where no revision is discernible in
the pencil substratum. Clearly those sheets on which Sophia's markings appear
are the last version on which her brother was able to work. . . . [Page 365.]

The now lost remainder of the manuscript? It may have served as
printer's copy while only the surviving Huntington and Houghton
sheets were recopied by Sophia. It's a comforting thought, as Moldenhauer notes, despite Sophia's probable doctoring of Thoreau's longhand. For if a full scribal transcription of the manuscript occurred,
Thoreau's intentions for 'Allegash' must be considerably distant from
the first edition's and the Princeton edition's texts. Whatever — Moldenhauer *constructs* his copy-text from the surviving draft sheets, and
the first-edition text when manuscript is not available, indicating in his

textual apparatus when the draft sheets or the first edition text serve as copy-text.

In emending this eclectic copy-text Moldenhauer touches all of the bases. He has clearly visualized each point at which Thoreau's intentions may have been thwarted, and when apparently awry readings arise he zeroes in on the possible stages at which the interference may have occurred: Sophia's hand in the last draft (see textual notes 158.32 and 264.8–11); compositorial misinterpretation of Thoreau's autograph idiosyncracies (202.23) and handwriting (291.26–27); house-styling of Thoreau's accidentals (196.3); and obvious spelling errors which Thoreau presumably would have corrected, or have wanted corrected (234.34). To further glean Thoreau's probable intentions he repeatedly makes good use of journal drafts and worksheet readings which preceded the lost final manuscript sheets. It is a risky business to even consider emending to such 'rough copy' readings, but in every instance Moldenhauer makes excellent sense. For example, when emending the first edition copy-text's 'singing', describing the sound of toads, to 'ringing', he more than adequately supports his decision: 'Although the copy-text's "singing" is plausible, Thoreau's usual term for the sounding of toads was "ringing," as the word appears in the manuscript draft, MJ, July 23, 1857. Two other drafts of the passage, MJ October 5, 1857, and a Houghton Library worksheet (b MS Am 278.5, folder 17B), have "ring of toads." Thoreau's initial *r* and *s* before *i* are often indistinguishable.' ('Textual Notes' 163.22.) A better example involves a near nonsense reading in the copy-text which is rendered fully intelligible by an addition from the manuscript journal. The scene involves a brood of ducks 'moving off in a long line, very cunningly.' The first-edition text immediately follows this with, 'Yet they bore a certain proportion to the great Moosehead Lake on whose bosom they floated, and I felt as if they were under its protection.' Thoreau's qualification makes no sense, until the copy-text reading is considered in light of a journal draft of this passage which contains a sentence that was probably omitted at some late, nonauthorial stage of transmission. Moldenhauer declares that since 'no later draft has been located, the editor can come no nearer to Thoreau's intention than the journal version of this passage' ('Textual Notes' 166.19–20), and he emends to include the clarifying sentence thus:

. . . moving off in a long line, very cunningly. The Indian thought that the mother had perhaps been killed. Yet they bore a certain proportion to the great Moosehead Lake on whose bosom they floated, and I felt as if they were under its protection.

In instances such as this we have Moldenhauer at his best.

As with 'Allegash', the 'Chesuncook' section poses a considerable copy-text problem because so many key stages of textual transmission are not extant. The essay was first published in three installments in *Atlantic Monthly* (1858), and so far as we know, Thoreau read galley proof for only the second installment. But no proofs survive; and Thoreau's marked-up *Atlantic* pages which served as printer's copy for the first edition have also disappeared. What does survive is eighty-seven consecutively-numbered pages of the fair copy Thoreau submitted to *Atlantic*. There are small gaps in this partial manuscript which served as *Atlantic* printer's copy — they are identified on p. 380 — but they are inconsiderable compared to the bulk that is available. And thus Moldenhauer confronts a situation similar to that of 'Allegash'. The extant sheets did not serve as printer's copy for the corresponding section of the first edition text, which contains Thoreau's later revisions; the revised *Atlantic* pages did. The result is that for the section of 'Chesuncook' represented in manuscript (roughly the first half), there are three forms of the text which might be considered for copy-text: the first-edition text which undoubtedly contains Thoreau's latest revisions, but certainly contains much more (the *Atlantic* editorial and compositorial interferences, Sophia's 'improvements' and errors, and Ticknor and Fields's tamperings); the *Atlantic* text, which obviously must be used as copy-text of the second half of the essay, but which includes that magazine's styling features, editorial alterations, and compositorial changes throughout; and the partial *Atlantic* manuscript printer's copy, which expresses Thoreau's original intentions for the first half of the essay prior to revision for book publication as the second section of *The Maine Woods*. Right. Moldenhauer wisely plays it safely and in harmony with the best of modern editorial theory. In the manuscript we have Thoreau's accidentals in pristine form, and that is the paramount consideration of copy-text choice. We have what Thoreau wrote, not what the *Atlantic* decided to publish. Consequently Moldenhauer constructs another eclectic copy-text. The printer's-copy *Atlantic* manuscript serves for the first half of the essay, except for the gaps when the published *Atlantic* text must be used; and the *Atlantic* text is copy-text for the second half because of its proximity to the lost section of fair copy. With this copy-text Moldenhauer emends forward so as to recover Thoreau's probable final intentions as may have been expressed in the lost marked-up *Atlantic* pages, the printer's copy for the first edition.

Moldenhauer thus takes the two steps necessary to determination of Thoreau's texts. He asks the two essential questions which usually lead to sound copy-text choice and sensible emendation of that basic text. The first is, what did the author actually write, and which text most fully and clearly indicates this? Thus we come to the partial *Atlantic* fair copy. It was not the author's final version, but it is the sole surviving version over which we know Thoreau exercised full control, especially in regard to accidentals. Fair copy for the second half is lost and thus the 1858 published text is closest to what Thoreau wrote, granted *Atlantic* house-styling, editorial revision, and compositorial interference. In the latter situation copious pre-copy-text drafts enable Moldenhauer, as in the 'Allegash' situation, to identify and eliminate the more obvious editorial alterations: see, for example, textual notes 123.10, 141.20, and 150.22. Having determined as closely as possible what Thoreau wrote in 1858, the next question to ask is, how — from available evidence — did Thoreau revise so that his marked pages reflected his final conception of 'Chesuncook'? And here it is needless to repeat that Moldenhauer again effectively wields his profound understanding of Thoreau in making the conservative emendations he does. I might only point to the textual note for 143.35 as another fine example of how well an editor can analyze his data to understand the probable motivations that seem to have led an author to alter his text.

In these three sections — 'Chesuncook', 'The Allegash and East Branch', and 'Appendix' — Moldenhauer fairly dazzles one with his erudition, and makes one start at considering the labor he has performed. He exhibits excellent sense as a critic and depth as a historian; and when these traits are blended with his editorial expertise, the results are striking.

In the 'Ktaadn' section of *The Maine Woods*, therefore, Moldenhauer surprises his reader. He stumbles and, for an unfortunate instant, establishes a link of kinship with the editor of the Princeton *Walden*. One of Shanley's faults in *Walden* is that he falls into an old trap. Editors have traditionally done themselves in by falling prey to an exaggerated regard for that holy of holiest notion, the 'author's final intention'. It has resulted in numerous editions which pay undue homage to the last version of a text published during the author's lifetime; it has repeatedly sent editors scurrying to choose a copy-text which stands as close as possible to the published text of a work when manuscript fair copy, galley proof, page proof, foundry proof — all manner of prior forms of the text are available. The great revolution in modern editing has been the gradual discrediting of this orientation by McKerrow, Greg, and Bowers; the means has been the idea that copy-text choice should be based upon proximity to the author's fair copy manuscript. With this orientation one can preserve the author's accidental usages, those features over which he usually exercises his fullest control in manuscript and which are most easily corrupted and lost during the normal processes through which a manuscript passes as it is readied for publication. The author's later revisions and corrections of substantive and accidental features are preserved by emending the copy-text to include those authorial alterations. As a theory it is remarkably simple, clear, and commonsensical; and, most important, it produces positive results, the results of which few people have disputed successfully.

Moldenhauer, as is demonstrated in his handling of the three sections of *The Maine Woods* already discussed, does not dispute this theory or its method. In fact, he employes them remarkably well. But in 'Ktaadn' the final intentions boogey man, and perhaps Shanley's example in *Walden,* seem to throw him off the track. The stemma for the essay is as follows: after writing a first draft in a notebook, the bulk of which survives, Thoreau prepared a fair copy manuscript which he sent to Horace Greeley who sold it to the *Union Magazine* for him; *Union Magazine* set the essay in type from that now lost manuscript and Thoreau seems not to have received proofs; after magazine publication, Thoreau made his corrections and revisions on pages cut from the magazine, twice; one set of corrected pages he appears to have 'presented to a friend or relative' (p. 359), and the other set, now lost, served as printer's copy for the first-edition book text. The line of textual transmission may be diagrammed accordingly:

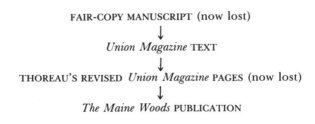

FAIR-COPY MANUSCRIPT (now lost)
↓
Union Magazine TEXT
↓
THOREAU'S REVISED *Union Magazine* PAGES (now lost)
↓
The Maine Woods PUBLICATION

Greg's theory of copy-text leads one to choose the *Union Magazine* text as copy-text because of its proximity to the lost fair copy. One would then emend it in light of the early draft material to determine any obvious house-styling of Thoreau's accidentals or egregious substantive blunders, and, if they survived, in light of Thoreau's final intentions expressed in the marked-up *Union Magazine* pages that Sophia sent to Ticknor and Fields. Also, one would certainly emend from the first edition text because it certainly contains at least some of those expressions of final intent. The set of corrected pages that Thoreau sent 'to a friend or relative' is, obviously, tangential to this stemma; yet it is this version of 'Ktaadn', preserved in NN-Berg, that Moldenhauer chooses for his copy-text.

Moldenhauer explains his theoretical basis for copy-text choice on pages 385–89. His statement is an orthodox one, based upon the CEAA's *Statement of Editorial Principles* of 1967.[1] Then he declares that the 'relevant forms of all four *Maine Woods* sections have already been identified, and the theory of copy-text on which this edition proceeds has been explained. That theory dictates the selection of the corrected *Union Magazine* "Ktaadn" pages in the Berg Collection as copy-text for the first chapter' (pp. 389–90). Well, no, it doesn't. But one can clearly see how Moldenhauer arrives at this conclusion:

> An eclectic or critical text is not an exact transcription nor an exact reprint of any particular printed form of the text. It is, rather, that one of the documentary forms of the text over which the author exercised the greatest degree of control (*e.g.*, a fair-copy manuscript, or a set of corrected proofs for the first printing if the fair copy is lost, or a first printed form if both the fair copy and corrected proofs have disappeared), as emended by the editor to reproduce as nearly as possible the author's intention. [Page 386.]

The terminology and idea of 'greatest control' worked well enough in the other three sections; the orientation quite naturally leads the editor to fair copy or the version of the text closest to it. But in the case of 'Ktaadn' it cannot apply in the manner in which Moldenhauer has employed it. Thoreau did exercise a great amount of control over the Berg pages; but these pages do not figure in the line of textual descent. They might, and should, be viewed as a relevant form of the text, tangential to the actual history of the text's transmission, which

[1] *Statement of Editorial Principles: A Working Manual For Editing Nineteenth Century American Texts* (New York: Modern Language Association of America, 1967).

may be used as an aid in determining Thoreau's final intentions — especially since the great majority of corrections and revisions in the Berg pages are duplicated in the first edition text. But these pages cannot serve as the copy-text itself. Actually, the extant version of 'Ktaadn' over which Thoreau exercised the greatest control is the uncorrected *Union Magazine* text. It was set from the author's fair copy which was *the* text exhibiting the greatest authorial control since it contained Thoreau's accidental traits in a pure state. It must be chosen as copy-text; the only other alternative at the present time is the first edition text, and one would have to be nearly blinded by the glitter of 'final intentions' to choose it. And even if the Berg pages were the setting copy, they could not be used as copy-text. The version of the text upon which Thoreau superimposed his corrections and revisions, the uncorrected pages, would still be closer to the lost fair copy.

Ironically, Moldenhauer's copy-text choice does not result in any objectionable readings in the Princeton 'Ktaadn'. Though his procedure is simply wrong, and potentially disastrous, I do not think that he would have established a different text. It is his method that gives reason for complaint. But even in this — to my mind — Moldenhauer the historian mitigates the error of the textualist. For in a table entitled 'Thoreau's Manuscript Revisions in the Copy-Text' he lists all of the variants between the *Union Magazine* text and the marked pages in the Berg Collection. The reader thus has a do-it-yourself list of all of the emendations actually made in the true copy-text. All he need do is conflate Moldenhauer's 'List of Emendations' and the revisions table. But should the reader have to do what is, after all, the editor's job?

With *Walden*, however, it is a do-it-again situation. There is no easy way to eliminate blemishes in this edition. It must someday be reconstructed from the ground up. Shanley not only makes mistakes in judgment — precipitated by the final intentions concern — but also in the matter of reporting the particulars of the textual situation. He clearly enough sets forth his procedure in his textual after matter, but he does not provide all of the information that would be necessary even if his copy-text choice were a defensible one. Unlike Moldenhauer, Shanley does not seem to realize the kind of data that he must closely examine and discuss. Moldenhauer consistently follows the CEAA's injunction to present the information that will 'make it possible for any reader of his text to follow him in his editorial choices and emendations' (*Statement of Editorial Principles*, p. 8). But even in this simple requirement, Shanley fails. *Walden* is an amateur-hour performance from the word 'go', and the consequence is distortion at every turn.

One of my early comments about *Walden* in this review alluded to the lyric, 'Things Are Seldom As They Seem', and I might again insist upon its aptness, as any textualist will begin to note early in the 'Textual Introduction'. The distortions begin on the first page, as Shanley writes, 'The text presented here is an unmodernized critical reconstruction'. (Page 379). Fine. It should be, but five pages later we read,

> The editor has changed five variant spellings in 925 [his copy-text] that were acceptable in Thoreau's day; (1) in each case the form in 925 is obsolete or archaic today, and not found in some current standard dictionaries, and therefore might be misunderstood; and (2) except in one case, the form adopted in this text was used by Thoreau in 924 [the *Walden* manuscript drafts]; a textual note is given in every case. [Page 384.]

This follows a two page discussion of why the editor 'has not regularized . . . spellings' (p. 382): 'Thoreau was largely indifferent to any choice between acceptable variant spellings' (p. 383). Thoreau's indifference and the needs of the modern reader accordingly result in the following modernizations (or are they regularizations? or both?): 'Bramins' to 'Brahmins' (4.19); 'dervis' to 'dervish' (135.31); 'crums' to 'crumbs' (225.28); and 'leger' to 'ledger' (279.27). And in the textual notes the reader of this 'unmodernized' text is in for even more surprises. I will simply quote one textual note:

> 46.34 caraway: It is thus in Bailey, Johnson, Walker, and N. Webster [the eighteenth and nineteenth century dictionaries which Shanley uses as standard references], and there is no separate entry of "carroway" [the copy-text's spelling] as a variant in the OED which does give "carrowayes" as an old variant in the entry "caraway." Here, as in the case of "Ranz" (158.18), "gerbille" (232.23), and "furring" (330.26), the editor has chosen to print the form of the word that will allow the ordinary reader to determine its meaning by reference to the dictionaries of Thoreau's day and the present. The textual variants and these notes will serve the historians of the language.

What seems to be going on here, to borrow a phrase from traditional moralists, is the divorce of the head from the heart. Shanley, however dimly, seems to know that modernization, for either the ordinary reader or the people who will actually examine his editorial practice, is a no-no. Thus the declaration of 'unmodernized'. Yet he cannot resist the feeling that something must be done for the Thoreau of 1971 and those ordinary people who keep reading *Walden*. In his note explaining his emendation of 'Bramins' to 'Brahmins' (4.19) this trait even more dramatically manifests itself. Shanley admits that, 'The form without the "h" may possibly be found today'; but he then goes on to note that it is not recorded in Webster's *Second* or *Third International Dictionary*, nor in a 1969 American dictionary, nor in two others published in 1966. One would not mind learning this from Shanley: it is an interesting fact. But Shanley is using this fact as a justification for his emendation; and that is simply not legitimate in an edition which terms itself 'unmodernized'.

The head-heart dilemma, however, results in far more serious distortions in Shanley's *Walden* when the question of choosing a copy-text arises. Shanley tells us in his first footnote of the 'Textual Introduction' that he has read the most commonly-accepted statements on copy-text theory (p. 380, n. 2). It is thus only fair to assume that he knows how modern editors should approach the problem. And yet his nineteenth-century editorial instincts work at odds with this knowledge. Rather than accept and employ the notion of copy-text choice based upon proximity to fair copy, Shanley gravitates toward a more 'final' version of the text containing Thoreau's corrections — and thus, so the story goes, a version of the text which more fully embodies Thoreau's intentions. Because Thoreau read *Walden* page proofs, because he corrected page proofs, Shanley reasons, those corrected page proofs most fully reflect all of his intentions for the book. With his 'final intentions' blinders firmly in place Shanley consequently directs his focus away from the text that an editor would presumably want to 'reconstruct' ('The text presented here is an unmodernized reconstruction' [p. 379].) That text is the lost fair copy which served as printer's copy, which a scholarly editor would want to recover and then modify in light of the author's *later* revisions and corrections. But Shanley's blinders will not allow him to see this clearly. Rather than choose his copy-text on the basis of proximity and then emend to include later authorial alterations, he uses a standard of apparent finality. He accordingly ends up emending a version of the text two stages removed from the lost fair copy.

The history of *Walden*'s textual transmission is as follows. By 1854 Thoreau had taken his text through seven stages in manuscript, the greater part of which is now preserved at the Huntington Library (HM 924). In the winter of 1854 he began transcribing version seven to a fair copy state, adding his final revisions. While he was writing against the press, sending his fair copy in sections to Ticknor and Fields, that house was sending him installments of page proof (HM 925) for correction. He corrected and returned the proofs and the majority of corrections, by Thoreau and the printer, were made before plating. The first edition was published on 9 August 1854. Diagrammed, the stemma of *Walden* through the first edition appears thus:

MANUSCRIPT VERSION SEVEN

FAIR COPY MANUSCRIPT (now lost)

PAGE PROOFS

CORRECTED PAGE PROOFS

FIRST EDITION PUBLICATION

With the fair copy missing, there are two approaches to copy-text choice one might consider, provided he is not hung-up on final intentions and can see clearly. Uncorrected page proofs is a most obvious first choice. But one might also try working with version seven, Thoreau's final working draft. The decision one might reach in this matter would depend upon an exhaustive analysis of the differences between the uncorrected page proof readings and those of the manuscript. Substantive differences would be of key concern since *someone* altered, added, and deleted substantive readings at *some* undetermined stage(s) between version seven and uncorrected page proofs. But most important — since copy-text choice depends upon a desire to retain the author's accidental traits — accidental differences would constitute the paramount consideration. Which version of the text gives a truer reflection of Thoreau's accidental idiosyncracies in the lost fair copy? That is the cardinal question to answer before the actual editing of *Walden* can begin.

I am afraid that no ready answer can be given here. For no one has yet performed the kind of analysis that would necessarily precede copy-text choice. This is a main reason for my earlier insistence that Shanley and Harding should have waited, and worked, longer before editing *Walden.* All of the data has simply not been collected, much less analyzed in depth, so far as I know. Version seven *is* close to the page proof version of the text. And it appears to have been the copy against which Thoreau read page proofs, when he did have occasion to check peculiar page proof readings. (There is no evidence to suggest that the fair copy was returned to Thoreau with the instalments of page proof.) But in the Princeton *Walden* the issue is merely side-stepped. Shanley does this in two ways. First, he keeps his discussion of the manuscript to an absolute minimum by repeatedly directing his reader's attention to his 1957 study of the seven versions, *The Making of 'Walden'.*[2] Unfortunately, *The Making of Walden* is not equal to the demands Shanley makes of it. It is a remarkable general study of how Thoreau developed his masterpiece; one gets a fine general idea of what happened; but it is too general in its analysis, and too limited in terms of the *examples* it presents, to be of significant aid to the editor of *Walden* or the reader of the Princeton edition.

The second way in which the editor absolves himself from the task of giving full attention to the manuscript is by a blunt declaration of its inability to merit consideration as copy-text:

The latest extant version of *Walden* in Thoreau's handwriting is version VII in 924, but it could not possibly serve as copy-text. It consists of pages written at various times over the course of eight years, 1846–54; interlineations and cancellations abound; some pages are missing. Further, when Thoreau wrote his copy for the printer he extensively revised phrases, sentences, and paragraphs, omitted and added material, and reordered material;[3] the result was a new (the eighth) version of *Walden*. [Page 380.]

The superscript '3' refers the reader to 'specific examples' in *The Making of Walden*. But, really, can a few examples suffice to disavow the prevailing theory of copy-text? Moreover, were these changes, and every other unspecified difference between version seven and the page proof text definitely made by Thoreau? Thoreau certainly did alter his text when readying fair copy; but just as certainly Ticknor and Field's editor, and their printer's compositors, introduced alterations of their own. Which are which? Shanley does not trouble to answer such questions. Here, and in *The Making of Walden,* he blandly takes it for granted that the differences between version seven and page proof result from Thoreau's revision, except for instances of compositorial misreading and compositional error.

Or, perhaps Shanley assumes that, since the fair copy is lost, we'll

[2] Chicago: University of Chicago Press, 1957.

never know for a certainty who was responsible for the differences. And so he gives up on the problem. But it is an editor's job to have to live sometimes with uncertainties and, in full awareness of them, to do the best he can, as Moldenhauer did with 'The Allegash and East Branch.' None of the reasons Shanley gives to support his claim that version seven 'could not possibly serve as copy-text' seems valid to me at present. None lets him off the hook of at least publically giving full consideration to the possibility, for version seven is simply not in so bad a condition as he suggests. Barring some gaps, a typed transcription of it can be made and employed for the investigatory work I have described. At least this is what Ronald E. Clapper clearly indicated in his 1967 dissertation, 'The Development of *Walden:* A Genetic Text', which Shanley never even mentions.[3] Clapper listed all of the variants between the 1906 Houghton Mifflin *Walden* (let this pass for the moment) and the seven manuscript versions; and in his 'Introduction' he declared that, 'For anyone with the desire and fortitude, the Genetic Text will enable him to construct the complete text of the manuscript at any one of its seven stages (except where leaves are missing from the manuscript) by referring to the footnotes in connection with the [1906 *Walden*] running text' (p. 5). One would never imagine that such is the situation after reading Shanley; at least I would not. But a transcript can be made. And before the next editor of *Walden* applies for a CEAA seal he must make such a transcript in order to determine if that last extant manuscript draft *can* bring us closer to Thoreau's accidentals — and therefore merits serious consideration as copy-text. If it cannot, the next editor of *Walden* ought to give a more convincing account of the reasons than Shanley provides: if he collates the manuscript against the page proofs he will be able to.

About uncorrected page proofs as a copy-text possibility there need be no uncertainty. If version seven is someday demonstrated by a competent textualist to be inadequate as a copy-text, uncorrected page proofs would be it. The choice is so obviously necessary that in any context other than a review of the Princeton Thoreau edition it would be silly to labor the point. The corrected page proofs contain two versions of *Walden:* one in the proofs before they were corrected, the other in the proofs afterwards. One was anterior to the other; one was closer to the lost fair copy not only in time but also in the priority of its readings, insofar as many of Thoreau's 'corrections' seem to be final

[3] Ph.D. dissertation, University of California at Los Angeles, 1967.

'revisions', as Shanley himself admits (p. 387). With this copy-text an editor would emend to include corrections of demonstrable printer's errors and Thoreau's alterations in the corrected version of page proofs. He would also evaluate each correction made on page proofs by Ticknor and Fields to determine if they coincide with Thoreau's probable intentions. Version seven, as well as Thoreau's other writings of the period, would be closely examined to determine instances of probable interference with the accidentals of the *Walden* fair copy. Emendations would also be derived from Thoreau's personally-marked copy of the first edition (at the Abernethy Library). What one simply must not do is what Shanley did: to leap over the manuscript and uncorrected page proofs to corrected page proofs, and state that 'The editor chose as copy-text the corrected page proof rather than uncorrected page proof on the grounds that corrected page proof enables one to come closer to Thoreau's final intentions in regard to accidentals as well as substantives' (p. 389). Corrected page proofs do give us Thoreau's corrections and revisions, but there is no way in the world in which anyone can legitimately claim that they bring us closer to the authoritative accidental traits, in toto, of the text.

I am willing to grant to Shanley the strong probability that Thoreau approved all of the alterations made by the printer, in the printer's hand, on the page proofs. (They are briefly discussed on pp. 384–92.) I recognize the fact that Thoreau did not stamp his feet, tear up the page proofs, and demand the return of his manuscript because of editorial and compositorial tampering. But 'final intentions' in regard to accidentals are not the primary concern here. Again, the real question is, what were the accidental features of the lost fair copy? Final intentions are significant when one emends a copy-text; the intentions expressed in printer's copy are what count before emending, when copy-text is chosen. And only someone especially naive in regard to the licenses assumed by editors and compositors, in Thoreau's time and our own, would hazard the presumption that page proofs represent faithful translations of Thoreau's accidentals into print. To presume this results in a distortion of what most certainly happened after Thoreau submitted his fair copy.

A future editor of *Walden* should do what Shanley did not do before choosing a copy-text: imaginatively reconstruct Thoreau's position as an author in 1854. Here was a fellow whose first book was an absolute bomb, and whose few periodical publications must have seemed ephemeral to any commercial publisher. He somehow wrangled a publishing commitment from Ticknor and Fields. And who was holding all of the cards? Certainly not this little known author of a 'Life In The Woods'. Thoreau died a relatively uncelebrated writer; and in 1854 he was far from the peak of what fame he did enjoy. In light of this construct it seems reasonable to assume that the editors and compositors of *Walden* would not balk at 'helping' the author along, at 'improving' his effort. Who would doubt that, at the very least, the people at Ticknor and Fields changed some punctuation and spellings? That was, and is, an editor's job; and it was part of a good compositor's job to correct a manuscript's variances from 'acceptable' usage. In short, the *Walden* of the page proofs was undoubtedly a collaborative effort, and Thoreau most probably did not hold the upper hand in the relationship. Moreover, Thoreau was rushed twice: as he prepared fair copy against a deadline, and later as he read proof without his fair copy before him. And he was not an especially proficient proofreader. Thus the fact that he read, corrected, revised, and noted printer's marks on the page proofs is not especially impressive. I am sure that Thoreau's book was not butchered in Boston; but I am equally sure that the page proofs were not verbatim transcriptions of the fair copy, particularly in regard to accidentals. Even without reference to Greg's theory of copy-text, or any theory at all, it seems manifestly evident that, because of the conditions I have attempted to picture, a critical editor of *Walden* must get as close as possible to that lost fair copy. Uncorrected page proof is as close as we can come now without more data on version seven; and even with the proofs we may presume that we are a good distance from Thoreau's accidentals.

Although Shanley seems more or less oblivious to the problem, I am not the first person to raise the terribly important question of what happened between the fair copy and page proof stages of transmission. A year before the publication of the Princeton *Walden* Philip Van Doren Stern mused over the subject in *The Annotated Walden,* a volume which, like Clapper's dissertation, Shanley does not mention.[4] A few selected statements by Stern will suffice to illustrate his healthy focus:

A comparison of the existing manuscript with page proofs shows that Thoreau's paragraphs were much shorter when he wrote them than they are as they appear in print. It is just possible that he consolidated them on the missing final draft for the printer, but it seems much more likely that some unknown person — probably a Ticknor and Fields editor — ran them together

[4] New York: Clarkson N. Potter, Inc., 1970.

until they became very long. Some go on for pages and make the unbroken text look unnecessarily forbidding.

This brings us to one of the greatest mysteries about *Walden*. Why did Thoreau cancel many thousands of words in the original manuscript?

The heavy hand of an editor or a printer can be seen in certain alterations of Thoreau's original copy as it was transferred from the manuscript to the printed page. This forgotten purist was responsible for putting words that might be considered slang in quotation marks. . . . This too-zealous corrector also wrote out Thoreau's Arabic numerals. . . . This has been done throughout the book.

Who decided what was to be changed or eliminated — Thoreau, his friends in Concord, some forgotten editor at Ticknor and Fields, or the compositor who set the type? Thoreau most probably made most of the decisions, for he was stubborn about permitting changes, as his dealings with other publishers reveal. [Pages 30–34.]

Stern's claim for Thoreau's authorial stubbornness is presumably based on one dramatic instance: James Russell Lowell's unauthorized deletion of the famous pine tree passage in 'Chesuncook', to which Thoreau reacted vitriolically. Stern, I believe, is exaggerating a bit here. But the man is on the right track. He raises the kinds of questions that Shanley glosses over, to the ruin of the Princeton *Walden*. The result is that we must still ask, what did Thoreau write? — the one question that a CEAA volume is funded to answer. Virtually ignoring version seven, passing by the uncorrected page proofs, and finally settling down on the corrected page proofs, Shanley leads us not only away from an answer but also away from the subordinate question that will reveal it someday. One wonders why he simply did not go on to use the first edition as copy-text. Then he would have the cosmetic, rather than critical, edition he almost fully achieved in the Princeton *Walden*.

What is to be learned from the failure of the Princeton *Walden*? First, it is obvious that a good deal of research is necessary before a critical edition of *Walden* worthy of the CEAA seal can be produced. A full collation of the page proofs and manuscript version seven should be published and the differences between the two versions thoroughly studied. The same treatment should also be afforded the two versions of the text in the corrected page proofs. The possibility of version seven being a viable copy-text choice demands long and hard discussion. If it proves inadequate to the task, a copy-text must be chosen with the aim of recovering Thoreau's accidentals, and not on the basis of 'final intentions': that is, uncorrected page proofs must then serve as the copy-text. If that copy-text is employed, it must be emended not only in the clear light of the three subsequent relevant forms of the text (corrected proofs, the first-edition text, and Thoreau's marked copy of the first edition) but in the even clearer light of version seven's accidentals so as to eliminate editorial and compositorial interference. In short, the Princeton *Walden* offers the valuable lesson of how *not* to edit *Walden*.

What the CEAA can learn from this unfortunate episode in its uneven history is to move more cautiously. Its vettors cannot be expected to be as knowledgeable about all of the particulars of each volume they examine as the editors who produce the volume. But — really — modernization of accidentals can scarcely escape notice. The vettors can also ask for more information when an editor claims that a very lengthy manuscript cannot 'possibly serve as copy-text.' And they can try harder to explain to an editor the kinds of textual tampering that regularly occur in editorial offices and print shops. It should also learn that 'seals' should not be awarded on the basis of majority rule. As I understand it, James B. Meriwether, the vettor originally assigned to *Walden*, rendered a negative judgment. This was, so Meriwether tells me, mainly because he suggested that if corrected page proofs simply *had* to serve as copy-text then the editor should at least provide a table listing all of the alterations made in the uncorrected proofs by Thoreau and the printer. The CEAA's *Statement of Editorial Principles* (p. 8) dictates such a table in a situation such as *Walden:*

Cancellations in pre-copy-text forms will normally be fully reported. Justifiable exceptions to this principle have developed and may develop in the future, but each case will probably prove unique in a number of respects and will have to be judged on its own merits.

There is nothing unique about the *Walden* problem, and none of the examples of exceptional cases described by the *Statement* apply. Shanley cannot argue that Thoreau paid such close attention to his accidentals and substantives when correcting page proofs and revised to such an extent that he created a new state of the text, thus making the uncorrected page proof readings unworthy of a full report. They *are* relevant; and Shanley should have made them available to his reader, just as Moldenhauer presented what he took to be pre-copy-text variants in the 'Ktaadn' situation. (Didn't these Thoreauvians ever get together to talk over such matters?) Shanley did not. And two other vettors were called in to break the deadlock. G. Thomas Tanselle and William H. Gilman voted in Shanley's favor and the CEAA 'seal' was awarded. This does not strike me as a proper procedure, especially when it involves certifying the disposition of my federal tax dollars. Meriwether was right; Shanley should have been obliged to redo his edition. Now someone else will have to.

The Maine Woods, then, needs a bit of patch-work before it can be termed a first-rate volume. *Walden,* one of the finest creations by an American writer, deserves the years of textual work that still must come. The Writings of Henry D. Thoreau has not made an especially fine beginning. But under the guidance of a new general editor, lost ground (as well as Thoreau's intentions) can be recovered. Achievements can be made. Hopefully the worst is over.

THE REGISTER OF
CURRENT PUBLICATIONS: 1974

THOMAS A. TENNEY

THE REGISTER OF CURRENT PUBLICATIONS IS A SELECTIVE RECORD OF in-print, separately published works — books, monographs, and pamphlets — judged of interest in the field of bibliographical and textual studies. Works for inclusion in the Register need not have been published in the current year, but they must be in print then. Only works that have been submitted by their publishers to *Proof* for examination by the compiler will be included. Works entered in the Register may be reviewed at length in *Proof,* and normally only those works will be selected for review.

   Entries in the Register are descriptive, not evaluative. They are arranged in thirteen areas, with each book listed only in its *major* area of interest. Since many works are useful in more than one area, users of the Register are urged to scan related areas when searching for a particular kind of work. Authors and titles of registered works are included in the volume index to *Proof,* but this is a *register* of publications, not a cross-referenced enumerative bibliography.

Each of the following subject areas into which the Register is subdivided includes facsimile reprints, except for the first group — Edited Primary Works — which are original editions prepared according to a textual theory.

1. Edited Primary Works
2. Reprinted Primary Works
3. Author Bibliographies and Checklists
4. Subject Bibliographies and Checklists
5. National Bibliographies and Checklists
6. Writing and Autographs
7. Printing, Binding, Publishing, and Bookselling
8. Copyright and Intellectual Property
9. Libraries and Book Collecting
10. Bibliographical and Textual Theory and Practice
11. Concordances and Indexes
12. Dictionaries, Rhetorics, and Guides to Language
13. Miscellaneous

1. EDITED PRIMARY WORKS

BRANDEIS, LOUIS D.

Letters of Louis D. Brandeis, ed. Melvin I. Urofsky and David W. Levy. 3 vols. Albany, N.Y.: State University of New York Press, 1971–1973. Vol. I, 1971: *(1870–1907): Urban Reformer.* xliv, 610 pp. (inc. frontis., plus 8 pp. illus.). $20.00. ISBN 0–87395–078–X (clothbound), 0–87395–178–6 (microfiche). LC 73–129640. Contents: Illustrations; Editorial Foreword and Acknowledgements; Introduction; Note on Volume I; Chronology, 1856–1907; Key to Letter Source Citations; Editorial Markings; Letters of Louis D. Brandeis, 1870–1907; Index. Vol. II, 1972: *(1907–1912): People's Attorney.* xxvi [xxiv], 750 pp. (inc. frontis., plus 8 pp. illus.). $20.00. ISBN 0–87395–091–7 (clothbound), 0–87395–191–3 (microfiche). LC 73–129640. Contents: Illustrations; Acknowledgements; Note on Volume II; Chronology, 1907–1912; Key to Letter Source Citations; Editorial Markings; Letters of Louis D. Brandeis, 1907–1912; Index. Vol. III, 1973: *(1913–1915): Progressivist and Zionist.* xxiv, 705 pp. (incl. frontis., plus 8 pp. illus.). $20.00. LC 73–129640. Contents: Illustrations; Acknowledgements; Note on Volume III; Chronology, 1913–1915; Key to Letter Source Citations; Editorial Markings; Letters of Louis D. Brandeis, 1913–1915; Index.

CALHOUN, JOHN C.

The Papers of John C. Calhoun. Vol. VII, 1822–1823. Ed. W. Edwin Hemphill. Columbia: University of South Carolina Press, 1973. liv, 609 pp. (plus frontis.). $20.00. ISBN 0–87249–288–5. LC 59–10351. Contents: Preface; Introduction; The Papers of John C. Calhoun; Symbols; Bibliography; Index.

EMERSON, RALPH WALDO

The Early Lectures of Ralph Waldo Emerson. Vol. I: 1833–1836. Edited by Stephen E. Whicher and Robert E. Spiller. Cambridge, Mass: The Belknap Press of Harvard University Press, 1966. xxx, 545 pp. (plus 8 pp. illus.). $18.50. LC 59–5160. The copy-texts were manuscripts. Contents: [Preface]; Introduction; I, Science (1, The Uses of Natural History; 2, On the Relation of Man to the Globe; 3, Water; 4, The Naturalist); II, Italy (Excerpts); III, Biography (1, Introduction; 2, Michel Angelo Buonaroti; 3, Martin Luther; 4, John Milton; 5, George Fox; 6, Edmund Burke); IV, English Literature (On the Best Mode of Inspiring a Correct Taste in English Literature; 1, English Literature: Introductory; 2, Permanent Traits of the English National Genius; 3, The Age of Fable; 4, Chaucer; 5, Shakspear [first lecture]; 6, Shakspear [second lecture]; 7, Lord Bacon; 8, Ben Jonson, Herrick, Herbert, Wotton; 9, Ethical Writers; 10, Modern Aspects of Letters); Bibliography of Principal Sources; Textual Notes and Variant Passages; Index.

FRANKLIN, BENJAMIN

The Papers of Benjamin Franklin. Volume 17, January 1 through December 31, 1770. Edited by William B. Willcox. New Haven and London: Yale University Press, 1973. ii, xxxii, 430 pp. (inc. frontis., 3 pp. illus., plus 1 p. illus.). $17.50. ISBN 0–300–

01596–8. LC 59–12697. Contents: List of Illustrations; Contributors to Volume 17; Method of Textual Reproduction; Abbreviations and Short Titles; Introduction; Chronology; [The Papers of Benjamin Franklin, January 1 through December 31, 1770; Index.]

LARDNER, RING

Caruthers, Clifford M., ed. *Ring Around Max: The Correspondence of Ring Lardner and Max Perkins.* DeKalb, Ill.: Northern Illinois University Press, [1973]. xxiv, 192 pp. (inc. 5 pp. illus.). $8.50 cloth, $5.00 paper. ISBN 0–87580–041–6 (0–87580–512–4, paper). LC 72–6919. Contents: Preface; Foreword; Correspondence; Afterword by F. Scott Fitzgerald ['from *The New Republic,* 11 October 1933, pp. 254–55']; Chronological Listing; Index.

PERKINS, MAXWELL

See Lardner, Ring, *Ring Around Max: The Correspondence of Ring Lardner and Max Perkins,* ed. by Clifford M. Caruthers.

REYNOLDS, JOHN HAMILTON

The Letters of John Hamilton Reynolds. Edited with an Introduction by Leonidas M. Jones. Lincoln: University of Nebraska Press, [1973]. xl, 82 pp. $8.50. ISBN 0–8032–0827–8. LC 72–90342. Contents: List of Abbreviations and Common Shortened References; Introduction; List of Letters; The Letters of John Hamilton Reynolds; Appendix; Index.

TENNYSON, ALFRED TENNYSON, BARON

Pfordresher, John (ed.). *A Variorum Edition of Tennyson's* Idylls of the King. New York and London: Columbia University Press, 1973. xxxiv, 1007 pp. $25.00. ISBN 0–231–03691–4. LC 73–4852. Contents: 1, How to Use This Book; 2, Alphabetical Key to Library Abbreviation Symbols; 3, Chronological Key to Printed Editions; 4, Introduction; 5, Some Early Notes on

Arthurian Legend; 6, A Discarded Idylls Passage; 7, Title Pages; VARIANTS: 8, Dedication; 9, The Coming of Arthur; 10, Gareth and Lynette; 11, The Marriage of Geraint; 12, Geraint and Enid; 13, Balin and Balan; 14, Merlin and Vivien; 15, Lancelot and Elaine; 16, The Holy Grail; 17, Pelleas and Etarre; 18, The Last Tournament; 19, Guinevere; 20, The Passing of Arthur; 21, Epilogue — To the Queen.

2. REPRINTED PRIMARY WORKS

BELKNAP, JEREMY

The Foresters, An American Tale. A Facsimile Reproduction with an Introduction by Lewis A. Turlish. Gainesville, Fla.: Scholars' Facsimiles & Reprints, 1969. xiv, 216 pp. $10.00. SBN 8201–1071–X. LC 71–100127. Facsimile of Boston: I. Thomas and E. T. Andrews, 1792. [Contents: Introduction; *The Foresters, An American Tale: Being a Sequel to the History of John Bull the Clothier. In a Series of Letters to a Friend.*]

CHANNING, WILLIAM ELLERY

The Collected Poems of William Ellery Channing the Younger, 1817–1901. Facsimile Reproductions Edited with an Introduction by Walter Harding. Gainesville, Fla.: Scholars' Facsimiles & Reprints, 1967. xxii, viii, 1026 pp. (inc. frontis.). $25.00. LC 67–21749. 'I have tried to include in this volume every poem of Channing's that has reached print. My basic texts are of course the seven volumes published during his lifetime . . . reproduced in exact facsimile and in chronological order. . . . followed by the texts of his uncollected poems presented in their chronological order of publication, and again, where possible, reproduced in facsimile.' (Page xx.) Contents: Introduction; *Poems* (1843); *Poems: Second Series* (1847); *The Woodman and Other Poems* (1849); *Near Home* (1858); *The Wanderer* (1871); *Eliot* (1885); *John Brown, and the Heroes of Harper's Ferry* (1886); Uncollected Poems; Index of Titles; Index of First Lines.

CRANCH, CHRISTOPHER PEARSE

DeFalco, Joseph M., ed. and intro. *Collected Poems of Christopher Pearse Cranch.* Facsimile Reproductions Edited with an Introduction and Index. Gainesville, Fla.: Scholars' Facsimiles & Reprints, 1971. xx, xii, 710 pp. (inc. 1 p. advertisement, 1 p. inscription by Cranch). $35.00. ISBN 0–8201–1091–4. LC 70–161930. Contents: Introduction; The Bird and the Bell, With Other Poems; Ariel and Caliban, With Other Poems; Poems (1844); A Poem Delivered in the First Congregational Church in the Town of Quincy, May 25, 1840. Note: There is no index in the volume.

DAVIES, SAMUEL

Collected Poems of Samuel Davies. Facsimile Reproductions, edited with an Introduction and Notes by Richard Beale Davis. Gainesville, Fla.: Scholars' Facsimiles & Reprints, 1968. xvi, xiv, 248 pp. (inc. frontis., 1 p. illus.). $12.50. LC 68–17019. Contents: Introduction; *Miscellaneous Poems, Chiefly on Divine Subjects;* The Appendix: Devout Ejaculations and Soliloquies; Uncollected Poems; Poems Ascribed to Davies; Notes.

DICKINSON, EMILY

Poems (1890–1896). A Facsimile Reproduction of the Original Volumes issued in 1890, 1891, and 1896, with an Introduction by George Monteiro. Gainesville, Fla.: Scholars' Facsimiles & Reprints, 1967. Three Volumes in One. xxii, 600 pp. [numbered 596] (inc. 4 pp. illus.). $20.00. LC 67–25640. Facsimiles of Boston: Roberts Brothers, 1890; Boston: Roberts Brothers, 1891; Boston: Roberts Brothers, 1896. Contents: Introduction; *Poems,* 1890; *Poems,* Second Series, 1891; *Poems,* Third Series, 1896.

DWIGHT, TIMOTHY

The Major Poems of Timothy Dwight (1752–1817) with A Dissertation on the History, Eloquence, and Poetry of the Bible. Facsimile Reproductions with an Introduction by William J. McTaggart and

William K. Bottorff. Gainesville, Fla.: Scholars' Facsimiles & Reprints, 1969. xvi, 558 pp. $20.00. SBN 8201–1059–0. LC 68–24207. Contents: Introduction; America: or, A Poem on the Settlement of the British Colonies; The Conquest of Canaan; The Triumph of Infidelity; Greenfield Hill; A Dissertation on the History, Eloquence, Poetry of the Bible.

GALLAGHER, WILLIAM D., ET AL.

Selections from the Poetical Literature of the West. Edited by William D. Gallagher. A Facsimile Reproduction with an Introduction by John T. Flanagan. Gainesville, Fla.: Scholars' Facsimiles & Reprints, 1968. xx, 264 pp. $10.00. LC 68–29083. Facsimile of Cincinatti: U. P. James, 1841. [Contents: Introduction; Text.]

HOWELLS, WILLIAM DEAN

Annie Kilburn: A Novel. St. Clair Shores, Mich.: Scholarly Press, Inc., 1972. [ii], 331 pp. $19.50. ISBN 0–403–01033–0. Facsimile of New York: Harper & Brothers, 1891.

REED, SAMPSON

Observations on the Growth of the Mind; with Remarks on Some Other Subjects. A Facsimile Reproduction with an Introduction by Carl F. Strauch. Gainesville, Fla.: Scholars' Facsimiles & Reprints, 1970. xvi, [ii], viii, 192 pp. $10.00. SBN 8201–1070–1. LC 78–100126. Facsimile of Boston: Otis Clapp, 1838. [Contents: Introduction; *Observations on the Growth of The Mind; with Remarks on Some Other Subjects.*]

SILLIMAN, BENJAMIN

Letters of Shahcoolin. Intro. by Ben Harris McClary. Gainesville, Fla.: Scholars' Facsimiles & Reprints, 1962. xxii, 152 pp. $6.00. LC 62–7013. Facsimile of Boston: Russell and Cutler, 1802. [Contents: Introduction; Text].

STOWE, HARRIET BEECHER

Annie Fields, ed. *Life and Letters of Harriet Beecher Stowe.* Detroit: Gale Research Company, 1970. [vii], 406 pp. $12.50. LC 77–102057. Facsimile of Boston: Houghton, Mifflin and Company, 1897.

TANEYHILL, RICHARD H.

The Leatherwood God (1869–70). A Source of William Dean Howells's Novel of the Same Name, In Two Versions. Facsimile Reproductions, with an Introduction by George Kummer. Gainesville, Fla.: Scholars' Facsimiles & Reprints, 1966. xvi, 86 pp. $5.00. LC 66–11025. Contents: Introduction; *The Leatherwood God* by R. H. Taneyhill (Cincinnati, Ohio: R. Clarke & Co., 1870); *"The Leatherwood God"* by R. King Bennett (Reprinted from *The Barnesville Enterprise* in *The Guernsey County Jeffersonian,* December 9, 1867; December 23, 1869; January 6, 1870).

TYLER, ROYALL

The Algerine Captive; or, The Life and Adventures of Doctor Updike Underhill, Six Years a Prisoner Among the Algerines. (1797). A Facsimile Reproduction of the London Edition of 1802 with an Introduction by Jack B. Moore. Gainesville, Fla.: Scholars' Facsimiles & Reprints, 1967. Two Volumes in One. xviii; Vol. I: xxiv, 190 pp.; Vol. II: xii, 228 pp. $15.00. LC 67–10272. Facsimile of London: G. and J. Robinson, 1802. [Contents: Introduction; Text.]

3. AUTHOR BIBLIOGRAPHIES AND CHECKLISTS

BERRYMAN, JOHN

Kelly, Richard J., comp. *John Berryman: A Checklist.* Metuchen, N.J.: The Scarecrow Press, Inc., 1972. xxxviii, 105 pp. (inc. 1 p. illus.). $5.00. ISBN 0–8108–0552–9. LC 72–8187. The Scarecrow Author Bibliography Series, No. 8. Contents: Preface;

Foreword: In Loving Memory of the Late Author of "The Dream Songs," by William Meredith; Introduction: The Epistemology of Loss, by Michael Berryhill; Chronology; I, Works by John Berryman; II, Works about John Berryman; Addenda; III. Indexes.

COZZENS, JAMES GOULD

Meriwether, James B., comp.; intro. by James Gould Cozzens. *James Gould Cozzens: A Checklist.* Detroit: Gale Research Company, [1972]. viii, 87 pp. (inc. frontis., 30 pp. illus.). $8.50. [Contents: Introduction; Compiler's Forward; Books; Contributions to Books and Pamphlets; Short Stories in Periodicals; Other Prose in Periodicals; Poems; Published Letters.]

DICKEY, JAMES

Ashley, Franklin, comp.; intro. by James Dickey. *James Dickey: A Checklist.* Detroit: Gale Research Company, 1972. xvi, 98 pp. (inc. frontis., 17 pp. illus.). $11.00. [Contents: Compiler's Note; Introduction by James Dickey; National Book Award in Poetry, 1966 Acceptance Speech; Books; First Book Appearances; Poems; Stories; Articles and Essays; Reviews by James Dickey; Interviews; Public Letters; Unclassified Separate Publications.]

DREISER, THEODORE

Salzman, Jack, ed. *Theodore Dreiser: The Critical Reception.* New York: David Lewis, 1972. xxxviii, 741 pp. (inc. 24 pp. illus.). $17.50. LC 73–78882. The American Critical Tradition. Contents: [General Editor's Preface; Contents; Introduction]; 1, Sister Carrie (1900); 2, Jennie Gerhardt (1911); 3, The Financier (1912); 4, A Traveler at Forty (1913); 5, The Titan (1914); 6, The "Genius" (1915); 7, Plays of the Natural and The Supernatural (1916); 8, A Hoosier Holiday (1916); 9, Free and Other Stories (1918); 10, Twelve Men (1919); 11, The Hand of the Potter (1918); 12, Hey Rub-a-Dub-Dub (1920); 13, A Book About Myself (1922); 14, The Color of a Great City (1923); 15, An American Tragedy (1925); 16, Chains (1927);

17, Moods, Cadenced and Declaimed (1928); 18, Dreiser Looks at Russia (1928); 19, A Gallery of Women (1929); 20, Dawn (1931); 21, Tragic America (1931); 22, America Is Worth Saving (1941); 23, The Bulwark (1946); 24, The Stoic (1947); Index.

GILL, ERIC

Peace, David, comp. *Addendum and Corrigenda to The Inscriptional Work of Eric Gill.* San Francisco: The Brick Row Book Shop, 1972. 38 pp. (plus gatefold). $10.00. Contents: [Preface; Introduction; Text]. *Note:* Accompanied by a one-page errata slip.

HAWTHORNE, NATHANIEL

Ricks, Beatrice, Joseph D. Adams, and Jack O. Hazlerig, comps. *Nathaniel Hawthorne: A Reference Bibliography 1900–1971. With Selected Reference Materials.* Boston: G. K. Hall & Co., 1972. viii, 337 pp. ISBN 0–8161–1021–2. LC 72–6535.$ Contents: [Preface]; Masterlist of Bibliographic Entries; Subject Index; Table of Abbreviations and Publications. 'A Few brief annotations have been inserted to indicate the area of study. Explication or critiques have not been offered. . . . Works whose titles reveal their subject matter, and works which have earned reputations as standard critical texts in Hawthorne scholarship are entered without comment. . . . Hawthorne's own writings, chronologically arranged, are divided into representative *Complete Collections;* representative *Partial Collections; Diaries, Letters, Notebooks; Romances, Collected Stories, Biography.* (Pages iii, iv).

LESSING, DORIS

Burkom, Selma R., and Margaret Williams. *Doris Lessing: A Checklist of Primary and Secondary Sources.* Troy N.Y.: The Whitston Publishing Company, Incorporated, 1973. x, 88 pp. $7.50. ISBN 0–87875–039–8. LC 72–87109. Contents: I, Works by Lessing; II, Criticism of Lessing's Works; Index. 'It will be noted that several items are not complete. These are entries which I have been unable to personally verify. They were cited in Dorothy Brewster's *Doris Lessing* (Twayne, 1965); I include them out of respect for that writer's scholarship.' (Page ii.)

MELVILLE, HERMAN

Ricks, Beatrice, and Joseph D. Adams, comps. *Herman Melville: A Reference Bibliography 1900–1972. With Selected Nineteenth Century Materials.* Boston: G. K. Hall & Co., 1973. xxvi, 532 pp. ISBN 0–8161–1036–0. LC 72–14197. $18.00. Contents: [Preface]; Table of Abbreviations and Publications; Masterlist of Bibliographic Entries (A., S. P. — Meldrum, Barbara ([entries 1–1730]); Melville, Herman ([entries 1731–2115.2]): Representative Complete Editions; Representative Partial Collections; Journals; Letters; Poetry; Reviews by Melville and Miscellaneous Pieces; Melville's Prose Writings; Menard, William — Zolla, Elémira ([entries 2116–3167]); Subject Index. 'The bibliography is comprised of two parts: a masterlist of bibliographic items, alphabetically arranged, the items consecutively numbered; and an index where references are numerically listed under works and various topics. . . . No attempt has been made to evaluate the critic's thought; the aim has been to bring together the bulk of scholarship directed toward Melville study. Brief annotations have been inserted to indicate the principal areas of study, or pertinent issues raised.' (Page v.)

ROETHKE, THEODORE

McLeod, James Richard. *Theodore Roethke: A Bibliography.* [Kent, Ohio]: The Kent State University Press, [1973]. xliv, 241 pp. $8.00. ISBN 0–87338–100–9. LC 72–158715. The Serif Series: Bibliographies and Checklists, Number 27. Contents: Introduction; Acknowledgements; Abbreviations; Biographical Notes; Awards, Memorials, Reminiscences, Tributes; I, Works and Materials by Theodore Roethke; II, Works and Materials about Theodore Roethke; Index of Names; Index of Poems and Prose Pieces.

SINCLAIR, UPTON

Gottesman, Ronald, and Charles L. P. Silet. *The Literary Manuscripts of Upton Sinclair.* Columbus: Ohio State University Press, [1972]. xxiv, 470 pp. (plus 4 pp. illus.). $12.50. ISBN 0–8142–0169–5. LC 72–751. Calendars of Literary Manuscripts. Contents: Foreword; Preface; List of Abbreviations; A, The Literary Manuscripts of Upton Sinclair; B, A Guide to the Letters of Upton Sinclair (Sinclair Letters in the Lilly Library; Sinclair Letters in Other Institutions); C, Related Manuscripts; Indexes.

Gottesman, Ronald. *Upton Sinclair: An Annotated Checklist.* [Kent]: The Kent State University Press, [1973]. xx, 554 pp. $15.00. ISBN 0–87338–114–9. LC 72–634010. The Serif Series: Bibliographies and Checklists, Number 24. Contents: Introduction; Acknowledgments; Part I, Upton Sinclair in English; Part II, Upton Sinclair in Translation and Foreign Editions; Part III, Selected Publications about Upton Sinclair; Part IV, Supplementary Material [Compiled with the assistance of Edward Allatt]; Appendix: Chronological and Alphabetical Listings of Upton Sinclair's Major Books; Index of Proper Names.

VALLE-INCLÁN, RAMÓN DEL

Lima, Robert. *An Annotated Bibliography of Ramón del Valle-Inclán.* University Park, Pa.: The Pennsylvania State University Libraries, 1972. xii, 401 pp. (plus frontis., plus 13 pp. illus.). $5.00. The Pennsylvania State University Libraries Bibliographical Series, no. 4. Contents: Forword; Preface; Illustrations; Part I, The Works of Valle-Inclan; Part II, Studies.

VONNEGUT, KURT, JR.

Hudgens, Betty Lenhardt, comp.; intro. by Vance Bourjaily. *Kurt Vonnegut, Jr.: A Checklist.* Detroit: Gale Research Company, 1972. xvi, 67 pp. (inc. frontis., 9 pp. illus.). $8.50. [Contents: Compiler's Note; Kurt (an introduction by Vance Bourjaily); Books; First Book Publication of Stories; Stories, Short Plays, and Poetry; Articles and Public Letters; Non-Fiction Books with Contributions; Book Reviews; Blurbs; Interviews; Juvenilia; Related Material; References and Ana.]

WAUGH, EVELYN

Davis, Robert Murray, Paul A. Doyle, Heinz Kosok, and Charles E. Linck, Jr. *Evelyn Waugh: A Checklist of Primary and Secondary Material.* Troy, N.Y.: The Whitston Publishing Company, 1972. viii (numbered 'iv'), 212 pp. $12.50. ISBN 0–87875–021–5. LC 77–155725. Contents: Introduction; Works by Evelyn Waugh; Works about Evelyn Waugh; Index.

4. SUBJECT BIBLIOGRAPHIES AND CHECKLISTS

BOOKS, SPORTING

Phillips, John C. *A Bibliography of American Sporting Books: Sport, Natural History, Hunting, Dogs, Trapping, Shooting, Early American Travel, Fishing, Sporting Periodicals, Guide Books, Forestry, Conservation, &c.* Ann Arbor, Mich.: Gryphon Books, 1971. [viii], 639 pp. $27.50. LC 75–153019. Facsimile of Boston: Edward Morrill and Son, 1930. Contents: Introduction; Part I, The General Catalogue; Part II, Conservation (A, General; B, Federal Conservation; C, State Conservation; D, Conservation in Canada); Part III, Periodical Publications, Pamphlets, Etc.

DRAMA

Greg, Walter Wilson. *A List of English Plays Written Before 1643 and Printed Before 1700.* St. Clair Shores, Mich.: Scholarly Press, Inc., 1972. xii, 158 pp. ISBN 0–403–00611–2. LC 76–131724. [Contents: Introduction; Hand-List of English Plays; Addenda; I, Index of Authors; II, Index of Plays.] 'First Published in 1900. (Page ii.) Note: Original publisher and place not given.

Mikhail, E. H. *A Bibliography of Modern Irish Drama, 1899–1970.* With a foreword by William A. Armstrong. Seattle: University of Washington Press, [1972]. xii, 51 pp. $4.95. ISBN 0–295–

95229–6. LC 72–1373. Contents: *Foreword* by William A. Armstrong; *Preface;* 1, Bibliographies; 2, Books; 3, Periodicals; 4, Unpublished Material.

FILM

Bukalski, Peter J., comp. *Film Research: A Critical Bibliography with Annotations and Essay.* Boston: G. K. Hall & Co., 1972. [iv], 215 pp. $12.50 U.S.; $13.75 outside U.S. ISBN 0–8161–0971–0. LC 72–3794. Contents: I, Film Research; II, Essential Works; III, Film Rental; IV, Film Purchase; V, Film Periodicals; VI, Using the Bibliography; VII, The Major Bibliography.

IMPRINTS

Bowden, Edwin T. *The First Hundred Publications of the Humanities Research Center of the University of Texas at Austin.* [Austin: The Humanities Research Center of the University of Texas, 1971]. 56 pp. (inc. 1 p. illus.). LC 70–63–002. Contents: Introduction; A Checklist of Publications of the Humanities Research Center; List of Titles; Index of Series.

PERIODICALS

Ward, William S. *British Periodicals & Newspapers, 1789–1832: A Bibliography of Secondary Sources.* [Lexington]: The University Press of Kentucky, [1972]. xii, 387 pp. $21.00. ISBN 0–8131–1271–0. LC 74–190536. Contents: Preface; Acknowledgments; List of Abbreviations; 1, General Bibliographies and Bibliographical Studies; 2, General Studies; 3, Periodicals; 4, People (A Selection of Collected Biographies, Biographical Dictionaries, and Biographical Essays; Individuals); 5, Places; 6, Special Subjects (Journalistic: Printing, Production, etc.; Advertising; Circulation and Reading Public; Freedom of the Press; Stamp Tax; Literary: Drama and Theater; The Essay; Fiction; Poetry; Miscellaneous): Index A, Authors; Index B, Subjects; Index C, Library Catalogs and Union Lists. 'In 1953 I published an *Index and Finding List of Serials Published in the British Isles, 1789–1832.* The purpose of the present volume is to provide a bibliography of the books and articles listed in that *Index.* '(Page vii.) 'My aim has been to include only second-ary materials . . . "primary" materials such as statutes, tran-scripts or evidence in libel suits, and so on, are not, for exam-ple, included under "Freedom of the Press." Neither are casual or perfunctory accounts in books included if an abun-dance of fuller accounts seems to render them superfluous. . . . Most of the annotations are brief and are limited to iden-tifying the relevant chapters or pages of the book or article in question. In such cases they are included in the bibliographical entry itself. Longer, descriptive annotations are set below the entry.' (Page ix.)

RELIGION

Berlin, Charles (ed.). *Studies in Jewish Bibliography, History and Litera-ture in Honor of I. Edward Kiev.* New York: KTAV Publishing House, Inc., 1971. [ix], 643 pp. (inc. frontis., 71 pp. illus.). $25.00. SBN 87068–143–5. LC 70–138462. Contents: Baron, Salo W.: A Collection of Hebrew-Latin Aphorisms by a Chris-tian Hebraist; Berger, Abraham: Approaches to Rabbi Nach-man and His Tales; Berlin, Charles: A Sixteenth-Century He-brew Chronicle of the Ottoman Empire: The *Seder Eliyahu Zuta* of Elijah Capsali and its Message; Berlin, George L.: The Jew-ish Labor Committee and American Immigration Policy in the 1930's; Braude, William G.: Maimonides' Attitude to Midrash; Chiel, Arthur A.: Ezra Stiles and the Polish Rabbi; Cohen, Martin A.: The Rebellions during the Reign of David. An Inquiry into Social Dynamics in Ancient Israel; Goodman, Philip: Jewish Bookplate Literature: An Annotated Bibliogra-phy; Gottschalk, Alfred: Ahad Ha-Am as Biblical Critic: A Pro-file; Greenbaum, A. A.: Some Notes and Conclusions about the Published Totals of the Soviet Census of January 15, 1959, by Y. Kantor. Translated and Annotated by A. A. Greenbaum. Gutmann, Joseph: Jewish Ceremonial Art: A Basic Bibliogra-phy; Kabakoff, Jacob: S. B. Schwarzberg (1865–1929)—He-brew Publisher and Bibliographer; Kaganoff, Nathan M.: Sup-plement II: Judaica Americana Printed before 1851; Kisch, Guido: An Innovator of Haggadah Illustration — Cyril Kutlik; Marx, Moses: A Bibliography of Hebrew Printing in Dyhern-furth 1689–1718; Meyer, Isidore S.: The Hebrew Exercises of

Governor William Bradford; Meyer, Michael A.: Christian In-
fluence on Early German Reform Judaism; Nemoy, Leon:
Studies in the History of the Early Karasite Liturgy: The Lit-
urgy of Al-Qirqisani; Neusner, Jacob: Some Early Traditions
Concerning Yohanan ben Zakkai; Noble, Shlomo: The Jewish
Woman in Medieval Martyrology; Parzen, Herbert: Observa-
tions on Maimonides' *Guide for the Perplexed;* Perlmann, Moshe:
"Talmudic Human Sacrifices", Egypt 1890; Pelli, Moshe: The
Methodology Employed by the Hebrew Reformers in the First
Reform Temple Controversy (1818–1819); Rabinowitz, Isaac:
A Rectification of the Date of Judah Messer Leon's Death;
Sarna, Nahum M.: The Order of the Books; Scheiber, A.: Bibli-
ographisches aus der Genisa; Schemlzer, Menahem: Rashi's
Commentary on the Pentateuch and on the Five Scrolls, Ven-
ice, Bomberg, 1538; Silberschlag, Eisig: Contemporary He-
brew Literature: Source of Untapped Values; Talmage, Frank:
David Kimhi and the Rationalist Tradition II: Literary
Sources; Voss, Carl Hermann: Letters from Stephen S. Wise
to a Friend and Colleague: Morton Mayer Berman: Weinstein,
Myron M.: A Putative Ceylon Rite; Wiener, Theodore: Ad-
denda to Yaari's *Bibliography of the Passover Haggadah* from the
Library of Congress Collection; Yerushalmi, Yosef Hayyim:
Privileǧos del Poderozo Rey Karlo (1740): A Neapolitan Call for
the Return of the Jews, and its Ladino Translation; Zafren,
Herbert: Dyhernfurth and Shabtai Bass: A Typographic Pro-
file; Zimmermann, Frank: A Suggested Source for Some of the
Substitute Names for YHWH.

5. NATIONAL BIBLIOGRAPHIES AND CHECKLISTS

CANADA

Lochhead, Douglas, comp.; Index comp. by Peter E. Greig. *Bibliography of Canadian Bibliographies.* Second Edition, Revised and
Enlarged. [Toronto and Buffalo]: Bibliographical Society of
Canada and University of Toronto Press, [1972]. xvi, 312 pp.
$20.00. ISBN 0–8020–1865–3. Microfiche ISBN 0–8020–
0195–5. LC 76–166933. Contents/Table des matières: Preface
to the second edition; Préface de la deuxième édition; Preface
to the first edition; Préface de la première édition; Introduc-

tion; Bibliography of Canadian bibliographies/Bibliographie des bibliographies canadiennes; Index. 'The major changes introduced in this second edition are an alphabetical arrangement of entries regardless of subject and a consolidation of indexes. As a result of the use of an alphabetical list and the subsequent renumbering of all items included, it should be pointed out that entry numbers do *not* correspond with those in the first edition. . . . The following categories have been omitted with a few exceptions: (a) bibliographies or catalogues on cards, unless a list is expected to be made available for circulation; (b) bibliographies included in a monograph, a thesis, or in a periodical article; (c) catalogues and price lists of publishers, booksellers, and second-hand book-dealers; (d) analytical writings on bibliography or on source material; (e) subject or name indexes; (f) directories, trade lists, biographical dictionaries, even though they include cursory bibliographies. . . . Lists submitted by students for library school requirements can often be useful, and we have listed all those brought to our attention. The library to which they were submitted is listed after the collation. It has not been possible to examine the great majority of bibliographies described. . . . The greatly expanded bilingual index provides an increased number of references both by subject and compiler.' (Pages xi, xii.) Note: also listed on a French title page as *Bibliographie des bibliographies canadiennes.*

GREAT BRITAIN

Mellown, Elgin W. *A Descriptive Catalogue of the Bibliographies of 20th Century British Writers.* Troy, N.Y.: The Whitston Publishing Company, Incorporated, 1972. xii, 446 pp. $17.50. ISBN 0–87875–022–3. LC 79–183301. [Contents: Preface; General Bibliographies; A Descriptive Catalogue; Index of Names]. 'In the *Catalogue* I have listed (in alphabetical order and with birth and death years and pseudonyms) all the British writers who, born after 1840, published the larger part of their work in England or Ireland after 1890 or thereabouts and who have been the subject of bibliographical study. I have included authors less by judging the nature and quality of their work than by considering which ones the users of this *Catalogue* might expect to find here. Thus I list only the better-known writers in the social sciences and the sciences, but I include all the imaginative writers and writers in the humanities whom I have been able to name and for whom I have been able to locate bibliographies.' (Page v.) 'Evaluation of the bibliography: When possible, I quote some authority; if the bibliography is the only one available, or if one should consult all of the bibliographies listed, there is generally no comment.' (Page vii.)

6. WRITING AND AUTOGRAPHS

No entry

7. PRINTING, BINDING, PUBLISHING, AND BOOKSELLING

Durrant, W. R., C. W. Meacock, and R. E. Whitworth. *Machine Printing.* New York: Visual Communication Books, Hastings House, Publishers, [1973]. x, 245 pp. (inc. 7 pp. illus.). $14.50. ISBN 0–8038–4671–1. LC 73–3040. The Library of Printing Technology. Contents: Editor's Preface by J. E. Reeve Fowkes; Acknowledgments; 1, Machine Design: Functions of a Printing Machine, Machine Construction, Principles and Methods of Offset Printing, Gravure Machine Principles; 2, Printing Surfaces: Letterpress, Lithography, Photogravure; 3, Inks and Printing: Ink Formulation, Rheological Properties and Drying Mechanisms of Inks, Design of Inking Systems; 4, Impression: Letterpress, Lithography, Gravure; 5, Makeready and Running: Principles of Sheet Feeding, Letterpress Makeready, Lithographic Makeready, Gravure; 6, Web Printing: Web Control, Web Offset, Accelerated Drying Systems, Pre-Printed Webs; 7, Ancillary Equipment: Quality Control, Ink and Colour Control, other Controls, Ancillary Operations; Appendix: Screen Process Printing, Flexography, Solvents and Roller Cleaning, Solvent Recovery, Relevant British Standards; Glossary; Index.

Gunther, Max. *Writing and Selling a Nonfiction Book.* Boston: The Writer, Inc., Publishers, [1973]. viii, 124 pp. $6.95. ISBN 0–87116–074–9. LC 75–188591. Contents: Introduction; 1,

What Makes a Good Nonfiction Book Idea? 2, Types of Non-fiction Books; 3, The Query Letter: Pre-Selling Your Book; 4, The Outline and Sample Chapters; 5, Planning and Organizing; 6, For Reference: Public and Personal Libraries; 7, Getting Facts by Mail; 8, Interviewing; 9, Three Elements of Style; 10, Making the Style Your Own; 11, The Job to Be Done by Chapter One; 12, Be Specific! 13, Fictional Techniques in Nonfiction Writing; 14, Finding a Good Title; 15, Putting It All Together; 16, Writer to Writer: Some Questions and Answers.

Hess, Stanley. *The Modification of Letterforms.* [New York]: Art Direction Book Company, [1972]. 150 pp. (inc. 68 pp. illus.). $7.95. ISBN 0–910158–03–7. LC 72–85237. Contents: The Modification of Letterforms; Shape; Illusion; Image; Continual Proportionals; Small Letter Proportionals; Space; Pattern; Equality; Slope; Surface; Prospect; Glossary.

McLean, Ruari. *Victorian Book Design and Colour Printing.* [Berkeley and Los Angeles]: University of California Press, [1972]. xii, 241 pp. (inc. 94 pp. illus., plus 16 pp. illus.). $40.00. ISBN 0–520–02078–2. LC 71–165234. Contents: Foreword to Second Edition; Foreword to First Edition; 1, The Background; 2, Whittingham and Pickering; 3, Novels and Gift Books up to 1850; 4, Colour Printing Becomes Commercial; 5, Colour Printing: George Baxter, Charles Knight, Thomas de la Rue, and Others; 6, Children's books up to 1850; 7, Henry Shaw's Coloured Books and Chiswick Press Colour Printing; 8, Early Lithography and Owen Jones; 9, The 'Illuminated' Gift Book; 10, Henry Noel Humphreys, Author and Illustrator; 11, The Advance of Chromolithography; 12, Joseph Cundall, Publisher and Book Designer; 13, From Yellow-Backs to the 'Sixties; 14, Colour-Printing from Wood: Vizetelly, Edmund Evans, and the Dalziels; 15, Colour-Printing from Wood: G. C. Leighton, Kronheim, Dickes, and Fawcett; 16, Styles in Nineteenth Century Publishers' Bindings; 17, The End of an Epoch; Index.

Moran, James. *Printing Presses: History and Development from the Fifteenth Century to Modern Times.* Berkeley and Los Angeles: University of California Press, [1973]. 263 pp. (inc. 35 pp. illus., plus 48 pp. illus.). $25.00. ISBN 0–520–02245–9. LC 72–75519. Contents: Introduction and Acknowledgement; 1, The Beginning; 2, Improving the Wooden Press; 3, The Stanhope Press; 4, The Columbian Press; 5, The Iron Press after Stanhope and Clymer; 6, The Albion Press; 7, Koenig and the Cylinder Machine; 8, The Bed and Platen Press; 9, The First Stages of the Cylinder Machine; 10, The Jobbing Platen; 11, The Cylinder Machine Takes Over; 12, Rotary Printing — the Background; 13, The Type-Revolving Machine and the Development of the Modern Rotary; 14, Reel-Fed Flatbeds and Sheet-Fed Rotaries; 15, The Rotary Press — Final Stages; 16, Apotheosis Deferred; Plates; Appendix I: Miniature, 'Toy', Amateur and Card Presses; Appendix II: The Proof Press; Bibliography; General Index; Index of Presses and Machines.

[Papantonio, Michael.] *Early American Bookbindings from the Collection of Michael Papantonio.* New York: Pierpont Morgan Library with American Antiquarian Society, Cornell University Library, Princeton University Library, University of Virginia Library, 1972. xii, 92 pp. (inc. 62 pp. illus.). $5.50. SBN 87598–037–6. LC 72–91710. Contents: Foreword; Introduction; Catalogue; Principal Bibliographical Citations; Index of Binders; Index of Previous Owners; Index of Authors.

Spencer, Herbert, ed. *The Penrose Graphic Arts International Annual 1973.* [New York: Visual Communication Books, Hastings House, Publishers], 1973. Vol. LXVI. 230 pp. (inc. 53 pp. illus., plus 2 transparencies and divider, plus 32 pp. advertisements). $22.50. SBN 8038–5793–4.

Thomas, David St. John and Hubert Bermont. *Getting Published.* New York: Fleet Press Corporation, [1973]. 188 pp. $6.95. SBN 8303–0116–X (American Edition). LC 73–179016. Contents: Introduction; Subject Matter and Approach; The Mechanics of Writing; The Physical Book; Your Manuscript; The Illustrations; Your Publisher; Your Contract; Authorship and Finance; Copyright; The Book Business; The Author's Library and Source Material; Specimen Contract; Author's Alterations; Index.

Young, L[aurence] C[arvan]. *Materials in Printing Processes.* New York: Visual Communication Books, Hastings House, Publishers, [1973]. xiv, 293 pp. (inc. 12 pp. illus., plus 8 pp. illus.). $15.00 ISBN 0–8038–4666–5. LC 71–38323. The Library of Printing Technology. Contents: Editor's Preface by J. E. Reeve Fowkes; Acknowledgments; 1, Introduction — The Nature of Materials: Elements and Atoms, The Structure of Atoms, Compounds and Mixtures, Linkages between Atoms, Dipole Moments, Gases, Liquids and Solids, Small Molecules and Large Molecules, Solutions and Dispersions; 2, Metals for Platemaking: The Lithographic Properties of Metals, Copper, Zinc, Aluminium, Magnesium, Chromium and Nickel; 3, Printing Alloys: Alloys, Oxidation Losses, Impurities, A Simple Equilibrium Diagram, The Structure of Solid Alloys, Tin-Antimony Alloys, The Ternary System, Tin-Antimony-Lead; 4, Polymers: Thermosets and Thermoplastics, Natural Polymers, Cellulose Derivatives, Synthetic Polymers, Thermosetting Plastics, Cold Curing, Printing on Plastic Films; 5, Paper and Board — Raw Materials: The Nature of Paper, Stages of Manufacture, Fibrous Materials, The Structure and Composition of Wood, The Manufacture of Cellulose Pulp, Non-Fibrous Materials; 6, Paper and Board — Manufacture: Preparing the Stock for Papermaking, The Paper Machine, Board Manufacture; 7, Paper and Board — Finishing and After Treatment: Calendering, Slitting, Trimming and Cutting, Conditioning, Coating, Other Finishing Processes; 8, Paper and Board — Classes: Printings, Writings, Wrappings, Boards, Specialty Papers; 9, Paper and Board — Testing Methods: Subjective Methods of Testing, Objective Methods of Testing, Sampling for Paper Testing, Humidity and Paper Testing, Paper Testing Methods; 10, Printing Ink — Drying Methods: The Nature of Printing Ink, Oxidation and Polymerisation, Absorption, Evaporation, Precipitation; 11, Printing Ink — Pigments: Types of Pigment; 12, Printing Ink — Vehicles: Oils, Resins, Solvents, Driers; 13, Printing Ink — Formulation and Manufacture: Formulation, Manufacture; 14, Printing Ink — Testing Methods: Tests on Printing Ink, Subjective Methods of Testing, Objective Methods of Testing, Tests Carried out on Prints; 15, Light-Sensitive Materials: Photographic Materials, Other Light-Sensitive Coatings; 16, Adhesives: The Nature of

Adhesion, Types of Adhesive; 17, Bookbinding Materials; Appendix A: Some Reference for further Reading; Appendix B: Selected List of Testing Equipment for Paper, Ink and Other Printing Materials with Names and Addresses of Suppliers in the United Kingdom; Appendix C: Standard Methods for Testing Paper and Printing Ink, British Standards Instituition (BSI), Technical Association of the Pulp and Paper Industry (TAPPI); Appendix D: Metrication and SI Units; Appendix E: Metrication and Paper Sizes, ISO Trimmed and Untrimmed Stock Sizes and their Inch Conversions; Appendix F: Metrication Applied to Paper Substance, The R20 and R40 Ranges of Basis Weights; Appendix G: Traditional Paper Sizes in Britain and the United States; Index.

8. COPYRIGHT AND INTELLECTUAL PROPERTY

No entry.

9. LIBRARIES AND BOOK COLLECTING

Brown, John Carter, Library. *Annual Reports 1901–1966.* Providence: The John Carter Brown Library, Brown University and The Colonial Society of Massachusetts, 1972. 8 vols., with a preface by Thomas R. Adams, Librarian; Introduction by Edmund S. Morgan; Index comp. by Dorothy G. Watts. $100.00. LC 13–26520. Vol. I: 1901–1924. lxxiv, 327 pp. [Contents: Preface by Thomas R. Adams; Introduction by Edmund S. Morgan; The John Carter Brown Library Annual Reports]. Vol. II: 1925–1935. xxviii, 420 pp. [Contents: The John Carter Brown Library Annual Reports]. Vol. III: 1936–1942. xx, 402 pp. [Contents: The John Carter Brown Library Annual Reports]. Vol. IV: 1943–1948. xviii, 406 pp. [Contents: The John Carter Brown Library Annual Reports]. Vol. V: 1949–1953. xvi, 376 pp. [Contents: The John Carter Brown Library Annual Reports]. Vol. VI: 1954–1958. xvi, 406 pp. [Contents: The John Carter Brown Library Annual Reports]. Vol. VII: 1959–1966. xviii, 426 pp. (plus 12 pp. illus.). [Contents: Annual Report. July 1, 1959; Annual Report, July 1, 1960; *The John Carter Brown Library Conference: A Report of the Meeting Held*

in the Library at Brown University on the Early History of the Americas.
Providence, Rhode Island, MCMLXI. Contents: Introduction;
Program for the Future Growth of The John Carter Brown
Library; The Use of Old Sources in New Ways, by Robert E.
Spiller; Early American History as a Part of the History of
Western Civilization, by Lewis U. Hanke; The Use of The John
Carter Brown Library in Fields other than History, by Durand
Echeverria; The Discussions; Participants. Report for July 1,
1960–June 30, 1965; Annual Report, July 1, 1966.] Vol. VIII:
Index, comp. by Dorothy G. Watts. 271 pp. 'The authorship
of the series is as follows: George Parker Winship, Librarian,
Reports for 1901–1915; Champlin Burrage, Librarian, *Report*
for 1916; Worthington C. Ford, Acting Librarian, *Reports* for
1917–1923; Lawrence C. Wroth, Librarian, *Reports* for 1924–
1957; Thomas R. Adams, Librarian, *Reports* for 1958–1966'
(Vol. I, p. vi). 'To read one of the Reports carefully is to realize
that . . . there is more design than meets the eye in the way
the author moves from one subject to another' (Vol. I, p. x).
'The range of subjects is enormous, from English piracy to
Pennsylvania printing, from Aztec languages to colonial
boundary disputes, from navigation to legislation. But the
disparity is embraced in the encompassing theme of the discovery of America and its effect upon the world' (Vol. I, p.
xvi).

Hechtlinger, Adelaide, and Wilbur Cross. *The Complete Book of Paper
Antiques.* New York: Coward, McCann & Geoghegan, Inc.
[1972]. 220 pp. (inc. 27 pp. illus., plus 4 pp. illus.). $6.95. SBN
698–10468–4. LC 72–79513. Contents: I, How, Why and What
to Collect; II, Display and Preservation; III, Paper, Prints and
Profits; IV, Brownies, Sunbonnet Babies and Other Such; V,
It's In the Cards; VI, Pretty as a Picture; VII, Hearts and
Flowers; VIII, A Message for Anyone About Almost Anything;
IX, Eye-Catchers; X, The Play's the Thing; XI, "All
Aboarrrd!"; XII, *The Old Farmer* Grows Money, Too; XIII,
Made to Order; XIV, It's Your Turn to Bid; XV, Sharps and
Flats; XVI, Ten Thrills per Page; XVII, A Funny Thing to
Collect; XVIII, How to Make Worthless Documents Valuable;
XIX, Leaping Back over the Years; XX, Where Do You Go
From Here? XXI, Fashions, Fads and Paper Dolls; XXII, Some

Sticky Matters; XXIII, And in Conclusion; Bibliography; Glossary; Index.

10. BIBLIOGRAPHICAL AND TEXTUAL THEORY AND PRACTICE

Gumbert, J. P., and M. J. M. De Haan, ed. *Varia Codicologica: Essays Presented to G. I. Lieftinck/l.* Amsterdam: A. L. Van Gendt & Co., 1972. Vol. I [of 4 vols.]. 112 pp. (inc. 26 pp. illus.). $31 single vol.; $96 for 4 vols. ISBN 90–6300–319–6. LC 72–78495. Litterae Textuales: A Series on Manuscripts and Their Texts. Contents: [Preface]; The Script of Corbie: A Criterion (T. A. M. Bishop, Hemingford Grey); Das Evangelienbuch von St.-Ursanne (A. Bruckner, Basel); La provenance du ms. Bruxelles 7666–71 contenant la "Clausula de unctione Pippini regis" (Maurice Coens S. J.†, Bruxelles); Further Observations on Durham Cathedral Ms. A.IV.34 (A. I. Doyle, Durham); Eton College Ms. 44 and its Exemplar (N. R. Ker, Edinburgh); The IJsselstein Manuscripts in the Orange-Nassau Library (P. F. J. Obbema, Leiden); Fragment d'un catalogue ancien de Groenendael ayant servi à la composition du répertoire collectif de Rougecloître (A. Gruisjs, Nijmegen); Gedanken und Erfahrungen bei der Katalogisierung von Handscriftenfragmenten (H. Butzmann, Wolfenbüttel); Le vidimus aux Pays-Bas septentrionaux (J. L. Van Der Gouw, Voorschoten); Index of manuscripts; [table of contents]. 'The forty essays in this volume and its three companion volumes are offered to Professor Dr. G. I. Lieftinck at the moment when his teaching at the University of Leiden reaches its official end. . . . The first volume presents work on Carolingian and Gothic manuscripts, on monastic libraries of the Netherlands, and on the material vehicles of the written word in general; as a parallel to this, we list a selection of the writings of Professor Lieftinck in the same fields (overleaf)' (p. 5). *Note:* contains erratum slip.

11. CONCORDANCES AND INDEXES

Naugle, Helen Harrold, ed., and Peter B. Sherry. *A Concordance to the Poems of Samuel Johnson.* Ithaca and London: Cornell University Press, [1973]. xxx, 578 pp. $13.50. ISBN 0–8014–0769–9. LC 72–13383. The Cornell Concordances. '*The Poems of Samuel Johnson,* edited by David Nichol Smith and Edward L. McAdam (Oxford, 1941), is here used as the definitive edition. But . . . *Poems,* edited by McAdam with George Milne (1964) in the *Yale Edition of the Works of Samuel Johnson,* Vol. VI, supplements the basic text. That is, both poems and variant readings in the Yale edition that do not appear in the Clarendon edition are indexed. The editions are designated by "O" for Oxford and "Y" for Yale with pagination to the volume cited.' (Page x.) Contents: Preface; Abbreviated Titles: English Poems (together with French and Greek); Abbreviated Titles: Latin Poems; Concordance to Poems in English; Frequencies; Concordance to Poems in Latin; Frequencies; Concordance to Poems of Doubtful Attribution; Frequencies.

Mann, David, ed. *A Concordance to the Plays of William Congreve.* Ithaca and London: Cornell University Press, [1973]. xxiv, 888 pp. $15.00. ISBN 0–8014–0767–2. LC 72–13384. The Cornell Concordances. 'This concordance [is] based on *The Complete Plays of William Congreve,* edited by Herbert Davis (Chicago and London: University of Chicago Press, 1967) . . . Although Davis' edition is unquestionably the best . . . it does have a few minor errors, mostly typographical. . . . Consequently, I have felt it advisable to compare his text with quartos . . . and I have made a few corrections. . . . Nevertheless, citations of page and line, act and scene, throughout, are to the authoritative Davis text.' (Page vii.) Contents: Preface; Concordance to the Plays of William Congreve; Appendixes (A, Stage Directions; B, Index of Common Words; C, Words in Order of Frequency).

12. DICTIONARIES, RHETORICS, AND GUIDES TO LANGUAGE

Baker, W. M., comp. *Bell's Acrostic Dictionary.* Detroit: Gale Research Company, 1971. vi, 277 pp. $10.00. LC 77–141772. Facsimile of London: G. Bell & Sons, Ltd., 1927. Contents: [Preface; Text.]

Kennedy, John. *A Stem Dictionary of the English Language.* Detroit: Gale Research Company, 1971. x, 282 pp. $15.00 LC 78–142547. Facsimile of Chicago, Cincinatti, and New York: The American Book Company, 1870. [Contents: Preface; Explanations; Alphabetical Word List; Alphabetical Stem List; Prefixes; Quotations.]

Rocke, Russell. *The Grandiloquent Dictionary.* Englewood Cliffs, N.J.: Prentice-Hall, Inc., [1972]. 175 pp. $5.95. ISBN 0–13–363291–1. LC 70–170028. Contents: Pre-Text; Table of Symbols; Pronunciation Key; One, Shapes, Semblances, and Resemblances; Two, Bodily Processes and Characteristics; Three, Nouns of Power; Four, Vibrant Verbs; Five, Adjectives and Adverbs of Power; Six, Shades of Meaning; Seven, Esoterica; Eight, Sesquipeds; Nine, Words of Whimsey; Ten, Wordmaking; Pronunciation Guide/Vocabulary Test; Index. 'The principal object is to assemble the most intriguing and challenging words actually *used* (not always printed, until now) to describe them in a comprehensible manner, to categorize them in an imaginative and unusual way, and, above all, to make this an entertaining and diverting journey into the backwaters of the English language, and only secondarily a scholarly dissertation.' (Page 14.)

Rose, Howard N., comp. *A Thesaurus of Slang.* Detroit: Gale Research Company, 1972. xii, 120 pp. $9.00. LC 72–167144. Facsimile of New York: The Macmillan Company, 1934. Contents: Introduction; I, Aviation; II, College; III, Detective; IV, Hobo; V, Lumberjack; VI, New England; VII, Newspaper; VIII, Oilfield; IX, Railroad; X, Sea-Fishing; XI, Sports; XII, Theater; XIII, Western; XIV, War.

13. MISCELLANEOUS

Erle Stanley Gardner: an Exhibit, September 1972. Austin: The Humanities Research Center, The University of Texas at Austin, [1972]. ii, 14 pp. (inc. frontis., 2 pp. illus.). [Contents: Erle Stanley Gardner; Case 1, Characters in Series; Case 2, Perry Mason; Case 3, Pen Names; Case 4, Non-Fiction: Travel and Adventure; Case 5, Foreign Publications; Case 6, Non-Fiction:

Law Enforcement, Criminology, and Penology; Case 7, The Formulas for Writing a Mystery Novel; Case 8, The Court of Last Resort].

Francis, Sir Frank. *A Bibliographical Ghost Revists His Old Haunts.* Austin: Published by the Humanities Research Center, The University of Texas at Austin, [1972]. 30 pp. Bibliographical Monographs Series No. 5.

Glick, Thomas F., ed. *Darwinism in Texas: An Exhibition in the Texas History Center April, 1972.* 'Austin: The Humanities Research Center,' [1972]. 40 pp. (inc. illus. front cover, inc. 2 pp. illus.). Contents: Introduction by Thomas F. Glick; Part II, Catalog of the Exhibition; Part III, Cranfill Debates an Evolutionist (J. B. Cranfill and John H. Jessen); Part IV, Dawson and Cranfill on the Days of Evolution (1922; Joseph M. Dawson and J. B. Cranfill); Part V, Darwinism and Dawson: A Memoir (1972; Joseph M. Dawson); Part IV, The Evolution Controversy: Remembrance and Reflection (Blake Smith).

Grimsted, Patricia Kennedy. *Archives and Manuscript Repositories in the USSR: Moscow and Leningrad.* Princeton: Princeton University Press, [1972]. xxx, 436 pp. $22.50. ISBN 0–691–05149–6. LC 73–166375. Studies of the Russian Institute. Contents: Preface; Acknowledgments; Note on Bibliographical Format; Transliteration Table; Abbreviations and Acronyms; Historical Survey; Procedural Information; Part A — General Archival Bibliography and Research Aids; Part B — Central State Archives of the USSR; Part C — Archives and Manuscript Collections of the Academy of Sciences of the USSR; Part D — Special Archives; Part E — Manuscript Divisions of Libraries and Museums in Moscow; Part F — Manuscript Divisions of Libraries and Museums in Leningrad; Part G — Republic and Local State Archives in Moscow and Leningrad; Appendix 1 — Research in Libraries; Appendix 2 — Reference Aids for Paleography and Ancillary Historical Disciplines; Glossary of Archival Terms; Author-Title Index; Subject Index.

Jordan-Smith, Paul, *et al.,* eds. *American Book-Prices Current 1970: A Record of Literary Properties Sold at Auction in England, The United States, and in Canada.* New York and London: Columbia University Press, 1970. Vol. LXXVI. xliii, 1501 pp. $40.00. ISBN 0–231–03706–6. LC 3–14557. Contents: Preface; Abbreviations; Auction Houses; Season's Sales; Named Consignors; Part I: Books, Broadsides, Maps & Charts; Part II: Autographs & Manuscripts; Section I — Illuminated Manuscripts and Manuscripts before 1600; Section II — Autographs & Manuscripts after 1600.

McCoy, Garnett. *Archives of American Art: A Directory of Resources.* New York & London: R. R. Bowker Company, 1972. x, 164 pp. $20.00. ISBN 0–8352–0598–3. LC 72–5125. Contents: Preface; Collections; Index.

McGrath, Daniel F. *Bookman's Price Index: A Guide to the Values of Rare and Other Out-of-Print Books.* Detroit: Gale Research Company, [1973]. Vol. VI. x, 694 pp. $38.50. LC 64–8723. Contents: How to Use this Book; Dealers Represented in this Volume; Guide to the Values of Rare and Other Out-of-Print Books.

Payne, John R., comp.; intro. by Alan Friedman. *Modern British Fiction: An Exhibit of Books, Paintings and Manuscripts November–December 1972.* Austin: The Humanities Research Center, The University of Texas, [1972]. 56 pp. (inc. 5 pp. illus.). [Contents: Compiler's Note; Introduction; Modern British Fiction].

Poulton, Helen. *The Historian's Handbook: A Descriptive Guide to Reference Works.* With the Assistance of Marguerite S. Howland. Foreword by Wilbur S. Shepperson. Norman: University of Oklahoma Press, [1972]. xii, 308 pp. $4.95 (paper). ISBN 0–8061–0985–8. LC 71–165774. Contents: Foreword; Preface; 1, The Library and Its Catalog; 2, National Library Catalogs and National and Trade Bibliographies; 3, Guides, Manuals, and Bibliographies of History; 4, Encyclopedias and Dictionaries; 5, Almanacs, Yearbooks, Statistical Handbooks, and Current Surveys; 6, Serials and Newspapers; 7, Geographical Aids; 8, Biographical Materials; 9, Primary Sources and Dissertations; 10, Legal Sources; 11, Government Publications; Index of Titles; General Index.

Pirie, Robert S., comp. *John Donne, 1572–1631: A Catalogue of the Anniversary Exhibition of First and Early Editions of His Works Held at The Grolier Club February 15 to April 12, 1972.* New York: The Grolier Club, [1972.] xvi, 44 pp. (inc. frontis.; plus 4 pp. illus.). $6.00 (paper). LC 72–92128. Contents: Foreword; Compiler's Note; Lenders to the Exhibition; Prose Works; Letters; Sermons; Poetry (John Donne and The Grolier Club; Musical Settings; Translations); Miscellany (Donne's Seals; Books Dedicated to Donne; Books from Donne's Library; Biography; Iconography; Memorial Verses; Modern Editions; Bibliography; Memorabilia).

Riley, Carolyn, ed. *Contemporary Literary Criticism: Excerpts from Criticism of the Works of Today's Novelists, Poets, Playwrights, and Other Creative Writers.* Detroit: Gale Research Company, [1973]. Vol. I. vi, 385 pp. $25.00. LC 76–38938. Contemporary Literary Criticism series. [Contents: Preface; Text.]

Sale Catalogues of Libraries of Eminent Persons: Poets and Men of Letters. [London]: Mansell with Sotheby Parke-Bernet Publications, [1972]. Vol. V, ed., with intros., by Stephen Parks. vi, 554 pp. (inc. 1 p. illus.). $21.00. SBN 7201–0300–2. Contents: John Dunton; Elijah Fenton; Joseph Spence; Laurence Sterne; William Dodd; Hester Lynch Piozzi. Vol. VI, ed., with intros., by John Woolford. vi, 363 pp. (inc. 38 pp. illus., plus 1 gatefold). $21.00. ISBN 0–7201–0301–0. Contents: Robert Browning; John Ruskin; Algernon Swinburne and Theodore Watts-Dunton.

Wynar, Bohdan S., ed. *Reference Books in Paperback: An Annotated Guide.* Littleton, Colo.: Libraries Unlimited, Inc., 1972. 199 pp. $4.75 (paper). ISBN 0–87287–046–4. LC 74–189257. Contents: General Works; Anthropology; Biology; Botany; Business and Economics; Collecting; Drugs; Education; Environment; Ethnic Minorities; Fine Arts; Geography; Geology; History; Journalism; Language; Law; Literature; Medical Sciences; Music; Mythology; Philosophy; Political Science; Psychology; Religion; Repair Guides; School Libraries; Science and Engineering; School Sciences and Area Studies; Sociology; Sports and Hobbies; Statistics; Theater, Movies and TV; Travel Guides; Zoology; Author and Title Index; Subject Index.

CONTRIBUTORS

CLIFTON WALLER BARRETT is the noted bibliophile whose library at the University of Virginia is a landmark of American literary scholarship.

FREDSON BOWERS, recently retired as Linden Kent Professor of English at the University of Virginia, is Editor of *Studies in Bibliography.*

JOAN St.C. CRANE is Bibliographer of the Clifton Waller Barrett Library at the University of Virginia.

FLOYD EUGENE EDDLEMAN is Professor of English at Texas Tech University.

LILLIAN B. GILKES is an independent scholar and critic residing in Tryon, North Carolina.

DAVID LEON HIGDON is Associate Professor of English at Texas Tech University and General Editor of *Conradiana.*

BRIAN HIGGINS is Assistant Professor of English at the University of Illinois–Chicago Circle.

ROBERT W. HOBSON is a graduate student in English at Texas Tech University.

JOHN BUSH JONES is Associate Professor of English at the University of Kansas.

JOSEPH R. McELRATH, JR., is Assistant Professor of English at Florida State University and Editor of *The Editorial Quarterly.*

HERSHEL PARKER is Professor of English at the University of Southern California.

NOEL POLK is Visiting Associate Research Professor and Bibliographer with the Southern Studies Program at the University of South Carolina.

HASKELL SPRINGER is Associate Professor of English at the University of Kansas.

G. THOMAS TANSELLE is Professor of English at the University of Wisconsin.

THOMAS A. TENNEY is Assistant Professor of English at the College of Charleston.

LAWRENCE S. THOMPSON is Professor of Classics at the University of Kentucky.

INDEX

An asterisk following page numbers identifies the entry as a reference to 'The Register of Current Publications: 1974'.

PROOF 4: THE YEARBOOK OF AMERICAN BIBLIO-GRAPHICAL AND TEXTUAL STUDIES is composed principally in Baskerville, with Caslon Old Style being used on the title-page. PROOF 4 was printed by offset lithography on Warren's Old Style paper, an acid-free book stock noted for its longevity. The binding, manufactured in a special finish for PROOF, is Holliston's Sturdite. Composition, photoengraving, printing, and binding were performed by Kingsport Press. The publisher certifies that extraordinary care has gone into the making of PROOF 4.

PROOF 4 was published on 14 August 1975 in a first printing of 1,000 copies.